Bitter Harvest Moon

D M Hanson

Published by D M Hanson, 2019.

BITTER HARVEST MOON

First edition. November 11, 2019.

Copyright © 2019 D M Hanson.

ISBN: 978-1916201613

Written by D M Hanson.

For the late Meg Freeman without whose help and encouragement
I would never have got started.

I would also like to thank the following:

Hilary Kirby, Rick Mills and Eve Savory for their comments and
advice.

Anna Kirby for German translations

Monica Janowski for help with editing.

Mike Kirby for help with the book cover.

And last but not least – Jocelyn Hanson.

Prologue

For the third or fourth time since she'd arrived, she checked the contents of her bag – yes, everything was there. She checked it once more, just to be sure, letting her fingers linger on the coldness of the bottle. Disturbed in her reverie, she became aware of people moving around her. She looked intently at their faces, but there was nobody there who knew her.

She glanced at her watch, and was surprised to discover how long she had been standing there – still, better to be too early than to be late. To be late would have been unthinkable.

She gripped the rail, resisting the temptation to look east. Instead she turned west – west towards the setting sun.

June
Westbourne Avenue

The two men struggling with the enormous wardrobe stopped and put it down. The larger of the two took out a large handkerchief and mopped his brow. There were so many better things to do on a hot sunny June afternoon than move heavy items of furniture. He glanced towards the Avenue's ornamental fountain – a pity someone couldn't set that going. The cool sound of falling water would have been welcome. "Better get on with it, I suppose," he said to his companion and, on the count of three, they lifted the wardrobe and carried it inside.

The two bay windows in the double-fronted house and the cast iron railings around the formal front garden gave the house a pleasing symmetry. The agent had described it as being on 'the healthiest side of town, kept free from smoke by prevailing winds'. On this beautiful day, a gentle breeze moved through the leaves of the trees planted a meticulous thirty-five feet apart in the wide grass verges. In the house's back garden, the breeze was less apparent, and the sun beat down on the head of the girl waiting impatiently on the lawn.

Emily Walker looked up at her bedroom window and sighed. She should be inside, not still standing here! Her mother didn't seem to be taking any notice. She sighed again, even more loudly.

"Emily, I heard you the first time. I'm afraid sighing like that won't make any difference. You have to be patient."

"Will the men be much longer?" Emily said, unable to keep the frustration from her voice. "They've been coming and going for I don't know how long and I can't wait any longer."

"You know what your father said. You're not to get in the way."

Emily knew full well her father's expectations, but that didn't make it any easier. She tried again. "We arrived ages before Edward and David, and they've both gone up to their rooms." She glanced upwards. "I could stay in my bedroom."

"That's enough, Emily! Your brothers' things came earlier. They haven't taken your trunk up yet. They'll tell us when you can go in, so I don't want to hear another word!"

Life was so unfair, thought Emily as she managed a meek, "Yes, Mother," in reply. She looked around her. The idea of a large garden had seemed so appealing. Large gardens were meant to be overgrown and mysterious, with dark corners and unexpected encounters. There was little chance of that here. She surveyed the bare lawn and large empty borders. Even the garden's one promising feature, a red brick wall, with ivy and honeysuckle scrambling over it, was disappointing. Nothing exciting lay hidden there. She tried to think of improvements. A summer house? Yes, a summer house would be a welcome addition. She had decided that morning to be a famous author and a summer house would be perfect to write her famous novels in. It wasn't long until her eleventh birthday and it would be nice if there was one here by then. She sighed, this time at the difficulty of persuading her father. Now if David or Edward wanted something, that would be a different matter! Fragmented voices drifted over the wall. A grown-up and someone younger were talking. What a shame, she could not make out what they were saying! She gave up and moved back towards her mother.

"Put your hat back on, dear. The sun gets terribly strong at this time of year, and with your lovely fair complexion..."

Emily groaned to herself. The best way of removing herself from the sun's rays would be by going into the house. She fixed her hat on at a jaunty angle as a minor rebellion and considered her hair. Perhaps she should wear it loose in future? It would be so much easier if it could be short like her brothers, but her mother would never accept that. She liked the ribbons on her bunches, if not the bunches themselves. Edward had pulled them hard that morning. If only he were two years younger than her, rather than older, life would be so much easier.

Silence from next-door suggested that the neighbours had gone in. Would they call round? No, that was unthinkable, especially on the first day. They would need a formal invitation. And then... yes, the best china would be displayed, the silver polished, the damask table napkins perfectly ironed! And food? Thinly sliced bread and butter, dainty sandwiches, madeira cake – or perhaps an orange cake? All arranged in an appetising way, on crocheted d'oyleys, on the best cake-stands. Thinking of food, Emily realised that she was not only bored, but hungry.

Her elder brother's arrival interrupted her thoughts. At last! David was carrying a camera and tripod. He was seventeen and only spoke to Emily when he had to. "Father says he wants a record of our first day. You can come in, but only after I've taken some photographs of everyone," he announced.

"Take mine first, David. I promise I won't move while you take it."

"Yes, go on, David. Please do hers first, she's been driving me to distraction. And it's such a lovely afternoon. If your father wants more pictures, we can come out again later."

Emily did her best to keep still until the photograph was taken.

"Can I go in now, Mother?" At the merest hint of a nod, Emily ran towards the back door.

"Walk, Emily!" called her mother in vain.

"At last!" she told herself, entering the house.

In the kitchen, Alice was preparing some food, but looked as if she would not brook interruption. Emily closed the kitchen door behind her, walked through a room cluttered with boxes and into the tiled hallway. The light that filtered through a stained glass window in the north-facing front door gave the hall a rather sombre appearance. The door opened and a serious-looking man walked in. Emily's father was nearing fifty, but his receding grey hair suggested that he was older. He was tall but walked with a slight stoop. On seeing Emily, he pulled himself up straight. He had never felt comfortable with his daughter.

"Ah, Emily! I see that you have come inside."

Emily wondered why adults said things that were so obvious.

"And are you going up to your room?"

"Yes, Father. I want to see where they've put my things."

Mr Walker paused, as if considering saying something, but instead cleared his throat. The conversation was ended. Emily turned to go up the stairs, resisting with difficulty the temptation to take them two at a time.

Her room did not disappoint her. It was charming! Though doubtless smaller than her brothers', it was a big improvement on her old one. Ivy had made the bed and put her clothes away. Emily glanced at the bed. You never knew with Edward around, but everything appeared to be as it should. She examined the room. She especially liked the pretty white-painted fireplace, though no fire was laid there as she was neither ill nor was it the depths of winter. Her old carpet square was not down yet and a strong smell of polish came from the dark stained floor. She looked up, trying to decide which of her pictures would look best above the fireplace.

The lace curtains were not yet up at the window and she could see her father and mother talking in the garden below. Much more interesting was the neighbouring garden. The branches of an apple tree obscured her view, but she could see a boy sitting underneath it. He looked about Edward's age and was engrossed in a book. What was he reading? She watched, hoping he would stand up and become more visible, but he did not move except for turning the page. Emily was always interested in what others were reading, but before she could speculate further Ivy came in.

"Your mother says that tea's ready, Miss Emily."

"I'll be down straight away, Ivy," Emily said. She looked round her room and smiled, her earlier frustrations forgotten.

#

Dear Aunt Eleanor,

Thank you for your letter. It was the very first letter to arrive here this morning, not only for me but for anyone! The first letter, by first post, on my first full day, in my first new house. Edward's letter didn't come till the third post.

Yes, yesterday was exciting though there were boring bits too. I have decided that I love this house, even though I wish the garden were more interesting. My room is lovely and Father has said I can have a new bookcase of my own. I am hoping that I might get some new books for it next month, when it's my birthday. I am sure there must be lots of good bookshops in London. Edward liked the copy of the Scarlet Pimpernel that you sent him for his. He says it is too old for me, but I think I am the best person to decide that. What do you think? The one bad result from his reading it though is that wherever you go he leaps out and shouts "They seek him here, they seek him there, they seek Edwardo everywhere." There are so many more places for him to do this here.

I would be surprised if Edward writes as promptly as me, but I should warn you, he will ask you about Shackleton and Scott. He believes they will have a race to the South Pole. Who do you think will be first? I said Shackleton even though I don't mind, let alone know or care who wins.

Mother seems happy about the move, even though lots of things aren't finished. She thinks we should all be pleased that we now live in a much pleasanter area. It is a nicer house, but I am not sure about it being a better area as none of my friends are here. David and Edward are pleased because more people from school live near here than near our old house in Coltman Street.

Coming to see you when you are home will be easier, which is a good thing. But you do have to be there to be visited! I am not sure what Father thinks. I was going to tell you a lot more about the house, but I will stop now, as this letter seems quite long already. Showing you round when you do come will be fun, and better than telling you here. I hope it will be soon.

Emily xxxxx

P.S. You aren't going to live in London for good are you? It's just that Father said to Mother that he didn't know why you didn't just stay there.

P.P.S. Any mistakes in punctuation and grammar are Miss Ferguson's fault. I am completely puzzled by colons and semi-colons despite her long explanation. I decided not to use either in this letter.

P.P.P.S. Are you able to come to Bridlington? Please say that you will.

P.P.P.P.S. I have decided to be an author! I hope you approve.

P.P.P.P.P.S. Is there a limit on the number of Ps you are allowed to add to P.S? I am not sure whether to ask Miss Ferguson.

P.P.P.P.P.P.S. She has not got a sense of humour!!

July
Westbourne Avenue

"Now, Miss Emily, don't be getting in my way. You can see I'm fair rushed off my feet. And your mother wants everything straight, what with Mrs Buckley from next-door amongst those that's coming round this afternoon."

The kitchen was Emily's favourite room. It was bright and airy and she liked the way the sun streamed in and reflected off the yellow-varnished paper on the walls. Alice worried about it getting too hot, but today it was ideal. It would also be where to be when the summer ended – warm and snug.

Emily was sitting at the large wooden table and had been studying *A Book of Household Hints* intently for several minutes.

"Alice? Have we got any essence of camphor?"

"Now why would you be needing essence of camphor?"

"It says here it's good for stomach cramps, so I wondered if we had any."

Alice sighed, realising that if she were ever to get on she would have to pay some attention first to the youngest member of the household. "And have you got stomach cramps then?" she asked. "Perhaps I should fetch your mother?"

"No I haven't, but I might have them." This seemed perfectly reasonable to Emily. "And Alice, you said you were always busy, and I was wondering whether you thought we needed more help? There's you and Ivy, but Father said to Mother that a young tweenie was only three and sixpence all found. So we might be getting someone else, mightn't we? But then he said you had to be careful about lice and loose morals. What did he mean by that, Alice?"

"I wouldn't know about that. It's not my business to go asking your father, though you won't find me complaining if your father is persuaded to buy one of them new gas cookers. That would be a fine thing."

Emily looked at the cast-iron range and shuddered. Ivy had to get up early and blacklead the grate, polishing hard until she brought up its current dull sheen. It was one kitchen task that was less than appealing.

"Now, I'm going to need that table. I've my baking to do."

"I'll come back in a while then, shall I?" Emily said rising from her chair. "I'm very good at testing baking... and licking spoons," she added, moving towards the door.

"We'll see about that later, Miss!"

Emily passed through the breakfast room into the hall, where Ivy was polishing the banister. Loathe to risk another dismissal, she decided not to interrupt her. The mixed aromas of linseed oil and vinegar told her that Ivy had done the floor. Trying not to incur Ivy's wrath by making any marks, she stopped and flicked through the cards on the hall table tray. It was still almost empty, but after this afternoon it would be closer to the overflowing effect that her mother so desired. Glancing through them, she knew what to expect; ladies' cards had names in the centre, the address bottom left, with the top corner turned down if they had been left personally. Gentlemen left two cards, but both much smaller. Her mother always stressed the importance of such details – including which room visitors should be shown into, who should rise first on leaving, and so on. It was both complicated and tiresome.

She tapped the barometer several times. Her father had acquired it recently, and she had observed him tapping it on entering and leaving the house. She wondered why he bothered, the dial as usual read 'changeable'.

"I hope that you aren't going to be leaving grubby finger-marks on that, Miss Emily. I've just polished it and I don't want your father complaining at me." Emily turned. Ivy, an attractive dark-haired girl, was watching her from the stairs.

"I'm always careful, Ivy," Emily replied, checking her fingers. She liked Ivy and went to sit on the step next to her. Ivy was easier to distract than Alice and Emily knew the best way. "Ivy, it was your night off last night, wasn't it? Where did you go?"

"Now, Miss Emily, that would be telling," Ivy replied. "And perhaps I shouldn't tell, what with you causing me extra work. The mess you make of your room sometimes! If you ask me, you don't understand the meaning of the word tidy."

The conversation was heading in an undesirable direction.

"I promise to try harder. I will!"

Ivy stopped, and glanced down at the young girl looking up at her. "Then, Miss, perhaps this time I will tell." She paused. "At first we thought of going roller-skating. I've heard your father say people shouldn't waste money on such things because it lowers the tone of the city. Now, Miss, I don't hold with that. It's only sixpence a session. It's just harmless fun. Mind you, don't tell him I said so. We were going to go roller-skating, but we went to the new Kinema Colour Palace on Anlaby Road instead."

Emily, who had only seen a bioscope at the fair, was impressed.

"It were much better than Princes Hall on George Street, if you ask me, Miss. I know that were first and they say it holds fifteen hundred when full, but this were plusher and better. It were showing three features." She paused, before reciting, with great emphasis: "*Choice Bouquets, The Elite of the Canine World* and *Rough Sea at Santa Lucia*. I know there's those who like dogs or flowers best, but for me it had to be *Rough Sea at Santa Lucia*. It was just like being there, Miss, it was. I felt proper seasick from watching it. And you know what, those in the shilling seats got free teas."

Unfortunately, before Emily could discover whether Ivy had been a lucky occupant of a shilling seat she heard a movement on the stairs above.

"Ivy, why aren't you getting on?" Mrs Walker demanded. "I don't think Mr Walker wants to hear you spend all your time gossiping rather than doing the work you are paid for. Now get on – or do you consider everything already spick and span?"

"No, Ma'am. I'm sorry. I'll get right on." To show she was serious, and to avoid further reprimand, Ivy moved away up the staircase, polishing vigorously.

"And Emily, why are you wasting your time here? Miss Ferguson is due within the quarter hour."

Emily's heart sank. The image of free teas in the shilling seats was replaced by thoughts of her governess' arrival. "I am ready, Mother," she replied, trying to deflect the criticism. She prayed this was Miss Ferguson's last lesson. Her mother had hinted that her education might be elsewhere after the summer. Girls much younger than her attended a new school in Marlborough Avenue, whilst others went to the High School.

"Make sure you are ready, Emily! I'm just going to check on Alice. I hope someone in this house is being useful."

Once her mother had gone, Emily gave a heartfelt sigh. Her brothers didn't have to suffer Miss Ferguson. Both were at Hymers College and Emily had attended several school prize-givings there. They learned such exciting things, she thought. On occasion, she'd persuaded Edward to bring books home for her, though she always had to run errands in return. But brothers expected this service from sisters anyway, and it was no use grumbling to her mother. No, it was only girls who suffered Miss Ferguson. Her main ability was to turn anything interesting into a matter of the utmost tedium. In her presence time moved at a glacial pace. Miss Ferguson made comments such as "Bookishness is a bad sign in a girl". When she told Aunt Eleanor about this, her aunt had replied "Poppycock!" and given her a copy of *The Jungle Book* to read. Thinking of her aunt, Emily couldn't help smiling. The jangling of the door-bell brought her back to the present. Why, oh why, couldn't she go to a proper school? Why couldn't she study proper subjects? Why couldn't she pass examinations and become a... She realised Miss Ferguson was talking to her.

"Good morning, Emily."

"Good morning, Miss Ferguson," Emily replied, before reluctantly following her nemesis into the dining room.

August
Bridlington

Tomorrow was their last day and it wasn't fair, thought Emily. Then she smiled despite herself. On such a sunny afternoon it was impossible to feel downhearted. The waves lapped gently on the beach, and out in the bay Bridlington's entire fleet of cobles, pleasure boats and skiffs was plying its trade.

Last Thursday, however, could not have been more different. Anyone venturing out on the sea then would have put their lives at risk. The day had dawned with a threatening, overcast sky. The absence of beach-bound donkeys at breakfast-time had suggested that the weather could be expected to deteriorate further. The strengthening wind had shifted into the north-east, bringing ferocious squalls that forced people to scurry for shelter.

That day, Emily watched from the imposed safety of her bedroom, which had a grandstand view of the proceedings.

A number of hats bowled along at high speed down the parade, accompanied by a few parasols. As high tide approached, waves pounded the sea wall, driving the water skywards in magnificent plumes of spray before plummeting down on the far side of the promenade. Some young men, hoping to impress their sweethearts, dashed along, timing their runs between waves to avoid a soaking. Several had misjudged it and been drenched. The full force of a wave knocked one clean off his feet, but two of his fellows rushed forwards and hauled him away from the edge. They passed beneath Emily's window, laughing and slapping each other's backs.

Rain swept in with ever-increasing intensity, driving the few remaining hardy souls away from the front. At its heaviest, land and sea merged as one.

By early afternoon as the tide turned, the ferocious sea eased, the black clouds softened to grey and a watery sun broke through. Emily and Aunt Eleanor negotiated the enormous puddles covering the promenade. Battened down stalls reopened, steam rising from their canvas roofs as the sun gathered strength.

"We deserve a treat." Aunt Eleanor pointed at Reuben Williamson's horse omnibus. "Come on, if we're quick we'll catch that one to the Old Town. Shall we risk upstairs? It may be somewhat wet, but we don't mind, do we?" Emily agreed with pleasure. On the top deck they could sit next to the driver.

Ten enjoyable minutes later they disembarked, only a little damp, in the Market Place. Aunt Eleanor led her past the Black Lion and into High Street, where a great variety of buildings, some grand, some small, hugged its narrow pavements. After a short while her aunt stopped. "Here we are."

Emily looked in bemusement at William Milner's ironmongery display of pots and pans. "No dear, behind you. A new kettle hardly qualifies as a treat." Emily turned and read the words on the sign above the shop door - 'J. Braithwaite - Bookseller'. There were so many books stacked behind the dusty panes that seeing inside was impossible. They crossed the narrow street and Emily circumnavigated the boxes obstructing the doorway.

"New and second-hand," Eleanor said. "Now, I think I know what I want, but one can never be sure. Have a good look around." Emily surveyed the overflowing shelves with some trepidation. "It's impossible to spend too much time in a bookshop." Eleanor smiled. "Your mother has never understood that. She likes to read, but she's never learnt to browse. She's always found it difficult to make up her mind when purchasing things, but that's not browsing. Your father – in more ways than one – is a different matter altogether."

It wasn't always clear what her aunt meant when talking about her family, but Emily loved the way conversations leapt around. It was as if her aunt were thinking out loud. Though sometimes confused, Emily enjoyed it. The important thing was that her aunt's company was so stimulating and enjoyable when compared to her parents'.

"What I like most about these places, Emily, is searching for a particular book and coming across something totally different. Finding what you didn't know you wanted is the real excitement."

This struck Emily as strange and complicated.

"But how do you do it, Aunt?"

"Always have a good rummage. Of course you may be disappointed – you won't always find a treasure. But too many people are stick-in-the-muds, Emily: they know what they like and like what they know. They miss out on gems by not taking risks. And not only with books, you know!"

"I'll try not to get stuck in the mud, Aunt," Emily said, before giving in to the smile tugging at the corners of her mouth.

Her aunt's smile suggested she'd said the right thing. "Let's see what we can find. I've something particular in mind – if Mr Braithwaithe has a nice copy of it. Your mother might think you are not old enough yet and that it's more suited for Edward, but we shall see about that. It is a very exciting read, though I might save it for your next birthday!"

How infuriating, thought Emily. Looking forward to a present was fun, but there were limits. She'd just had her birthday, so that meant waiting almost a year.

"Don't look so serious, dear." Eleanor laughed. "Perhaps Christmas might be possible. Now, pick something for yourself, but by someone you've never read before," adding, with a twinkle in her eye, "and something unexpected for me perhaps."

Her aunt's condition ruled out E.Nesbit and Frances Hodgson Burnett and finding something for her aunt would not be easy. The bookshop was small and poorly lit but the atmosphere was welcoming. The proprietor, presumably Mr. J. Braithwaite, sat at a small table, writing by the light of a lamp. Emily was tempted to seek his advice, but decided to rely on her own instincts.

There was no obvious logic to the way in which the books were arranged, so she started in the darkest, most mysterious corner. The gilt lettering on a black leather-bound book caught her eye. The little book with its raised bands on its spine seemed full of potential and its title, *Scrambles amongst the Alps 1860-69,* certainly sounded more promising than its neighbours - *How to lay out a Small Garden* and *Old Age Pensions and the Aged Poor*.

She opened it at random, to see a startling engraving entitled 'In attempting to pass the corner I slipped and fell'. A man was hurtling backwards down a vertical snow slope, followed by his hat and stick. Emily read the accompanying text; 'I whirled downwards ... striking my head four or five times ... a leap of fifty or sixty feet ... brought me to a halt... on the verge of a precipice... ten feet more would have taken me in one gigantic leap of eight hundred feet onto the glacier below.' Emily gasped. Goodness, this was it. This adventurer's derring-do would entrance her Aunt.

Flushed with success, she sought her own prize. She concentrated on books with pictures engraved on their outsides, a common characteristic of books in her collection. Her aunt's strict rules disqualified her first choice, *Sara Crewe* by F. Hodgson-Burnett. She'd just decided she wasn't very good at browsing when she found it – the book she wanted herself. At the bottom of a jumbled-up, higgledy-piggledy box lay *Castle Blair*. She opened it and read the first paragraph:

'It was raining hard. Night had closed in already round Castle Blair. In the park, the great trees like giant ghosts loomed gloomily indistinct through the dim atmosphere. Not a sound was to be heard but the steady down-pour of the descending rain, and, from time to time, a long, slow shudder of trees as the night wind swept over the park.'

She especially liked the idea of trees as giant ghosts. She had never heard of the author, Flora Shaw, but she was sure she would keep her entertained.

She took her choices to her aunt, who was deep in conversation with the proprietor.

"I've found some books, Aunt. I just hope the one for you is suitable."
Emily was having second thoughts. What if her aunt had read it, or disliked
it? She hadn't checked the price; what if it were too expensive?

"Don't worry," Eleanor replied. "I'm sure you've chosen well. Give your
books to Mr Braithwaithe."

They returned on Mr Williamson's bus and found a shelter on the Es-
planade.

"Shall we see your choices?" Eleanor asked, smiling.

Emily clutched them, unsure which to display first. "This is for you," she
said.

Her aunt carefully unwrapped the parcel. "Splendid! I haven't read it,"
she exclaimed. "Mr Whymper's famous account of his exploits on the Matterhorn! Fascinating! And there's even an inscription, a little faded but in a
precise hand. 'For James Mahoney. In thanks for your care and fidelity with
my designs, E.W. London 1871'. You've found me a real treasure. But what
did you choose for yourself?"

Emily passed her selection over. "I tried to follow your advice, and it
took my fancy. Do you know it?"

"Yes, it's quite enchanting and I'm sure you'll enjoy it. I had a copy when
I was young. I shall look forward to discussing it with you when you've read
it." She took out her small pocket watch. "Look at the time. Your mother
will be becoming agitated, so we should be getting back."

The beach now could not be more different from that Thursday morning. Edward was at the shoreline, whilst her parents were nearby. Her aunt
had disappeared somewhere, and David was attending the cycling meet at
the Recreation Ground. At least he wasn't in one of those silly walking
races, like the one held for grocers last week. She'd never seen such a collection of men – pumping their arms and legs in such an eccentric manner,
and all with red perspiring faces, knobbly knees and large stomachs sticking
out above long baggy shorts. She started to laugh out loud at the memory,
before seeing that her father was asleep. He, having had a good lunch, continued snoring in his deckchair.

The sand felt cool between her toes. Thank goodness she'd been allowed to take her shoes. and stockings off. Her father must be so hot,

dressed in the same thick worsted suit, high stiff collar and tie that he wore to the office.

Emily always felt slightly nervous when their paths crossed. At home, her father spent long hours at the bank and in the evening he retired to his study and smoked cigars. They generally met only at meal times at the weekend, where Emily was not expected to contribute to discussions or ask questions – such as why was the bottle of Lee and Perrins sauce for his personal use only?

On holiday, there were more opportunities for uneasy meetings between them. Their conversation about the Waterloo Pierrots she'd seen at the children's corner was typical. She'd described their fine black and white costumes and their funny antics. Instead of responding he'd asked her about the Municipal Orchestra concert at the Floral Hall. Emily had spent her time there studying the display of large ferns and palms which appeared to be growing out of Miss Elsie Hope's head. However, she had agreed that the soprano's performance of *The Jewel Song* was 'a musical delight'. At least he was happy for her to enjoy the seaside entertainments, and Aunt Eleanor's company, yet she also remembered that incident from last week.

#

Her father's raised voice drifted out of the doorway. "These are unfit to be on sale to any decent members of the public. They are quite disgraceful!"

Intrigued, Emily stopped examining the bric-a-brac in the shop window and listened hard.

"I don't like them either, but it's nothing to do with me." An unknown female voice answered. "You'll have to ask…" Emily strained to hear, as the words became indistinct.

"Mother?" Emily said. "I know I said I didn't want any postcards, but perhaps I do. Edward's inside choosing some, so I thought I might go in and…"

"No, Emily you can't!" her mother interrupted. "In fact, I think we should wait for your father elsewhere."

Before she could act on this, a new voice, this time male, spoke.

"Yes, I *can* see. A gentleman wearing civilian clothes is kissing a young lady wearing a regulation bathing costume. I am not sure what harm there is in that! *You* are the first person to complain. In fact, it is one of the most popular cards we stock so I suggest you take your custom elsewhere!"

Moments later, her father appeared with Edward in his wake.

"Clara, take the children back to the hotel. I will join you later." He took a few steps then turned. "I am going to find a constable... disgraceful, quite disgraceful." With that, he strode away down the street.

"Emily! Edward! You heard what your father said. We shall return to the hotel." Her mother set off before either of them could respond. Emily regarded her mother's back in frustration. What had happened? She glanced across at Edward. He smirked at her with a self-satisfied smile before drawing his fingers across his lips. Then he repeated the gesture.

"Beast," she mouthed.

He seemed delighted by this and raised a single finger to make a shush sign.

She could not think of a response so glared at him and stuck her tongue out.

"Emily! What are you doing?"

"Sorry, Mother. Nothing."

Edward grinned at her.

Even a few evenings later, sitting in the lounge of the hotel, Emily was still none the wiser. The more she asked Edward, the more he pretended that it was a big secret and he wasn't allowed to tell. She put her book down as she became aware of her aunt speaking.

"Clara, if Alfred wants to waste his afternoon in the magistrate's court, that's up to him. It all strikes me as a little ridiculous. They were just harmless postcards, after all."

"Well, the magistrate agreed with Alfred, Eleanor. A shilling fine for the girl and ten for him." Her mother paused. "Emily, look at the time. It's well past your bedtime. Upstairs, now please."

"Mother, it's not that late."

"Emily! Bedtime!"

She rose and the rest of the conversation remained unheard.

#

Now, at half past two, bedtime was a long way away and Emily decided to see what Edward was doing.

"May I paddle, Mother?" she asked. "Edward's there so I'll be all right." She placed her favourite white beret on her head, rolled up her skirt and, with her white petticoat just above her knees, set off to negotiate the larger family groups and the uncomfortable areas of pebbles between her and the sea.

She stopped near her brother, who acknowledged her but made it clear he was not to be interrupted.

"I'm doing an experiment, so don't disturb me, Emily!"

Was this linked to his oft-quoted ambition to be a scientist? She considered offering her services as an assistant, but seeing the intense concentration on his face, decided not to. He was counting silently to himself, then as a wave washed up on the beach he moved to its high point.

"What are you doing, Edward?" she said, risking his wrath. When no reply came, she repeated the question.

He realised he would get no peace unless he answered. "I'm estimating where every tenth wave will reach on the sand. Now, go away!"

The sand was wet, cleansed by the receding tide. It was perfect for building sandcastles. Edward had explained at breakfast his plans for the competition on their last afternoon. He had a complicated, elaborate design in mind, involving a model of the harbour as well as a castle. Emily was looking forward to the tide returning to demolish his creation.

She pressed a foot down. Why did the sand around her feet change from wet to dry when she did that? She dug her heels in, pushing her feet in until they disappeared. Edward said that large toe-pinching crabs lurked under the sand. Unlike last summer, she didn't believe him. The waves washed around her feet, each wave edge made up of tiny frothy bubbles that popped until none were left. She ventured out a little further holding her petticoat and jumping as the waves came in. She looked back up the beach. Her father, now awake, was talking to her mother. Emily's mind went back to the conversation that had taken place in the hotel lounge before lunch. Her father had been speaking to her aunt.

"I'm afraid, Eleanor, you won't be surprised to hear that I believe that your views on this, as on many other issues, fly in the face of common sense. Just look at that ribbon you're sporting. Purple, white and green! I thought you favoured their red, white and green competitors? I saw their blessed caravan down on the promenade. Some woman on the step spouting forth and a whole series of propaganda tracts on display. It's a fine thing when a person on holiday can't escape such nonsense."

"You won't be attending then?" Eleanor replied. "The vanners' meeting is at half past six by the lamp-post outside the Britannia Hotel. I'm sure Miss Gardner and Miss Robertson would welcome your views. They're good speakers, you know. You might find the views of a recent Cambridge History graduate illuminating. Consider it to be an agreeable aperitif before dinner! I would be quite happy for you to accompany me."

"I shall not be attending. Lamp-post indeed! The only thing I would gain from going is indigestion. I am not the least bit surprised that you know these women. The next thing I'll hear is that your blessed doctor friend is holidaying here."

"You mean Murdie? No, she's far too busy, and not just with campaigning and meetings. If you need proof, Alfred, of the advantages of a quality education for girls, then look no further than the city's first female GP."

"That's all very well, Eleanor. I was talking about what's best for girls from comfortable circumstances. The demands of being educated for the drawing room are completely incompatible with what is required to educate someone for the wider world. I do admit, however, that those suggesting too much learning damages the brain fibres that control women's femininity may be misguided."

"We can agree on that last point, Alfred. But Emily should have been at a proper school long before now. And she's had that dreadful woman for far too long!"

"I'm sorry, Eleanor, you are going too far there," her mother interjected. "She came with the highest recommendations and we've been more than satisfied. Alfred has, however, decided that Emily can start at the High School after the summer."

Emily was startled to receive such important news like this. Before she could react, her father continued. "Yes, I am happy for Emily to start at school, but certainly not for her to damage her chances of marriage by going on to higher education. I know that's what you recommend, Eleanor, but in my opinion it's a most outlandish view."

The gong had rung at that point, and the conversation in the dining room had moved on to other topics.

She watched the waves lapping past her legs. A new school! Just think of that!

"Emily!" Edward shouted. "Mother says come on out. Aunt Eleanor is back and she's found something exciting for us to see on the South Beach. Hurry up!"

Emily made her way back, and once she had dried her feet and put on her shoes and stockings, she accompanied her family along the front and round the harbour past the now deserted quays. Earlier in the week, they had overflowed with women busy cleaning, gutting and packing fish into barrels of salt. They had been a strange sight, and had sounded even stranger. Gaelic speakers, following the herring, her aunt had said. And now they were all gone.

"Come on, Emily. Don't dawdle," her mother said.

"Yes, we don't want to miss it because of you, do we?" added Edward.

Emily hurried after her brother, still unsure what 'it' was. After a few minutes they stopped where a poster proclaimed 'The Dangerous and Amazing Exploits of the Famous Professor Gaudion'.

"This way, we'll get the best view from up here," Eleanor announced. "And Alfred, I hope you won't be too affronted if you let me pay our sixpences."

"By all means, Eleanor," he replied. "No, by all means."

Their sixpences duly paid, Emily followed her family through into the New Spa Gardens.

September
Westbourne Avenue

Emily walked back up the Avenue with her mother. Emily enjoyed shopping, but there were eight drapers on Princes Avenue and her mother had been overcome by indecisiveness in each one. Her search for curtain material had finally ended when they had returned to the first shop and purchased the attractive pale chintz that Emily favoured.

Nearing home, they overtook Mr Roper, the milkman. His horse, Tommy, a grey, was Emily's favourite amongst the many that she regularly saw, so she hurried on to find an apple for him. Having retrieved one from the barrel in the scullery, Emily found that she wasn't the only person interested in Tommy. Mr Barber, who gardened for them and for several neighbours, was busy with his shovel.

"Morning there, young Miss," he said, unbending his back and stretching. He grinned at her.

"This here is for next door's roses. Very particular they are about their roses, so nothing but the best, and this is some of the best," he said, offering her a view of his steaming bucket. Emily, not wishing to be impolite, peered in, wrinkling her nose before turning her attention to the horse.

"He likes sugar best, if you've got any," a voice from behind her said. "At least he used to."

The boy from next-door was leaning over his garden gate. It was the first time she'd seen him since that brief glimpse on the first day. He was a couple of years older than her and his pale complexion was in stark contrast to his dark hair. He had a pleasant smile and, best of all, he wasn't regarding her in that superior way her brothers and their acquaintances sometimes did.

"He likes anything sweet," she answered, as the horse took the apple from her outstretched palm. She patted him one last time then watched as Mr Roper fitted Tommy's nose-bag on. She crossed the verge and went over to the boy. "You're Robert, aren't you? You were sitting under your apple tree, the afternoon we moved in. I haven't seen you since, though. I'm Emily, by the way."

"I know," Robert began. "And I've just come back. At the start of the holidays, I was at my Aunt Edith's on the South Bank and I caught measles."

"How horrid," Emily replied. Catching measles was serious. At best, it meant an unpleasant couple of weeks in a darkened bedroom, and everyone knew of someone who'd been seriously ill or even died of the disease. "Was it very bad? You do look pale."

"I was quite poorly," he said, suggesting it had been a severe case. "I spent most of the summer there, with convalescing." He paused. "And you're right about me being pale – my father said he thought he'd seen a ghost." He added with a laugh, "So I look in the mirror every morning to make sure I haven't disappeared." Emily found herself joining in with his laughter. "But I wouldn't have missed this summer, even with the measles, what with the great excitement in New Holland."

Emily could think of nothing worth catching measles for.

"Do you get the *Mail*?" he said. "It was in last week." Before he could continue, her mother came out of the house and interrupted the conversation.

"It's Robert, isn't it? Are you feeling better? Your mother said you'd be back in time for school."

"Yes, much better, thanks, Mrs Walker. I missed the first few days, but I'll soon catch up. My mother says the colour is finally coming back to my cheeks."

"I'm glad to hear that, Robert." She smiled. "Is she in? She called earlier. I said I'd help her on Hospital Saturday."

"Yes she is. I'll go and find her." He reappeared a few moments later. "She says please do come in, and bring Emily too, if she'd like to."

"Well, Emily?"

"Yes please, Mother," she replied following her in. Whereas her mother went into the drawing room, she and Robert were given shortbread and freshly made lemonade to take into the garden, where Mr Barber was busy amongst the roses. He stopped, wiped his brow, puffed and gave them a meaningful look. "Fair thirsty work and no mistake, this is. A man could get parched."

Robert who got on well with him, knew a strong hint when he heard one. "Would you like a glass of lemonade, Mr Barber? I can fetch another glass."

"Very thoughtful of you, Master Robert. I wouldn't say no to a drink and if there's any shortbread, I might manage some of that too."

"I won't be long, Emily," Robert said, smiling. "There's some things I want from my bedroom too."

With Mr Barber refreshed and back at work, Robert and Emily sat on the bench encircling the apple tree. He passed her a page from a newspaper.

Emily scanned the headlines. 'Maniac with Two Razors... Brother tackles him' caught her eye. No, it wouldn't be something gruesome like that. "Oh, you mean this," she said. "'Dropped From The Skies... Balloon on New Holland House... Aeronauts Kiss Each Other.'" There was a drawing of two men and a large basket stuck on a roof.

"You saw them? Was it your aunt's house? Was anyone hurt? And who are the men?"

He'll think me hare-brained, she thought, as the questions came out in such a rush.

"Shall I tell you what happened?" He grinned. "Or you can always read about it instead."

"I *could* take it home. Edward would be interested. Have you met him? But he's out, and I don't know where. He never tells me anything, which is very unfair, so perhaps you should tell me first."

He smiled, "I agree. I'll tell you. You can borrow it for your brother. I haven't met him yet. I'm at the Grammar School." He took two objects out of his pocket and placed them on the bench. "It was two o'clock on the Saturday afternoon. I was in the fields behind my aunt's house. She's keen on fresh air, so I was outside as I was feeling better, and that was when I saw it... a large balloon coming straight towards me. It wasn't high, fifty, perhaps seventy feet, from the ground and it only just cleared a line of trees."

"Were you by yourself?" Emily interrupted.

"No, a few others were about. As it came closer I saw two men inside the basket. They'd thrown out cords, perhaps two hundred yards long with large metal grapples on the ends, one of which caught in a hedge. Both men were shouting, but I couldn't understand. It wasn't French; I've done some at school so I can recognise it. But they were very excited. You know why?"

Emily shrugged and looked puzzled.

"You've been to the South Bank? The ferry?"

Emily shook her head.

"You should. It's best at night when there's a full moon. The men were only a few hundred yards from the river. Sam Wrack, the butcher's assistant, was nearest. He and some others grabbed one of the lines and everyone shouted for them to descend. But then the grapple came loose! Everyone, except Sam, let go and he was soon twenty foot in the air. You should have heard him scream!"

Emily was transfixed.

"He didn't know whether to hold on or not. Luckily the balloon descended again and he was able to let go. But he had a young lady companion and her clothes caught in the grapple. She had a lucky escape, except," he paused, "her skirts were torn off."

Emily's hand shot to her mouth. How dreadful!

"Do go on, Robert."

Robert sipped his lemonade. "The wind shifted and the balloon drifted towards the houses in Summercroft Avenue. Everyone ran after it, shouting. It was so exciting. And then it crashed into a row of cottages, knocking all their chimney pots off. There was soot everywhere. It came to rest with the basket hanging down one side of the house and the balloon on the other – that's what's in the picture. Unfortunately it wasn't my aunt's house. Of course," he laughed, "she might not agree. The aeronauts were agitated and the balloon had collapsed. One tried climbing through the bedroom window, then someone put ladders up. When they reached the ground, they kissed and hugged and everyone cheered."

"What were you doing?"

"Cheering, like everyone else. But guess where they'd come from?"

Emily thought. "Lincoln?"

"No. Paris! All the way from Paris! Just think of that: all the way from Paris!"

Emily was unsure how far away Paris was, and whether it was an unusual feat to travel from there by balloon, but she tried to look impressed.

"But you said they weren't French."

"It's true. They weren't. They were Italians. And before you ask, look at this."

He gave her one of the items on the bench. On a page torn from a notebook was written in scrawled handwriting: 'Alfred Von Willer, Ettore Cianetti, L'Elfe 1850m3'.

"Are those their names? But there are three. Von Willer, Cianetti." She glanced at Robert. He wasn't laughing at her pronunciation. "L'Elfe. But the numbers?"

"L'Elfe is the balloon's name; 1850 its size. And yes, those are their names. When they left the garden, they were signing pieces of paper and I had my notebook with me."

Emily had her own small autograph book and felt jealous at his having captured signatures from such exotic creatures. "Carry on, Robert," she said.

"They spoke some English. It was a race. They'd reached four thousand feet when they crossed into England. Think what the earth must look like from up there. And how far you could see!"

Emily hazarded a guess. "Would it be miles? Hundreds of miles?"

"And it's in the paper. They came second. Some Canadians or Americans who landed near Whitby won, but my aeronauts came second!" It was as if he was sharing in their achievement. "And that's what I want to do."

"What? Land on top of a house in a balloon?"

"No, Emily. Don't be silly. Be an aeronaut and see the world from up there, like the Italians. Have you read *The First Men in the Moon*?"

"No, but Edward's keen on that sort of thing."

"I'd go in a special airship." He laughed. "I know there's no air! But I'd see what's on the far side of the moon."

"But wouldn't it be dark?"

"Only when it's a full moon here. It would be fun. You can come too if you like. But I haven't the foggiest idea of how to become an aeronaut; so don't worry about packing for it just yet. Here, look at this." He gave Emily a rectangular piece of grey silk. "It's part of the balloon. Everybody took some, until a constable turned up." Robert puffed out his cheeks impersonating the policeman. "Everyone here is to stop their peculations... this instance! I thought of giving the silk back, but it was such a prize and the Italians didn't mind. I'm thinking of framing it, with the autographs, for my bedroom wall."

Emily thought of describing the two samplers she had on her wall, but then remembered something he would be interested in. "I saw a balloon recently too," she began. Good, she had his attention. "We go to Bridlington for our holidays and my Aunt Eleanor took us all to the New Spa. The gardens were crowded, but I still had an excellent view. A French Professor, Edward would remember his name, it began with G, had a balloon. Gaudion, I think. It was tied to something but it rose up into the air, and when it got really high, he jumped out and came down on a parachute and landed with an enormous splash in the sea. Edward counted and he took twenty-nine seconds to come down; Edward likes details like that. Anything to do with numbers. Mother says when he was little, he used to count to a hundred to himself, but over and over again and then he'd announce he'd reached ten thousand or some such figure. So if Edward said twenty-nine seconds, it *was* exactly twenty-nine seconds. The Professor was picked up in a boat and everyone clapped and cheered and even though he was dripping wet, he bowed like this. I normally only curtsey."

She performed the lowest bow she could. Robert clapped as she came back up, making her feel both embarrassed and pleased.

"I wish I'd been there, Emily. What an amazing spectacle."

To Emily's disappointment, her mother then came out. "We should be going, Emily. And Robert, do come round soon and meet Edward. Now Emily, thank Robert for his kindness."

"Thank you, Robert, for the lemonade and biscuits ... and for the balloons."

Back at home her mother gave her a puzzled look. "What did you mean about balloons, Emily?"

"Mean, Mother? Nothing, of course, though I might go in an airship to the far side of the moon one day."

October

Westbourne Avenue

Dear Aunt Eleanor,

Thank you for your letter. I was worried that you might not get mine, but Mother says she knows an address where you will be at some point and she will send it there. A caravan sounds so exciting. You are lucky. I wish I were there too. Mr Barber has been worrying about early October frosts so it must be a bit chilly at nights, but I could pack extra clothes if I ever had the chance to stay in a caravan.

I'm glad you liked my last letter about school. It's hard to imagine that Miss Ferguson ever existed! You will be pleased to know that I still love it. I have been given a rather odd essay to do for homework – about 'Root vegetables'. We have a week and are allowed to change the title a little so I have decided on 'Why root vegetables should stay in the ground!'. I could have asked Mr Barber for ideas, but I made the mistake of mentioning it to Edward instead. He has been so irritating ever since. Little notes have been appearing under my door. They say things like 'Perfectly Perfect Parsnips' and 'Terribly Terrific Turnips'. The most recent says 'You Can't Beat Beetroot!' I tried my best to ignore them, but he kept putting PSRV at the end. It was so annoying. Everyone knows it's RSVP (Répondez s'il vous plaît). After the latest one I had to say something to him. He looked at me as if I had escaped from a lunatic asylum, and said, 'Emily, I wasn't expecting a reply. I thought you must know that PSRV means 'Please Save Root Vegetables.' And with that he burst out laughing. I was so annoyed. I was more annoyed with myself than him though, for being caught out again.

I have suggested to Alice that she writes a book of recipes. I don't see why she shouldn't, do you? She is a very good cook, after all, which is something which we should all be thankful for, as Mother says. I offered to provide a list of ideas. I was a little disappointed that she wasn't more enthusiastic. She should do it in alphabetical order - A for Apple Cake, B for Bread and Butter Pudding (I know it's not everyone's favourite, but it's mine), C for Chicken (Roasted), D for Damson Jam and so on. I would be grateful if you have any suggestions for X and Z. The title could be 'Alice's Alphabetical Cookery Book'. I will let you know if she ever agrees.

Is it worth my trying to persuade Mother, (well, Father really), that we should have a cat? Now that we've moved it seems ideal. What is the point of a larger house when you can't fill it with things that you like? I think describing a cat as an unnecessary, pointless expense is missing the point, don't you? Edward would like a dog and David would like a motorbike, so I have no great hopes of help from them. I have thought of some possible names for a cat, just in case. Everyone chooses such boring ones, Blackie, Ginger and so on. I have decided on Pudding, but would call her Pud for short. She would be a tabby. I love them. Oh dear, I might have to wait until I am old and grey or at least thirty until I can have one. Have you ever thought of having one? You are away too often, I suppose. Ivy said her sister had a problem with vermin and they were looking for a good mouser. Weren't you saying something to Father, when we were away, about the ends justifying the means? I think it means if you wanted a good thing to happen then you were allowed to do less good things to get it. Would it be wrong to attract some vermin in order to get a good mouser here?

Perhaps you can tell me what you think when you write (if you have time) or when I next see you. I hope the rest of your caravan trip goes well. I think you said something about it being a good idea for people to do as many different things as they could, if they ever had the chance. I have never been in a caravan – though, with the nights drawing in, Alice does not think it is a good idea and if I am honest Mother is unlikely to either.

Your affectionate niece,
Emily
xxx

P.S. I have just read what I have written and I have not said much about why root vegetables should stay in the ground! I hope you don't mind. I hope to see you soon.

P.P.S. I shall keep a copy of my essay for you!

August 4th, 1914
Westbourne Avenue

"How are you this morning, Ivy?" asked Emily, coming downstairs for breakfast. "Did you manage a good day yesterday?"

"Yes I am, Miss. Fine, that is. And as to yesterday... our plans were all disrupted, so we ended up going to that Hussars display. Very good, it were. One Hussar cut right through a hanging sheep with one blow of his sword. It were already dead, Miss, in case you thought it wasn't. Still, I wish North Eastern hadn't cancelled all its excursions. Put paid to me and Bert's trip to Filey. How stopping day trips can have anything to do with all this, I don't know. But if they say they need excursion trains then they must know best. It's very strange, Miss." Ivy shook her head.

Emily agreed. Things were moving so fast. The *Mail* had published its first ever Sunday edition, and 'Great War by Land, Air and Sea' had been emblazoned across last night's front page. "I know, Ivy, I have been reading about it, but we're not at war yet."

"Well, I'm sure I don't know what'll happen, Miss, and maybe nothing'll come of it, but whatever Mr Asquith or that Kaiser fellow does, one thing that won't change is this cleaning, so if you don't mind, Miss..."

"Sorry, Ivy, I'll get out of your way".

Was Ivy right to think there might not be a war? Edward's copy of *The Riddle in the Sands* was full of spies and German plots to invade England, and his copies of *Magnet* consisted of stories of brave young men going off to war, overcoming great hardship before emerging victorious. Perhaps Edward saw himself like that, but he was away, bossing around all those younger School Scouts in Weltondale.

Her mother and David were in the breakfast room.

"Father's left early, Mother."

"Yes, dear. These extra bank holidays mean more rather than less work, so he's gone in even though they're closed."

"If everyone presumed they've got extra days off, that would be chaotic," David said. "It's hardly what the government has in mind. Maintaining stability is imperative." He sipped his coffee. "Bound to be dreadful problems. I mean who'll replace all these reservists being called up?"

Since returning from Oxford, David sounded more and more like her father. Hearing them discuss the Bank Rate was not a positive development. But he wasn't her father!

"You're against it then, David? Alice's family were at Paragon Station at five o'clock on Saturday morning giving a good send-off to her brother and the rest of the naval reservists." Emily saw she'd surprised him, because he seemed lost for words. Challenging him was quite satisfying.

"I'm sure David didn't meant that at all, Emily."

Her mother sounded a little flustered, but David soon regained his composure. "No, Mother, I'd hate Emily to think I don't support any necessary measures in a national crisis." Believing this to be the end of the matter, he resumed spreading a thick layer of marmalade on his toast.

"So should we go to war then, David?" she continued, risking maternal disapproval.

Her brother brushed away a crumb from the corner of his mouth. "Undoubtedly. War's inevitable, unless Germany withdraws from Belgium today. And that won't happen. Germany's set on the path of war. I agree with Father that a war will be a struggle between morality and barbarism."

"So it's a clash between polar opposites who..."

"Emily, do get on with your breakfast rather than worrying about such things."

"Yes, Mother, but David said..."

"Emily!"

To all appearances calm descended, though Emily's thoughts were anything but. How would a war affect them? She felt guilty that her first concern was next week's trip with Aunt Eleanor. Convincing her father to let her go had been hard enough. "An unwarranted indulgence. A seaside holiday should be enough!" Would he consider it unpatriotic to go?

"Mother... do you think?" No. Better not to ask. The way she'd been glancing at David – was she worrying? David had been, and Edward still was, in the Hymers Cadet Corp. Edward looked so smart in his scarlet tunic and dark blue trousers, but wouldn't he be too young to join up? How many men would they need? Perhaps there were enough reservists? Alice had said men from all walks of life were being called up; The Three Aeros trapeze artists had not appeared at the Palace Theatre for that very reason.

She wanted to tell Robert about the missing acrobats, but he was at his aunt's. He'd enjoy speculating about how trapeze artists might be used by the armed forces. And what about Robert and the close friendship that had developed between them? Robert enjoyed her company and considered her capable of intelligent conversation. If she asked questions, it wasn't proof of female stupidity. Unlike Edward, he would concede defeat when bested in an argument. She regretted telling school friends about this as since then she'd suffered endless teasing about her passion for Robert. Did she have a passion? How was she meant to know? If she did, it was nothing like what she'd read about in novels. There was no-one to discuss it with. Her mother was the last person she would ever dream of asking – and even if she did, her mother's main preoccupation when giving advice was to emphasise the importance of things like not drinking too much tea when visiting someone's house so as to avoid social embarrassment.

"And what are your plans, Emily?" her mother asked, interrupting Emily's thoughts.

"I'm meeting Aunt Eleanor in the park later, but nothing besides that."

"Could you call in at the grocers? The delivery boy forgot Alice's flour. And check with her that nothing else is missing. Edward's back from camp this afternoon."

After breakfast, Emily returned to her room. On a day like this, she was glad that it was at the rear of the house. She pushed the net curtains to one side and enjoyed the sun streaming in. How the view had changed since that first day! The greatest difference lay in the middle distance where the roofs and upstairs windows of new houses in Marlborough Avenue were visible. Nearer to her, the garden was now well established. Mr Barber was busy at work tying in the sweet peas. She must pick some for her room; their heady aroma was intoxicating.

She turned, lay down on the bed and surveyed the samplers on the wall. Her mother's was downstairs, but these were her grandmother's and great grandmother's. She'd met neither, but had heard stories about them. The samplers were a connection. The smaller and simpler was her grandmother's, but Alice Bradwell had been only five when she produced her fine red and green stitches, whereas Elizabeth Read's more complicated black and white endeavour was the work of an eleven year old. Both were superior to Emily's. She'd never pick out twenty-seven tiny stars, each with a hole at its centre, just to make the inch-high letter *N* of *INDUSTRY* like Elizabeth had. She must finish hers, and someday it might hang on some other girl's wall who might daydream about Emily Walker and what she was like.

"Now I need to get ready to go out," she announced, to no-one in particular.

In the hall her mother was busying herself with a flower arrangement.

"Have you checked with Alice?"

"Yes, Mother. She wants some cocoa essence and some syrup of figs, as well as the flour. She's pleased with the new gas cooker, isn't she? It took ten minutes to get away. She insisted on showing me, and she's always complaining about me doing all the chattering."

"She ought to be, what with the expense and the mess of taking the range out. Can you tell your aunt she's welcome to return with you, or to call tomorrow afternoon if that's more convenient – and don't dawdle in any other shops."

At the end of the avenue, Emily turned right into Princes Avenue. Clarkes, the grocer, was near the corner with Spring Bank, in the parade of shops opposite Botanic Gardens station – or Cemetery Gates, as older residents still called it. It was neither the nearest nor the cheapest, but according to her mother it stocked a superior quality of goods. Also, it attracted a better class of customer than its competitors!

The queue in Clarkes seemed endless. One woman's order came to the enormous sum of thirteen pounds, seventeen shillings and sixpence. When it was Emily's turn she explained about the missing flour, not forgetting Alice's extra requests.

"Afraid we've run out, Miss, but more's ordered and the lad'll bring it then. It's gone up a penny, though. And we can't get sugar anywhere – if we do get it, it'll be fourpence, even fivepence a pound." Emily promised to pass the information on. Her brothers both had a sweet tooth, so wouldn't like this news.

A tram in its fine crimson and white livery came towards her as she walked back towards the park. She had an urge to jump on, imagining travelling to somewhere exotic in a literary special – perhaps an Austen special to Netherfield via Mansfield Park and Norland Park – or, better still, in a University special, that might drop her off at London, Girton or Newnham. The tram passed her, heading for the more prosaic King Edward Street terminus in the city centre.

Plenty of horse and carts were about, interspersed with the occasional motorcar. David had a brochure for the Saxon, which claimed to be the world's best cheap car. Unfortunately the hundred and five pound price tag meant that for the foreseeable future, the collection of temperamental motor cycle parts strewn about the floor of a friend's old stable in Victoria Avenue would remain his sole form of motorised transport.

Emily stopped near the railings encircling the Park Grove fountain. As always she glanced up at the sculptured birds on the first tier. Although they were of the same design as those near her house, there was something special about this set of four: standing, waiting, erect with heads held high, cormorant-like, with especially steely, sinister glints in their eyes. The fountains weren't working, but she felt that the birds could come alive, swooping down on anything that took their fancy. Some small trick of the light had placed the idea in her head years ago, and even now that original impression sometimes resonated with her.

She turned and walked down Park Grove taking the route she followed to school, though it would be a few weeks before she put on her blue serge tunic and yellow-trimmed navy blazer again.

She'd been thinking how they must be feeling today, so stopped and looked through the gates at a building of greyish brick: the French Convent. None of the nuns, refugees from growing French anti-clericalism seven years previously, were visible, just a few shrubs and the gravel forecourt leading to the front door.

As a non-Catholic, Emily was excused the early Masses before breakfast every Wednesday morning, and the extra Religious Instruction lessons, but could take the extra Saints Days holidays. She was fond of most of her teachers, even Mother Marie de l'Enfant Jesus, whose impenetrable English accent had made learning French so hard to begin with. Despite this Emily had progressed so well that it was suggested she might study further. Her aunt had excellent German, so perhaps there was a family affinity for languages, but Sister Philomena, the Order's first English postulant, was encouraging Emily towards literature, a direction in which she was happy to be pushed. Emily herself had wondered whether it was possible to combine the two. Discussing this with her parents would not be easy. Her mother's support in persuading her father would be vital, but her belief that the most valuable part of Emily's education came from the half a guinea spent a term on extra Elocution, Deportment and Music was not encouraging. This seemed less important today. One sister came from Moineville, close to the German border. What would she thinking about the news? All the nuns would be in chapel praying, praying to the same God as nuns in Berlin or Vienna. Emily walked on. Hearing a Hornsea-bound train on the level crossing behind her, she realised she'd turned into Park Road without noticing.

Her aunt was near the grand entrance from Beverley Road, with its triumphal arch, and greeted Emily with a kiss.

"I'm not late, Aunt, am I? Have you been waiting long?"

"My feet have been considering putting down roots, so I might end up joining these fine trees." Eleanor smiled. "Experience has taught me that though my favourite niece has many fine qualities, accurate timekeeping isn't amongst them."

"Oh Aunt. That's so unfair." Emily pointed at the part of the French Convent overlooking the park. "I've never been late for school. And Aunt, my guess is that you found something to do, or someone to talk to. I was once told it was impossible to waste time, only opportunities. Now, who said that?"

Eleanor laughed. "I'm pleased you have such an excellent memory, and yes, I was having an interesting conversation with Mr Rees about the difficulties of establishing exotic plants in the conservatory. But let's take our walk."

Emily took her aunt's arm. They set off along the path bisecting the park, passing Mr Rees, who doffed his hat. He cut a distinguished figure, in his fine uniformed jacket with its six finely polished buttons. His smile, fine grey beard and well-tanned face suggested he was of a kindly disposition, but underneath lurked a temper he'd vent on any transgressor of the Park's lengthy list of rules and regulations.

"It wasn't all my fault, Aunt. Being late. I had an errand first. I had such a wait in Clarkes! One woman seemed to be buying their entire stock."

"Yes, Emily, I know. It's not just Clarkes. A woman bought all the dustbins in my ironmongers to fill with flour. I've heard some places are putting limits on what people may spend." She paused. "Unlike much of the populace, I find the current prospect a thoroughly depressing one. There will be ample opportunity for discussing that in the future, however."

Emily was unused to her aunt being so serious.

"So to cheerier things," continued Eleanor. "Passenger services will be running, if a little disrupted, and we'll catch the eight o'clock train. Now think of everything we might do."

Emily dismissed her worries about her father vetoing their plans. "Yes let's do that, Aunt, and shall we see how Mr Rees' plants are faring?"

As they passed the statue of a young Queen Victoria, an acquaintance of her aunt's came hurrying towards them. "Eleanor?" she said. "Excellent, you've saved me an errand. You haven't forgotten the meeting?"

"No, Murdie, I hadn't. It's more important now than ever." She gestured towards Emily. "You've met my niece?"

"The one you wanted in the choir. Yes, I think so." She smiled at Emily. "Must get on, Eleanor. Lots to do! Seven-thirty." And with that she was gone.

"Who was that, Aunt?"

"Dr. Mary Murdoch. A wonderful woman." Before Emily could ask anything, she found herself shepherded into the conservatory, where the discussion turned to her aunt's plans for their trip. By the time they were outside again she'd quite forgotten what she'd meant to ask. They crossed the cast iron bridge which spanned the small serpentine lake. Emily stopped in the middle and leant over. A solid wall of greenery surrounded her. She looked down. Her reflection regarded her from a crystal clear still-ness more typical of an autumnal morning after the first frost than early Au-gust. She was aware of the murmur of people's voices, children's shouts, a dog's high-pitched yapping, her aunt standing next to her, but as she stared, these faded away and she felt drawn to her mirror self. People on ships, she'd heard, had urges to throw themselves overboard, but she wished to preserve the girl in the reflection, not join her. The light behind the girl darkened as a large cloud passed in front the sun. The mirrored surface rippled in an accompanying breeze and the reflection distorted out of all recognition.

"Are you all right, Emily?"

She shuddered. "Yes, thank you, Aunt. I'm fine."

"Are you sure?"

"Honestly, it was nothing. Nothing at all."

They left the bridge, followed the path around the lake and went onto Princes Avenue, where Emily waited for her aunt's tram to arrive.

"Thank your mother for the invitation, Emily. I'll call tomorrow."

Her aunt stepped up into the tram and Emily watched it accelerate away into the patch of sunlight sweeping towards her. The breeze died away as the sun came out.

Back in the park, the lake was once again still, but the reflected girl re-mained lost in it forever.

#

"Edward!" She hadn't heard him approach until he'd put his hands over her eyes. "You're back."

"It's a Painted Lady, Emily, the butterfly you were admiring." He smiled and stepped away from her. "*Cynthia cardui*, if you want its proper name. And it's probably flown here from Spain. They're strong flyers. Amazing for such a small creature."

Emily was unsurprised by his knowledge. She'd seen him with his butterfly net and his killing jar. They looked so much better alive and flitting from flower to flower than pinned out in his neatly labelled collection.

"Did you enjoy ordering all those youngsters around at camp?" She smiled. "I know how they feel. Some of us have had to put up with that for a whole lifetime."

Edward laughed. "What are you referring to, Emily? It's you who's always got her way in this household. Most sisters would be grateful to have a brother who's always fetching and carrying, doing their bidding, treating them with the utmost kindness ... ouch!"

Emily moved as if to pinch him again.

"I surrender. I do." Edward held his hands up in supplication. "And I solemnly declare that I'm the most obnoxious brother any poor girl ever had the misfortune to suffer."

"I'm glad that you've finally realised it, Edward." He gave her one of his most winsome smiles. "In recompense, my best future endeavours will ensure I never irritate you again."

"Hmm, I'll give you the benefit of the doubt," Emily said, her expression suggesting total disbelief. "Did you have a good time?" she said. "You've certainly caught the sun."

"Have I? I hope it doesn't start peeling." He ran a finger along his nose, rubbing off some fragments of loose skin. "That's the outdoor life for you. Still, it was worth it." He sat down in a garden chair and picked up the sampler she'd been working on.

"You've nearly finished. I told mother you'd be old and grey before you did." He studied it. "I don't know what they teach you at that school of yours, but you've missed out J in your alphabet."

"What do you mean, I've missed out J? No! Have I? No, of course I haven't. Edward, you are awful." Emily sighed. It would be different when he started University; no-one would tease her in quite the same way.

"What an expression! You'd think you weren't pleased to see me."

Emily hadn't realised her face was betraying her feelings, but fortunately he'd misinterpreted them. She'd hate him to think she would actually miss him. "Don't be silly. I don't know what you can mean." She smiled. "I can suffer a little more detail about last week, and I'll stop you if you get too boring!"

"I meant it about the outdoor life. You should try it, a week under canvas. But aren't you're going away soon?"

"Aunt Eleanor and I set off on Saturday morning," she replied.

Edward grinned. "There you are. Take a tent. Mr Harrison would lend me one. It would save them packing them all away." He laughed. "I can picture you both struggling to get it up. Perhaps I should come and supervise you."

The idea of camping appealed to her, but like many things it was one of those opportunities she would never have. "That's really thoughtful, Edward. I'll tell her we shall be a party of three. It will mean changing our arrangements, so don't get your hopes up too high. I'd hate to think of you left behind in a flood of tears on Saturday morning." She pursed her lips and shook her head from side to side. "Poor, thwarted Edward."

"Perhaps it's for the best," he replied, taking a step backwards, "I'm not sure I could cope with your snoring, anyway."

Before she could think of a suitable riposte, her attention was distracted. "Look, more of those butterflies." She watched as the Painted Ladies circled each other, spiralling upwards before disappearing next door.

"Seriously, Emily, I'd hate to miss all the excitement. It was terrible, being away and unsure of what's been happening. We saw the army cyclists in town. They looked so splendid in their knee breeches and uniforms with black bugle buttons. Mr Harrison said they were the 5th East Yorkshires. They're so lucky! I wonder where they'll be going?" He sighed. "It'll be over before I get a chance to join in."

"You can't give up the opportunity to go to University! Aren't you excited? I am so envious."

"I suppose I'll go. Don't look so worried! Who knows who'll be wanted? But it's a great shame; I could study any time. Ah, here's Mother."

Their mother came out, deep in conversation with Robert's mother.

"Lady Nunburnholme," Mrs Buckley was saying, "has appealed for kettles, towels, basins, brushes, bedding, anything that might be of use. The collection point's on Spring Bank. Perhaps Alice could find some things?"

"We must have items to spare," her mother replied. "I'll tell Alice. In fact, Emily, can you find her and ask her? Anything we might do without... Edward, there you are..."

Emily left them in conversation and went inside in search of Alice.

#

Emily was brushing her hair in readiness for bed and thinking about the evening. Her father had been preoccupied with various minutiae concerning the bank. He'd wired the Bank of England with his concerns about possible panics and shared his views with all the family. "The most patriotic thing nervous people can do is to act with British level-headedness and leave their unwanted capital where it is." Then he'd spotted a letter in his evening newspaper. "Listen to this," he'd said, adjusting his spectacles. "From a Miss Isabella Richardson... 'All women's suffrage societies be urged to use their organisation for the help of those who will be sufferers from the dislocations caused by this likely war.'" He looked at his wife. "So even Mrs Pankhurst's friends are abandoning their egotistical self-interest to recognise their patriotic duty? Hard to believe but some of these women have a modicum of sense. Pity your sister isn't here to enlighten us on her views." He'd returned to his paper and Emily's mother's comment about her sister being genuinely patriotic had merely produced an explosive mixture of a cough and snort.

Emily placed her brush on her dressing table, picked up her book and got into bed. She started to read, but when she'd read the same page twice without taking it in, she gave up. Her brothers were still out. David had said news of a declaration of war would reach the *Mail* offices in Whitefriargate first. Her mother had been unhappy about Edward going, but he'd been persuasive. Emily sighed and turned out the lamp, but sleep was some time in coming.

#

Loud voices on the landing woke her. She got out of bed and opened her bedroom door. David had disappeared into his room but Edward was outside his.

"Edward. It's you!" She could see his face was flushed with excitement.

"Isn't it magnificent, Emily?" he said, almost breathless in his exhilaration. "I was there when the news came. You should have seen it, you should: the crowds, the cheering, people throwing their hats in the air, the shouts of 'God save the King'. It was magnificent." He shook his head as if in disbelief, "But you'd better get back to bed before mother catches you, and I'll catch it as well for waking you."

He was right. "Goodnight then, Edward, and sleep well." Emily went back into her room. Trying to get to sleep for a second time, Edward's words, as he opened his door, came back to her: "Goodnight Emily. Just think what an adventure we are setting out upon!"

October 20th, 1914
Westbourne Avenue

Dear Edward,

I know you haven't been at University long and haven't had a chance to send letters yet, so I'm writing even though I should be learning the endings for the Past Historic. Here you are - être in the passé simple - je fus, tu fus, il fut, elle fut, on fut, nous fûmes, vous fûtes, ils furent. Without cheating too! When I am racing through Madame Bovary at top speed it will prove to have been all worthwhile. Sorry, I forgot that you hated French, but I do love speaking it. There are some Belgian refugees in the city so I may get to speak it to someone other than a nun.

You must be busy. I am looking forward to hearing about all the interesting things that you have been doing. I have high hopes of you. Please don't disappoint me like David did! Oxford must be a far more exciting place than he ever suggested. He made it sound more like dreary rather than dreaming spires. Imagine being at Christ Church and not being at all interested that Charles Dodgson was there! I am sure he never gave it a second thought that he was rowing on the river where the Liddell girls first heard the stories about Alice.

It's now twenty-five minutes later. Mentioning Alice reminded me of when Aunt Eleanor took us to Beverley to see the carving of the White Rabbit in St Mary's, so I got the copy of Alice from the bookshelves. Then, of course, I got distracted and started reading. The White Rabbit is so good, I might ask Aunt Eleanor if she would like to go again, as it was such a long time ago. Wasn't your favourite one the Mad Hatter and the March Hare forcing the Dormouse into the teapot? I always liked the picture of Alice meeting the Dodo. But I have been disciplined and put the book down! At least until I have finished this letter et mon leçon de français. I hope you appreciate this, by the way.

David said Oxford was full of bluestockings. He made some rude remarks about 'Girton girls' but that has not put me off. It does seem unfair that women cannot be granted a degree there. Do let me know what Manchester is like. If I get the chance I will be an eccentric student, though a hard-working one of course, but no-one will call me a bluestocking. I should apologise to David because he did actually say a few interesting things about the women students. Did he tell you about the lecturer who walked into a lecture room at Oxford or Cambridge, and saw only female students were present? He announced that as no-one was there, he would not be lecturing and walked straight out again. It's hard to believe. I hope Manchester has no-one as dreadful as that!

David said a woman used to take her pet white rat to lectures, though I suppose the only rats you see are pegged out, waiting dissection.

Are there any female science students? If there are any, perhaps they paid more attention when their brothers taught them about the constellations. I did like the names of some of them though. I used to like saying Camelopardalis, the giraffe. Wasn't it hard to find? And Pegasus, the flying horse, that was the one you could use the stars from the square to find the Andromeda galaxy, wasn't it? I haven't forgotten everything, have I? I would go and have a look now to refresh my memory, but it's raining hard so the celestial heavens will have to wait.

The house seems quiet now as David is always out. They are still training locally. He thinks it won't be long before they go away to camp. We saw him marching in town with everyone else. There were meant to be around four thousand of them. Marching and drilling seems to be what he spends most of the time doing. The Lancashire Fusiliers are camped around the running track on your old school field and have their headquarters in the pavilion!

Robert wants to join up too, but you probably know that as he said he was writing to you. He is determined to be a flyer, though from what he says it is not that easy to get accepted. I hope you will not do anything impetuous.

What exciting things have you have missed? I've been to a couple of meetings of the Dickens Fellowship with Aunt Eleanor. No, don't groan. They were interesting. Even you would have enjoyed the readings from 'Sketches by Boz' and the second meeting was about the songs in his work. Do you remember Edith Watson? Her brother was in the year above you at Hymers. She sang about eight or nine and she was surprisingly good. And that's an opinion from someone once described as 'tone deaf with as much chance of singing in tune as a rusty gate!' I know you are much more musical but that was still an unwarranted criticism.

What else has happened? Russians have been in the city! The source of this information is Ivy and she got it from Millie next door. You know the long platform next to Anlaby Road in Paragon Station? The one built for all those poor Eastern Europeans on their way from the docks to Liverpool and on to the New World? The other day it was full of Russian troops! They were all herded onto the train, which left with its blinds pulled down. One of the Russians left the platform, because according to Millie the penny-in-the-slot machine was jammed by a rouble. Believe it or not, some of them were stamping snow off their boots. Snow all the way from Russia! In October as well! Robert says Millie must have heard someone talking about 'where are the rations?'. She is a scatter-brain. I was in the milliner's yesterday and somebody swore that Russians had landed in Aberdeen and were seen buying vodka in York station!

It is hard to know what to believe. I read about the Mayor of Brauns-berg in East Prussia ordering people to shoot stray cats so that they can turn their fur into body belts and mittens for their army. Would they do that?

I've done my bit to provide better clothing for our Tommies, without the use of cats! I say I, it should be we, as Charlotte, Sarah and Ann helped too. We raised £1 13s 4d collecting at school for the Cardigan Jacket Fund. A pure woollen jacket costs 8/- so we have paid for four and guess what - our names will be sewn in, so Emily Walker will be going to France. Mother took us all to a concert in aid of the fund last Sunday at the Eureka. I am sure you have never heard a juvenile mandolin band play the Marsellaise. At least it was in a good cause. And they have raised £263 so far.

Mother is busy organising the household. I shouldn't say it but she finds having both you and David away dreadfully hard, so even if you can't find time to write to me, please do write to her. She was bemoaning the fact that she hadn't heard from you when I went into the kitchen this afternoon, but on seeing me she switched the conversation to the new threepenny tax on a pound of tea. But do write. The number of deliveries has been cut but that's still half a dozen times a day that she's hoping for a letter.

Father is the same as ever. He has had another letter published. This one's about alcohol. I know you have always read them. I would send you the cutting, but it's gone into his collection. I always wonder how he de-cides on how to sign them. This one is from 'Temperance'. I thought you might like to read a little. The original is much longer and would take too long to copy.

'An evil force is in our midst. It demoralises our soldiers and lessens their efficiency. It degrades our women and is robbing the country of its resources. It is the Demon Drink. Night after night, people are becoming hopelessly intoxicated. Young men who should be happy to drink God's pure air on the drill field are being led astray. The Russians have banned vodka and it is no coincidence that they are sweeping the enemy from the field. Drink robs us of our strength. I urge that something is done as expe-ditiously as possible'.

What do you think? At least it's better than that one about whether women should be allowed to take poodles into cemeteries. I have just seen the time so I had better stop, si je vais finir mes devoirs de français,

ta pauvre sœur affectueuse
Emily
xxx

P.S. Remember I expect lots of exciting information about life at the University of Cottonopolis.

P.P.S. Read Mrs Gaskell. I love her novels and she is from Manchester.

P.P.P.S. Ecrire à la mère aussi vite que possible!!!

November 12th, 1914
Westbourne Avenue

Dear Edward,

I was really pleased to get your letter. I am glad you are settling in well. The food sounds good, but you must be looking forward to Alice's cooking next month. It was interesting about the female students. I suppose fewer men means more opportunities for women. I am in my usual quandary about whether to approach Father or not about what to do when I finish school.

Have you heard from David? He is pleased that they are only a short train ride away from here. He got his uniform only two days before the move and he did look smart in khaki. I was even allowed to use the camera to take his photograph!

He is not impressed with some of his training though - preparing to fight the Boer war, not this one, he says. He has to be out on parade earlier than the men. He's got more to learn, but he likes his platoon sergeant, who is an ex-territorial and is a great help and knows much more than David. This week he had to give a talk to the men about a topic of interest. I thought he might choose some dreary financial topic, but he talked about his rowing and it was quite popular. It's a good job he has always been so fit and keen on sports as he has had to go on innumerable route marches.

Mr Barber was here this morning, digging. I never realised that he lives near where Father has his lodge. He was upset though as someone has been shooting his pigeons. And this after applying to the police for a licence to keep them! I felt sorry for him as he is normally so cheerful. They always seem unattractive things to me, not that I would say that to him. From the way he talked, the pigeons were his pride and joy. I had thought his life revolved around vegetables.

The Defence of the Realm Act is important but why on earth we need a list to remind us about it is beyond me. Father even read it to us all in a serious voice. Ivy caught my eye whilst he was doing this and I had great difficulty not breaking into a fit of giggles. At least I now know not to loiter under any railway arches or use invisible ink when writing to anyone abroad! I considered writing this letter in invisible ink as I remembered you were keen on that sort of thing. Wasn't there a piece about how to do it in one of your magazines? I have had a go, without help. See below!

If you want any future letters in invisible ink then please remind me how to do it. I am not sure that it has worked.

Emily

xxxx

P.S. Thank you. Mother was pleased. Two letters too!

P.P.S. Do not give bread to ducks or horses (Father's list). I will test you when you come home.

June 6th, 1915
Westbourne Avenue

Emily shook her head as the depressing sound of the buzzer penetrated into her consciousness. There it was again. She didn't remember falling asleep. Count! One... two... three. No mistake. A five second blast, a short silence, then another blast. She sat up. Grey light seeped into the room so she couldn't have been asleep long. She got out of bed and drew the curtains back a little. The mist had thickened since earlier. She was just able to make out the time on her clock. Three minutes past ten. She sighed. She'd only been asleep for a few minutes.

She struggled into her clothes in the semi-darkness. Was it another false alarm? It had been one o'clock when she'd got back to bed the previous Friday. That was two alarms in a few days. That hadn't happened since the sinking of the *Lusitania* a month ago.

There was a knock at the door.

"Emily? Are you awake? Didn't you hear the buzzer?"

Emily smiled. Even the dead in nearby Spring Bank cemetery would have heard it.

"Yes, Mother. I heard it and I'm nearly dressed. I'll be down in a few minutes."

Robert might be here by now too. He'd been due back on leave that evening, though she hadn't expected to see him until tomorrow. She peered behind the curtains into his back garden. She might see a Zeppelin tonight as well. What would that be like? Frightening? Her mother would think so - a visitation from the devil! Exciting? Perhaps. Robert would think so.

Her door opened. "For goodness sake, Emily! What are you doing standing there by the window? You know what your father said."

"Yes, Mother. We assemble downstairs and then all go out to the fountain." It still surprised her that her father was prepared to disregard Government guidance to stay indoors if there was a raid. "One minute, Mother. I promise. And yes, I agree with Father. I don't want the house to become our encompassing tomb either."

Her mother's sharp intake of breath made her realise that she shouldn't have repeated her father's words.

"Mother, don't worry. This will just be another false alarm." She pointed at the anti-Zeppelin hand grenade hanging in the corner. "We won't need to use any of those." The newspaper advertisement's claims that they were 'a bargain at seven for thirty shillings!' and that 'a little child could play safely with them!' would hopefully remain untested.

"Look! I'm ready and I wasn't even a minute, and yes, I've remembered about avoiding the buckets on the landing." There was one of sand and one of water on every floor.

Her father was waiting at the bottom of the stairs.

"Emily. Here's your respirator."

"Thank you, Father." She examined it. Horrid, rubbery smelling thing, she thought.

"You remember what to do with it?"

"Yes, Father. I'm to wait until I notice a peculiar and irritating smell before using it." She did worry that this might be too late. Poison gas! She shuddered. Rather a bomb falling on her head than that. If it were needed, she hoped that the respirator would be more effective than the cotton wool pads dipped in washing soda that most people were relying on.

"Now, Emily. Alice is making some hot drinks. Can you help her bring them out when she's done them? And have you seen David anywhere?"

"I'm here, Father," her brother said.

David was home from his camp near Hornsea. Since enlisting, he had improved, she thought, and there might even be some interesting conversation with him.

"David, can you check the street-lights, please? Emily. The drinks."

"Yes, Father. I'm just going."

#

It was a warm still night. A thin veil of mist drifted around her as Emily looked for her brother in the large crowd milling around the fountain. What strange stages of dress and undress they were all in. Like a misplaced street carnival. She looked down at herself, and laughed – she was no better. She spotted David a bit further away, under a lamppost. He had a group of young assistants who were shinning up to pull down the levers that cut the gas supply. The Avenue would remain in darkness even if the all clear came soon.

She moved towards him. "David! Your cocoa."

"Thanks, Emily," he said. "Just what I needed before finishing the rest of these lamps."

Her duties complete and not having been given any further instruction, Emily wandered back towards the fountain. There was no sign of Robert. Perhaps he hadn't come.

As the lights were extinguished, her eyes gradually became accustomed to the gathering darkness. Some people had brought out blue-shaded lamps and these cast small palls of eerie blue light. She moved around picking up snippets of conversations.

"Charlotte's got German measles." "No, he said it's Belgian Flush."

"They'd got green tea, best quality, not rubbish, but you should have seen the queue!"

"I don't care how long they've been here. Ask yourself where their sympathies lie."

"One's using a weather vane to signal to them. Overcharges for his sausages as well."

Did they believe that Mr. Kress or some other local pork butcher was guiding in a Zeppelin to drop its bombs on their neighbourhood?

Good. There was Robert's mother. She would know about Robert. She moved closer and listened to what Mrs Buckley was saying.

"It must be a real possibility. Mrs Keates was in Flamborough on Friday and one came in after dark. Her brother-in law's at the coastguard station and they fired at it with their rifles. He thinks they recognised the headland from their maps."

"Did they drop any bombs, Mrs Buckley?" Emily asked.

"No, thank God, though they may have done so elsewhere." She took Emily's arm, moving her away a little. "Now, Emily. I know Robert's here somewhere, shall we find him?" Her voice was a mixture of the confidential and the conspiratorial. "He's very much looking forward to seeing you."

Emily was glad the semi-darkness covered her flushed reaction.

"Your mother said that David's here. Such a shame about Edward. It is a pity he didn't enlist in a local regiment. It would be a comfort for your mother knowing both her boys were together. David has other friends out at Hornsea, hasn't he?"

"Yes. He joined up with his two best friends at the City Hall. But Edward's always been a little different. And, yes, my parents were disappointed."

"Can't imagine what the lad's thinking of," her father had said. "A Lancashire regiment, of all things! I knew Manchester wasn't a good choice. And who knows what sorts he'll be mixing with? At least we know about David."

He had written to the *Mail* about his concerns about 'young men of good birth having to herd with all the types now enlisting. Men should live, sleep and train in company of others of their own class. The wielder of the pen with his fellows, the docker with his.' That the Commercial Battalion was formed a week later he considered a direct consequence of his correspondence.

"Robert didn't know anyone at first," Mrs Buckley continued, "but there was no shaking his determination to be a flyer."

"Yes, he's always wanted to do that," Emily replied. "But how long is he home for?"

"Forty-eight hours. His train was late. He was hardly through the door when this business started. Look! Isn't that him with David? I'm sure you'd rather talk to him than listen to me."

"I always enjoy talking to you, Mrs Buckley," Emily paused, "but perhaps ..."

"You go, dear. I'll see him later."

She hadn't seen Robert for several months and never in uniform. Men in khaki were common, but his blue double-breasted tunic was a rarer sight. Had he seen her? More importantly, she thought, would he be pleased to see her? At that moment, he glanced up. He said something to her brother, then walked towards her. He stopped with a click of his heels and gave her a smart salute.

"Shouldn't really do that," he smiled. "Not sure whether you're a commissioned officer or not. But if this fits, that would be a start." He took off the little forage cap set jauntily over one ear, and placed it on Emily's head. "There!"

"No," she laughed, giving it back, "it suits you so much better. And you've had to earn it." She pointed to the simple pair of wings on his left breast.

"I haven't earned anything yet. Anyone can tootle around an airfield a few times in an old Bloater. I did have a go in a Morane the other day and they're tricky little brutes, those French monoplanes... I'm sorry, Emily, even in this light, your face!"

"We always have bloaters in Bridlington, but why fly smoked herrings?"

Robert laughed. "No, it's my fault spouting Flying Corps lingo. Bloater is the nickname of the BE 8. It's what we train on. My mother could fly one. Stability Janes, you can't turn them over. I'll fly something else over there. Manoeuvrability is the key and there aren't many German aircraft trying to shoot you down over North Yorkshire."

There was an edge to his voice. Could any training prepare you for an enemy trying to kill you? Up there alone in the air, she thought. Freedom, but a fragile one.

"I'll start on two-seaters, so I won't be alone. I'll have an observer. You're right about feeling free: flying's everything I dreamt it would be."

She must have spoken out loud.

"Whoever he is, Robert, I hope he's good at observing."

"I'm sure he'll be first rate. What worries me most is not being up to it. Letting people down. Living with myself if I left my comrades in the lurch. They try to weed people out who might flunk it, but the whole selection process was very odd. What would be the most important question you'd ask someone who wanted to be a flyer?"

"Are you afraid of heights? Why would you make a good flyer? Something like that, I suppose."

"No, my interviewer asked, 'Do you ride?' Not what I was expecting at all. Why ask that? I'd done a bit at my aunt's." He shrugged. "People say flying is all about a good seat and sensitive hands. Whether that's true or not, plenty of chaps ride to hounds and suchlike. But enough about me. What have you been doing with yourself?"

"Oh, this and that, nothing important. School's as good as over. I still cling on to ideas of going to university." She gave a heartfelt sigh, "Cling on by my fingertips. It's all so frustrating and disappointing. This war's probably put paid to that. I have tried discussing it with father, but he's impossible. He's annoying. Unreasonable. He hasn't completely ruled it out... yet, so I might give it another go... next year perhaps. I might at least try and discover what's required. I don't know... there again, it's not much of a sacrifice when you think about other people's. I shouldn't complain. Life goes on."

"The papers are optimistic, Emily, and this won't go on forever. You could get the chance to go later."

"I just feel a bit useless. I need to think about the future. There must be more worthwhile things to do. Our mothers never stop. You should see the piles of khaki wool. It's like a factory they've set up: knitting socks, mittens, balaclava helmets. And now Ivy's gone to make munitions at Rose Downs, there's more to do at home. I thought of doing something similar, working in one of Queen Mary's sweat shops – that's what Aunt Eleanor calls them. You should have heard father when he read about women wanting to join up."

Was he nearby? She glanced around, before giving a passable impersonation. "Soldiers in petticoats, quite preposterous. These misguided, light-headed things should go home, sit still, and knit."

Robert laughed. "I hope he never catches you, Emily, but he has a point. I hate the idea of women fighting."

"I think I agree with you. But he's just so annoying. He always dismisses any suggestions women put forward. As to being useful, mother wouldn't approve of me doing something like Ivy. She wants me to learn shorthand, typing and bookkeeping at Wards on Spring Bank. That's just so, so dull. Make myself useful at home or bookkeeping... the height of my ambitions these days. I'm sorry, here I am going on, and you're only here for a short while."

"Please, do go on, Emily. You're a refreshing change. Even when you're moaning."

"If you're sure, and I'll try not to moan. Oh dear, here comes my mother."

"Emily. Mrs Green's over there. Her daughter's been doing secretarial classes..."

Please don't make me talk to her. Robert, say something!

"Robert, you don't mind if I borrow her for a few minutes? It would be so useful for Emily to find out more." Without waiting for an answer she took Emily's arm. Emily gave Robert a helpless look. Mother! Please let this not last too long!

After what seemed an interminable few minutes, she extracted herself.

"How was it then, Emily?" Robert asked, when she returned. "I watched you – you seemed very diplomatic." He laughed. "I hope you've signed up for advanced shorthand."

"No. I have not! And I have no intention of doing so. I am joining the British Grenadiers instead! Father is annoying, but Mother sometimes can be... I just wish she'd... but enough of that. Robert, you've obviously missed me most terribly in my brief absence." She gestured. "There don't seem quite as many people around now." The crowd had thinned a little, as had the mist.

"They're convinced it's another false alarm, I should imagine. Disappeared like the mist seems to be doing."

Yes. It was a little clearer, she thought.

"Did you hear something, Robert?"

There was a general conversational hubbub, but she was sure. She strained her ears. Yes. There it was. A clear, whirring noise, intermingled with clanging bells.

A nearby voice said, "Be quiet! Ssh... listen!"

An intense bright illumination filled the sky beyond the city, a shocking contrast to the surrounding gloom. Bright, bright light.

Emily raised her hand to her mouth. My God! It's happening. "Robert? What... what?"

"They're dropping flares," Robert said. He sounded calm. "Getting their bearings. It was quite foggy down by the river when my train came in, but if it's lifted, it'll be clear as day, looking down from up there."

Darkness returned. Emily scanned the sky, her eyes trying to re-adjust. Then she saw it. There, against the backdrop of the night sky. A long, grey-ish-silver cigar-shaped object. How big, how high, how far away was it? She let out her breath. She realised that she must have been holding it in.

Robert shaded his eyes with his hands.

"It must be over five hundred feet long. Probably a class M or N. They'll have developed more advanced types since the war started. There isn't a country in the world which can compete with Germany when it comes to airships. Some people dismiss them as gasbags but that seriously underesti-mates them: Count von Zeppelin has achieved incredible things." The ad-miration in his voice was undeniable. Few around them would appreciate hearing any German praised in this way.

Emily was aware of other voices.

"If I'm going to die, I'll do it in my own home, thank you very much."

"Come on, if we set off now we can be out in the country. Bloody Fritz won't bomb us there!"

But most people stayed and stared at the airship. Fascinated.

Emily took Robert's arm. "I once saw a rabbit mesmerised by a stoat," she said. "The stoat gambolled and cavorted in front of it and the rabbit just watched... until the stoat leapt and bit into its neck. Spellbound, then dead." She gestured at the people around her. She could not take her eyes off it either. "It's hardly moving."

"There's no wind," he answered. "It might make fifty miles an hour. It'll be at three to four thousand feet, possibly higher. Listen!"

A series of dull thuds was followed by explosions.

"My guess is they're over the docks. It's an obvious target. I wish I were closer."

"Don't do that!" a man shouted. Emily turned.

There was the brief, bright flare of a match.

"Idiot!" another voice responded. "Who are you to tell me what to do? The Germans are never going to see it from up there." Further explosions drowned the rest of their exchange.

The airship edged towards them. The noise of its engines grew louder and more persistent, except when drowned out by intermittent explosions coming from the direction of the city centre.

"Murderers!" someone shouted. Other curses were flung into the night sky.

Emily could see Alice. Her family lived at the town end of Holderness Road, near where the bombs must be falling. Her mother had her arm round her.

"Robert, look!" The airship's surface was changing colour, from silver to yellow to orange.

"They've been dropping incendiaries." Robert said. "The fires burning over there are reflecting off it."

"It's going to miss us." It was David. "Its course is taking it towards our old house. It will be using the river as a guide."

"I heard what might have been gunfire, but apart from that the city seems defenceless," said Robert.

David looked towards the city centre. "Father's concerned about the bank. It will be chaotic if it's been hit. All those accounts to sort. Terrible. Still, the safes should stand up to a few German bombs."

Emily couldn't resist responding, "As long as the bank's money is secure, that's the main thing. How awful if anything has happened to it!"

"That's not fair, Emily," Robert said. "David and your father aren't just concerned about that."

"I'm sorry David. It's just... oh... never mind."

"Father's asked me to go inside to check a few things," David continued, unperturbed.

"Robert, you said you'd like a closer look?" Emily turned to David, regretting her barbed comment, "Edward's telescope? Did he take it away with him?"

Edward's insatiable interest in anything mathematical or scientific included astronomy. His Crichton Day or Night single-draw marine telescope was his pride and joy. He spent ages polishing it, ensuring its brass had a wonderful burnished patina. Emily had rarely been allowed to use it, but hadn't minded, having little desire to identify Jovian moons.

"No, he didn't. It's in the attic where he last used it, but I don't think..."

"Oh, David," Emily interrupted. "Robert would like a chance to see more. Wouldn't you, Robert?"

"Emily, I don't mind. I don't want to..."

"Don't be silly. David's a tiny bit curious too, aren't you?"

"Perhaps I should ask Father..."

She took her brother's arm and before he could protest steered him and Robert towards their house. "There's a blue light on the hall table and I've got my respirator. So don't worry, David. Come on Robert. Up the stairs."

The attic was more of a walk-in cupboard. A skylight in the sloping ceiling gave access to the roof, and underneath it Edward had constructed a simple platform. With the skylight open it was possible for two people to look out. Emily had been dismissive of the idea of setting the telescope up in the attic, thinking that the back garden ought to be good enough for star-gazing. Now, though, she saw that there was an unparalleled view across the roof tops. The telescope was on a small table with a notebook and a book of charts.

"Here, Robert, can you take the lamp? How do I look by blue light, by the way?"

"Divine, of course."

"I'm not sure about that!" Divine, she thought!

Emily lifted up the telescope. It was quite heavy and cumbersome. "Edward had a thing for it to go on, but I can't see it. Do you want to go first?"

"No, I can wait. Rest it on the edge of the skylight. Here, let me help you." His hand was almost touching hers. "See if you can see the gondolas." She trembled. Was that due to the close proximity of the Germans or of Robert?

She brought it into focus. The Zeppelin hung in the south-western sky. "I can see two gondolas hanging underneath it. Really well, and there are some... figures... people, I'm sure. And above the front gondola... a letter and a number... an L and it could be a nine. Yes, L9. The gondola's got brighter – no it's not that, light's escaping from underneath it. Would there be a door there? There it is again. That could have been something falling. Yes, there it is again."

It took a few moments to connect what she'd seen with the explosions she now heard. "Robert! How dreadful!" He had his hand on hers. "You'd better have a look." She let her fingers slip away from his. "There's his..." tripod was the word, "tripod in the corner. It would be easier using that."

Robert studied the airship, taking in as much detail as he could. "It's an excellent view. She's turned away and is heading back. That's another she's dropped. We are going to be spared even if some poor beggars over there aren't so lucky." He lifted his head away from the eyepiece. The blue flickering lamplight played across them, casting their shadows against the wall. "You'd better tell David to come before she passes out of our line of sight."

David, she thought. Please stay downstairs doing some tedious task Father has given you.

"Emily?"

He had a smile on his lips. Was he going to touch her? Yes. The fingers of his right hand gently caressed her cheek. What should she do?

"Robert? Emily?" It was her brother, but only on the stairs, thank goodness. "Father thinks you should be back outside."

She made her decision.

"We'll be down in a minute, David."

#

Shortly after half past midnight, Kapitanleutnant Heinrich Mathy of the Imperial German Navy ordered a course set to return them to their sheds at Hage. He stood, stiff and straight, behind his helmsman and surveyed the scene from his control cabin. He congratulated the men around him and sent the same message to those working in the engine room in the rear gondola. The seventeen men under his command were exhilarated at such an excellent night's work under their inspirational captain.

Mathy had been unable to bomb London, his original target, due to strong headwinds over the North German coast and then poor ground visibility over southern England. He had worried about anti-aircraft gun defences as he'd made his approach along the Humber at between eight and ten thousand feet, but apart from ineffective fire from the light-cruiser Adventure, which was in dry-dock for repairs, the defences had proved non-existent. And as to the Royal Flying Corps, he was contemptuous of their ability to threaten him. He had remarked in the mess that morning: "As to an aeroplane corps for the defence of London, it must be remembered that it takes time for an aeroplane to screw itself up as high as a Zeppelin, and by the time it gets there the airship would be gone ..."

In complete control, he had descended unhindered to a perfect altitude for his attack and dropped thirteen high explosive and more than forty incendiaries over the city, leaving behind some forty to fifty demolished houses and shops, and twenty four people dead.

At two-thirty, the L9 was well out over the North Sea.

At two-thirty, Emily was in a confused and fitful sleep.

At two-thirty, some of Emily's neighbours were still in the countryside, only returning at daybreak.

At two-thirty, serious and widespread rioting broke out across the city.

June 7th, 1915
Westbourne Avenue

Why was it so hard to wake up when you had to, whereas when you didn't need to ... Emily sighed. She was surprised that a few hours' sleep, filled with a succession of vivid dreams, hadn't left her more tired. She punched her pillows to plump them up and let her head drop into them, enjoying the sensation of sinking down. Countless thoughts whirred round and round in her head. Trying to get back to sleep was pointless, so she pulled back her covers and swung her legs out of bed.

"I didn't expect you down as early as this," her mother said, as Emily entered the breakfast room. "You've remembered you don't have to go in?"

"To school? Yes, I know. It's annoying but I was awake and I feel fine – but you're looking tired, Mother." And looking worried too, she thought. Of course, David goes back to Rolston camp this morning.

"I didn't sleep much, Emily, and I don't want to talk about last night at the moment. Your father, of course, slept like a lamb."

Emily glanced at her father. He was deep in conversation with her brother. Their words drifted over her.

"It's a scandal! Taking money from the pockets of investors to redistribute in higher wages, war bonuses and allowances amongst the non-investing classes."

"I couldn't agree more, Father. And what do they do with it? Waste it on flashy, unhealthy and degenerate pleasures!"

Emily picked up a piece of toast. The sheer injustice was self-evident. If only money spent in public houses could be converted into small war-bonds, then the war would soon be over!

"Good luck then, David." Her father had stood up. "I'm off now. Should have left earlier to check on things, but I didn't want to miss you this morning. No telling how long it might be." He looked at his wife. "Enough of that anyway." He reached out and shook David by the hand "Yes, good luck and do your duty."

Did his voice have a slight quaver as he said that? Emily thought.

As if aware of this unfortunate lapse, he spoke to her, as if addressing an employee at the bank. "Your mother seems unduly perturbed this morning. If she is determined to meet her sister later then you will accompany her."

"Yes, Father, of course." He gave the slightest nod of his head to her mother and left the room.

"I'm catching the half past eleven train, Mother," David said. "Perhaps we could all walk down together?"

"That would be nice, David. Emily, if you can be ready before eleven, then?"

"Yes, Mother. I might be out in the garden as it's such a beautiful morning."

#

When Emily did go outside, Mr Barber was busy in the vegetable patch. He was bent over sowing something in the raked beds. Hearing her approach, he straightened up and pushed his cap back.

"That's what I like to see, Miss. A lovely smile! Have you come to give me a hand sowing these runner beans? I've started some off in pots, but these here are my insurance."

"I've a little unexpected free time, Mr Barber," she said, "so maybe I should do some digging for you."

He paused as if giving this serious consideration. "I'm afraid you're hardly dressed for that, but I hear there are lasses doing suchlike round-abouts." His expression made it clear what he thought of this notion. "You can keep me company while I get these last ones done, if you wish." With minimum effort he completed sowing the row.

"It's changed this year, hasn't it? The garden."

"It has that, Miss. And yours isn't the only one round here to do so either. More for me to do as well. Cabbages for chrysanths and parsnips for petunias. And just look at those parsnips. Going to be a fine crop."

She considered saying that she'd rather eat petunias! Just thinking of the smell of parsnips being cooked made her feel queasy.

"You're sure the..." she struggled to think of the pests that Mr Barber was wont to wax lyrical about, "root flies won't get them?"

Mr Barber ignored the note of hopefulness in her voice.

"Don't you worry, Miss, they'll be fine. And it's carrots that get the root fly. It's canker you've got to watch out for with parsnips. Go all soft they do."

Better pray for an outbreak of parsnip canker then, she thought. No, after last night's raid that was too frivolous a request. She changed the subject.

"Did you and Mrs Barber see the Zeppelin?"

"No, Miss, I didn't. I heard the buzzer, but Mrs Barber said there was no way she was traipsing out in the street after last Friday night and the Kaiser could do his worst; if she was going to die then it would be in her own bed. And we both slept like logs, I'm pleased to say."

"I'm glad someone did, Fred Barber." Emily saw that Alice had come out. "You can pick me some broad beans, that's if you're not too busy gabbling. And make sure they're nice young ones," she added, handing him a small basket. "Emily, your mother says she's going into town at ten to, so you'll need to get ready. She's pleased she can walk down with Mr. David. And your aunt's expecting her after that."

"Here, these should do you. Perfect they are. Pinched out the tips nice'n early, so not a sign of blackfly. But you're looking a bit frayed at the edges this morning, Alice."

"My nerves are quite shredded," she replied. "My sister and her family live over there." She gestured in the direction where they'd seen the Zeppelin. "I popped a letter in the first post, so I should hear back today. Mrs Walker has given me some of her Dr Cassell's tablets, so they should help with these anxieties." Emily was dubious as to how one tablet could cure 'the sleepless and nerve-torn' whilst preventing 'premature decay, nervous debility, wasting disease and all forms of paralysis' but she kept her thoughts to herself.

"I'm sure they'll help, Alice," she said.

"I hope so. But who knows what'll happen? Millie next door says the butcher's boy heard a music hall was hit and everyone was killed."

"But Alice, a music hall performance at midnight?"

"Who knows who helped them to," she struggled for suitable words, "commit murder by night. Yes. Murder by night," she repeated. "And Millie's sure there's plenty only too willing to do the Kaiser's bidding. And she says no alien's property was hit last night." With that she headed back to the kitchen.

"Well Miss, she's het up and that's no mistake. But there's plenty who've every right to be het up this morning. Anyway don't think me rude, but I'd better get on. Mustn't waste this fine weather and I've next door to do too."

"And I should be getting in, if I'm going into town," Emily replied.

Her mother was looking at the photographs on the sitting room mantelpiece. The most recent, the pictures of her brothers in their uniforms, were in pride of place. Many people had such photographs done by professionals, but in Emily's opinion, these taken by members of her own family were far superior – less stiff and awkward, more natural. It would be nice to have a photograph of Robert, or even of the two of them. No, that would be impossible. She'd never hear the end of it.

"Emily," her mother said, noticing her. "You're ready. David's just packing his last few things and then we'll set off."

#

"You will let us know how you're getting on, David," her mother said as they neared the station. "I just wish you were," she faltered.

"Defending the Holderness Coast for the whole war? I know, Mother. I understand." He paused. "Mind you it's not safe there either, a mud cliff collapsed into the North Sea recently when some German miners tunnelled into it... Mother, I'm sorry, please don't look so alarmed. It was a joke."

"You're sure, David?"

"Of course I am, aren't I, Emily?"

Emily nodded.

"Come on, give me a kiss – and you, Emily, too. And please don't hang around. Look, there's a tram coming. I don't want you to keep Aunt Eleanor waiting."

After they'd boarded the tram, her mother dabbed at her eyes and gave Emily a brave smile. "We're meeting your aunt on Monument Bridge. I need some material from Davis's and we can have lunch at Fields. I'm sure everything in town will be fine."

"Mother, what's happening over there? I wish they'd sit down." People on the far side of the tram were standing.

"That's it! Teach them a good lesson," a woman's voice cried.

"Emily, it's not seemly. Do sit down. Whatever it is, it's not our concern."

The tram gathered speed and the other passengers retook their seats. By the time they had passed the Infirmary in Prospect Street and reached the terminus, Emily had put the commotion to the back of her mind. She smiled at the conductress as she stepped down from the tram. Strange how soon novelties became commonplace, she thought.

They walked across the square towards the Monument, the Dock Office's clock showing that they were several minutes early. A wagon, laden down with beer barrels, came towards them onto the bridge that spanned Princes and Queens Docks. A single forlorn-looking bay horse struggled with its load. One of the dishevelled men in charge of the wagon caught her eye. He looked as if he'd been sampling his wares, a view reinforced when he shouted something unintelligible in their general direction. Her mother tensed next to her. His target seemed to be a small group of foreign-looking men. A snatch of French made her think they might be Belgian refugees.

The man shouted again and waved his arms, until his companion grabbed him and pointed towards the policeman who appeared cemented between the tram tracks in the centre of the bridge. The policeman, oblivious of the gesticulating drayman, examined his stomach as if anticipating his forthcoming lunch. The wagon's progress took the man out of earshot and to Emily's eye the foreigners did not appear disturbed.

Beyond them, the more distant view was obscured by the lighters and barges tied up in the dock. She looked up. William Wilberforce could do with a clean, she thought, though if she'd stood in one spot for eighty years, she'd need sprucing up a bit too.

"What a pleasant surprise!" Emily turned to see her aunt. "I wasn't expecting you, Emily.

"It was the raid, Aunt. It meant a free day."

Both sisters were in their forties, but Eleanor looked younger, making the age difference between them appear much greater than the eighteen months it actually was. Eleanor was tall and slim, whereas Clara was shorter and had a more homely figure. In outlook and temperament they were worlds apart. The measured and the impetuous. The pragmatist and the idealist. The pessimist and the optimist.

"Take my arm, Emily," Eleanor said. "Tell me what you saw of the Zeppelin. I'm sure you're a more reliable witness than your mother."

Whitefriargate was too narrow for trams, but plenty of carts moved up and down, and a sharp eye was needed when stepping off the pavement. At the corner with Parliament Street, they passed Emily's father's bank. When little, she'd imagined him counting vast heaps of gold coins in the bank's vaults. She had asked once if she could see these wonders, but he had talked at length about regulations and inappropriateness. She had not understood, but knew there would be no visit.

Her aunt collected a book she'd had rebound at Screetons, and her mother made enquiries at the hatters nearby. It was turning into Lowgate that Emily noticed the changed quality to the air. There was a distinct, persistent carbon smell, reminiscent of the coal cart but even more so, though her mother and aunt did not seem to detect anything unusual. There was always a miasma of smells in this part of the Old Town, but nearing Holy Trinity church it became pungent and unavoidable.

Her mother gasped as they passed the church. Where Edwin Davis's had stood was a scene of devastation.

Emily knew that bombs would cause great damage, but the actual scale of destruction was shocking. Nothing remained of the city's finest drapers. Smoke and dust rose from a chaotic jumble of bricks and masonry and hung in the still air above the ruins. Fire smouldered in a number of places within the debris. Pieces of darkened, twisted metal stuck out at strange angles, while a single pillar stood in bizarre and splendid isolation amongst the chaos.

"And it was such a lovely shop," she heard her mother say. It was hard to imagine now that it had gone... the greeting from the floorwalker in his splendid frock coat; his polite request for the required department; the chair to sit on whilst materials were brought; the fine, broad staircase to the upper floor; the beautiful long polished wooden counters behind which everything was displayed. And now this. Nothing. Apart from something colourful that caught her eye.

"Emily, you shouldn't get any closer. In fact, there's very little point lingering. We've seen enough of the devil's work."

"Now Clara," Eleanor said, "a few minutes. It's not as if we're the only ones."

Small groups of people clustered around. A motor car pulled up near the fire engines and a grand woman with an authoritative air got out to survey the scene. I'm no different, Emily thought, a ghoulish sightseer.

The splash of colour was no longer visible, as a policeman stood in the way, like some strange doorman positioned in the original but now non-existent shop entrance. Behind him, a small group of soldiers stood on one of the heaps of rubble. They looked exhausted, their faces blackened by the smoke. One took out a packet of cigarettes and offered them round, calling to the policeman in a hoarse, worn voice. The policeman looked as if he would have liked a smoke, but being on public duty he shook his head.

Emily moved closer, as her mother was now not actively discouraging her. Between the policeman and the soldiers were some rolls of cloth, still smouldering. Next to them were the lengths of brightly coloured ribbon she'd seen earlier.

"I wouldn't get too close, Miss," the policeman said, "nor your companions." Despite initial reservations her mother was also taking a closer look, and surprised Emily by speaking first.

"It's a miracle the church wasn't hit, officer." She gestured towards the pitiful remains of the shop. "This is terrible."

"That's true, Madam. But if God's providence helped spare it, he got help from mere mortals as well." He pointed towards the soldiers and to other policemen nearer the church. "The Lord gave us a still night and I'm thankful for that, because we wouldn't have stopped the fire spreading otherwise. We sprayed the stained glass windows to stop them cracking."

"You've done a fine job, officer," Eleanor added. "And if you don't mind me saying, you look in need of a rest yourself."

He sighed and pulled out his pocket watch. "I am due to be relieved in twelve minutes, to be exact, and I'll be off home to my bed – but I'm lucky, others have had to go down there." He pointed. "I hope you're not thinking of going down Queen Street. The whole street's been devastated and there's dead down there, but we can't be everywhere at once."

Emily wondered if the policeman on Monument Bridge shouldn't have been here too, but they had so many duties, and fighting fires was just one of them.

"Now ladies, if you wouldn't mind!"

"Constable," Emily found herself saying, "you see that small roll of red ribbon?" She'd been unsure about asking, but he seemed an amiable character. "Can you see it? About six feet behind you, there..." A slight note of pleading entered her voice. "Could you get it for me? I'd be so grateful."

"Emily! What do you think..."

"Mother! Please. It's important." She tried to gauge the policeman's reaction.

"Well, Miss, strictly speaking," he paused, "taking that might be thought of as looting, and if I gave it to you then I could be up on a charge of aiding and abetting." He rubbed his chin. "But I don't see how Mr Edwin Davis will miss one little bit of ribbon, what with everything else he's missing this morning. If your mother doesn't object that is?"

"You don't, do you, Mother? There's something important I have in mind and it won't do any harm."

"Well, Emily, I'm not sure." Emily interpreted her indecision as positive.

"So it's all right then." She directed her remark at the policeman, who, after a few seconds' thought, picked his way across a pile of masonry, rescued the ribbon and presented it to her.

"Here you are, Miss. I don't know why it's important, but I'll trust you'll make good use of it." He grinned at her. "Don't you go telling my Superintendent."

"I won't, I promise. And thank you. Thank you very much."

The ribbon was a little dirty and singed at the edges, but its colour shone out. Emily opened her purse and secreted it inside.

#

The tram lurched to a halt throwing Emily and her aunt forward.

"Are you alright, Aunt?"

"I'm fine, Emily – apart from losing my hat, that is."

"What do you think's happened? There must have been an accident."

Before her aunt could respond, a man descended from the upper deck and addressed everyone.

"The whole road's blocked. There's hundreds out there. This tram's going nowhere fast." And with that he jumped off. Emily looked at her aunt.

"Come on, Emily, let's see what's happening. Upstairs is a better view, I think."

Emily followed her aunt up the stairs and sat down in the vacant front seat. The road was blocked by a mass of people. The majority were women and children and their attention was directed towards a pork butcher's shop. The crowd emitted an angry resonance like a furious swarm of bees.

"I was in there only a few days ago," Eleanor said. "We've always bought meat from Mr Weiss. He's such a decent hard-working man. My accent always amused him if I spoke German. He was only saying the other day about missing being interned by the skin of his teeth, as he was fifty-six in April. One of his sons married a local girl and another has enlisted. The poor man! I just hope that he and Mrs Weiss aren't in there. I'm glad your mother went straight home."

A thin, raffish-looking man stood with his back to the shop, facing the assembly. His voice did not carry, but he was haranguing all who would listen, waving his arms as if conducting some imaginary orchestra. His words were greeted by a chorus of cheers. Emboldened, he turned, and to a roar of approval hurled himself with great force against the shop door. The plate glass shattered.

"It's because of last night, isn't it?" said Emily.

The crowd, let off some invisible leash, surged forward, then scattered as a number of missiles fell amongst them. A moment later, whoever had launched the salvo found their range. One struck a small pane in an upstairs window. A second hit the large main window, puncturing a hole where the words 'Finest Pork' had been whitewashed on in an ornate script, leaving a forlorn 'F... ork'. Yet another stone produced a fleeting pattern, like cracked ice on a pond, before the next completed the work. As the glass disintegrated, a cheer went up, not only from those outside, but also from a middle-aged man on the top deck. Emily felt her aunt tense. The man was not unlike her father in appearance, and dressed in similar sober fashion. He rose and with an expression of suppressed rage on his face said 'Damn Germans', before heading down the stairs and disappearing from view.

The smashing of the window removed the crowd's remaining inhibitions. A small group forced the door open, and as many as could squeezed through. Some ignored the broken glass and grabbed what they could through the window.

"Shouldn't the police be stopping this, Aunt?" said Emily. "Look at her!"

A ruddy-faced woman held the hand of a small child in one hand, whilst brandishing a string of sausages above her head in her other, as if displaying a sports trophy to a group of admiring spectators. She passed close to the tram, an exultant expression on her face. Her child stumbled in her wake, desperate to avoid being dragged off his feet. He was crying, but his mother seemed unaware of this. Finally, he lost his footing and his mother stopped long enough to smack him hard on the legs, all the while hanging on to her prize. Others followed her, laden down with spoils ranging from the edible to the useless.

"We should leave before anything else happens," Eleanor said.

"It's not far to walk," Emily replied. "And the worst seems to be over."

"Disgraceful! Where have the authorities got to?" Eleanor said. "Come on, time to get off."

They'd only gone a few yards when a new roar went up. Emily turned. She could not see the shop-front, but the upstairs windows were visible. The man who'd made the initial assault was kicking out the window's remains, his hefty boot unleashing a shower of shards of glass and broken bits of wooden glazing bars. He addressed those below.

"Just you wait a minute and don't disappear. The occupant is away, but I hope he's pleased with the improvements and renovations we're kindly making, and that when he scuttles back from whatever hole he's in, he'll be pleased that yours truly is levying no charge."

Many of the women beneath, who were the worse for drink, roared their approval.

"We've got some fine entertainment, especially for those in the expensive seats." He gesticulated at those immediately underneath him. "Don't worry," he continued, gaining confidence, "the hoi polloi at the back won't miss out either." He then disappeared from view, before reappearing with a second man. Together they were manhandling what Emily could see was a piano. With some difficulty they lifted its leading edge onto the window sill. The man surveyed them.

"These Germans'll have to serenade the Kaiser on a penny whistle after this," he announced to general laughter.

"Give us a tune first, Bill," someone shouted. "Go on, bash something out."

"But you'd better do it double quick before the Old Bill gets here, Bill," another person shouted, to even greater merriment.

Emily was shocked. A person's home was being destroyed, yet it was being treated like music hall entertainment. The people around her must be neighbours or customers, and here they were, looting their local butcher's shop. She glanced at her aunt. She had never seen her look so angry. Would she intervene with some quixotic gesture?

"Aunt..." Emily stopped as a few notes came from the piano. Though not accomplished, the man had mastered the rudiments well and wasn't put off by the keyboard's awkward angle.

"How about a Florrie Forde song?" someone shouted. The first bars of 'I Do Like To Be Beside The Seaside' were instantly recognisable and followed by 'Down At The Old Bull And Bush'.

"And now," announced the pianist, "to conclude this short recital." He played a verse of 'Hold Your Hand Out You Naughty Boy' before removing his cap with a flourish and holding his hand out to the delight of the crowd. "Some gentlemen in blue are on their way to spoil our fun, so if you at the front could move back, we'll finish our work. This piano needs retuning and after all, if a job's worth doing, it's worth doing..." The man paused for dramatic effect, so the crowd could join in with "Well!" With that, he and his companion levered the piano further over the edge. The piano teetered on the brink, before a final heave forced it out.

"We have definitely seen quite enough, Emily. Thirty years, Mr Weiss has been here. Thirty years! Come along."

Emily followed her aunt. Visions of the piano falling in a graceful arc and exploding in a strident chorus of discordant notes filling her troubled mind.

\#

Twenty minutes later, Emily was standing in front of a large bookcase in her aunt's drawing room. The tranquillity was in sharp contrast to her thoughts: the Zeppelin, the devastation in town, the riot... and then there was Robert.

"Rather a meagre offering today, I'm afraid," said her aunt, placing a tray on the ornate side-table near the window.

"It looks lovely, Aunt."

"Do choose a book, Emily. You know how much it delights me when you do."

Emily angled her head to read the titles, looking for any new additions. Upstairs many more books lined bedroom walls, as well as various other nooks and crannies, but her aunt's current favourites were here. Her eye was caught by the copy of *Scramble in the Alps* that she had chosen that afternoon all those years ago in Bridlington. She smiled. Its neighbour was a slim volume she had not seen before. She prised it out.

"What's this, Aunt?"

"I'm glad you've spotted that," Eleanor replied. "I picked it up recently. I'd meant to tell you. Not my normal choice, but the name rang a bell, and then, when I saw the title, it seemed an ideal companion for Mr Whymper."

Emily opened the book and flicked through a few pages.

"Is it by that gentleman we met on holiday last August?"

Her aunt smiled. "Yes. Hardly what I'd expected when we set off for our walk."

#

"The young man at the hotel told me it's a pleasant stroll if we go up Trout-dale," Eleanor said. "And it's such a lovely afternoon."

Halfway between the Borrowdale Hotel and Grange Bridge, they turned left onto a narrow track. This wound its way round before emerging into a wide hidden valley dominated by a large crag at its head. A stream meandered across the valley floor and trees clung to its delightful wooded slopes.

"I'm so pleased Mrs. Arthur Severn has given us permission to visit Brantwood on Friday," Emily said, referring to the letter her aunt had received on their arrival.

"I had a booking at the Waterhead Hotel anyway, as there's so much else to enjoy around Coniston," Eleanor replied. "Yes, it was excellent news. Oh, look, Emily!"

Emily glimpsed a colourful bird as its undulating flight took it away into the trees. "Wasn't it striking, Aunt?" The bird didn't reappear, but a rapid drumming noise reverberated around the valley. "A woodpecker! A pity Edward isn't here. He'd know exactly what sort." She paused. "But there would be disadvantages..."

"Emily, if only you could see your face! It's as if you've bitten into the sourest of sour lemons," Eleanor said, laughing. "I agree about Edward, things would be very different. I love your brother most dearly, but with his complete lack of interest in the Lake Poets, having him accompany us around Ruskin's home – let alone visiting Southey's grave – sounds a recipe for disaster."

"He'd enjoy the boat trip we're going to make up Derwentwater to St. Kernigens, though," said Emily.

Emily dismissed Edward from her mind as ahead and above her she heard voices. "Aunt!" she exclaimed. "Can you see them? Up there!" She pointed at the crag. "There! Two people climbing." She glanced at her aunt. "No, to the right. High up, there's a very steep bit." Her aunt peered vaguely. "They're below that, above those sloping rocks. Come on, perhaps we can get closer." Without waiting to see if she were being followed, Emily took a narrow path winding up through the trees. After a short steep climb, she emerged above them. Pausing to catch her breath, she was relieved to see her aunt not far behind.

"I knew my stoutest shoes would come in useful, though there are times when I wish skirts weren't so cumbersome," she said on reaching Emily. "Oh it is a most excellent view."

One of the men was climbing diagonally down a large, sloping slab of rock, whilst his companion payed out the rope that joined them.

"Well Emily, I pray he does not slip, as even with the rope he'd..."

"Swing like the pendulum on a clock," Emily finished for her. To Emily's relief, no such mishap befell him, and she watched in fascination as his companion climbed down towards him. He passed him and then climbed the large rock pinnacle rising above them. The terrible events on that first ascent of the Matterhorn came into Emily's mind. It must be strange to be only one short step from disaster! Watching was thrilling. The economy of movement with which he gained ground was almost beautiful. Emily was spellbound.

As she watched, he reached the top. Realising that he was being observed, he waved to them before raising his cap.

"We should be making our way back, Emily. He's at the top, after all."

"But Aunt, it's quite early and anyway how often can we see something like this at home?"

"Well," Eleanor began, "a few minutes then."

"Thank you, Aunt. I'm sure it will be worth it."

They watched as the second climber ascended to his companion. They stood together for a moment at the top before disappearing from view.

"On occasion, Emily, I enjoy seeing impetuosity rewarded, but we must set off back now."

They picked their way down the slope. At the stream, Emily looked back and saw that the two men were making much faster progress and would soon overtake them. One carried a rope and the other a tripod and camera, resting against his shoulder. In heavy three-piece tweed suits, neat collars and ties, they looked dressed more for church than for mountaineering. There was a strong family resemblance between them.

As they drew level, the younger, who sported a luxuriant moustache, doffed his cap. "Ladies! A lovely afternoon, don't you think?"

"Delightful," Eleanor replied.

"What is it like?" Emily interrupted, before stopping.

"Emily! I don't think..." but before she could finish, the elder said, with laughter in his voice, "No, ma'am, please let the young lady continue." He turned to his companion, "We're in no rush, are we, Ashley?"

"No, George, not at all," he replied, and addressed Emily and her aunt.

"May I introduce myself? I'm Ashley Abraham and this is my brother George."

"Eleanor Alsop, and this is my rather forward niece, Emily, who may wish to continue her questioning?" She raised her eyebrows at Emily.

Emily worried about saying something silly. No, she'd just say what she was thinking. "You both looked so balanced as you climbed. It was so delicate how you moved across and over the rocks. It looked so natural... and I do so envy you; it must be so exciting." To her great relief they both looked pleased, if a little surprised.

"How perceptive," the younger brother answered, "Don't you think, George? I wasn't expecting such a thoughtful analysis of how to climb well." Emily wondered whether he was making fun of her, but he seemed quite serious. "Shall we continue the conversation on our walk back?"

Despite their modest description of their exploits, it appeared they were pre-eminent members in their field. The camera and tripod formed the mainstay of their livelihood. Emily had asked about working in such perilous situations.

"Don't feel sorry for the photographer, Emily," George replied. "It's the climber who has it hard. Four seconds! Four seconds when he must stay perfectly still. A single movement and the plate's ruined."

As they reached the end of the track, the younger brother turned to her aunt, and to Emily's great delight and surprise said, "George and I have been thinking... your niece seems so enthusiastic about climbing. Perhaps tomorrow she might wish to try some rocks near here? I can assure you that she would be quite safe."

Emily looked at her aunt, trying to judge her reaction.

"Certainly not Troutdale Pinnacle." He pointed back. "The first ascent of that was only a few months ago. No, just something easy." Emily looked at her aunt beseechingly...

#

"Climb when you're ready!"

Emily ran the palm of her hand across the rock, cupping her hands so the tips of her fingers rested lightly on the rough-textured granite. It was warmer and dryer than she'd expected, the result of several hours of strong morning sun. She took her hands off the rock and rubbed them together vigorously, before blowing on them. She glanced up at Ashley Abraham, forty feet above her at the top of the small outcrop. She remembered his instructions. "Don't hug the rock. Three points of contact. Take your time."

She looked at her feet. The stout boots with their nailed soles felt odd, but she was glad they'd found some to fit her. She looked up again. "Climbing," she called. She moved her right foot up onto a small in-cut ledge a foot or so off the ground. Balancing her left hand against the rock level with her waist, she pushed up, straightened her leg and found she could reach up and grasp a large handhold. She was off the ground! And going up! As she climbed, the rope snaked sinuously upwards away from her. She'd worried that she might freeze, cling to the rope and be afraid to move up or down. She smiled. There was no danger of that.

"Excellent, Emily," Ashley said. "First rate! Just feel the rock." Before she knew it, she was standing at the top. She waved to her aunt below. Emily felt exhilarated. She'd experienced something she'd never known before. Immersing herself in a good book was an escape, but this was different. This was a sense of freedom.

"Here's George," Ashley said. "We planned a little surprise, if you'd like another try."

George Abraham was standing next to her aunt, the camera and tripod resting against his shoulder. "Can you can manage to keep completely still for four seconds, Emily?"

#

"It's marvellous that you've found a copy," she said. Looking for her erstwhile climbing partners, Emily turned to the photographs at the back of the book. One plate, entitled 'Skye. Climbing the Bhaister Tooth by the Great Western Precipice', was magnificent. Three tiny figures were marooned in a vast enormity of rock, completely dwarfed by their surroundings.

Emily sighed. How she longed for that sense of freedom again. "You still have the photograph, Aunt?" she said.

"I'd hardly discard such a treasured possession, would I?"

"I so wish I could take it home."

"I know, dear, but come and sit down," Eleanor said, "and drink your tea before it gets cold. Tell me your plans for this evening."

"The theatre! I'd quite forgotten." She crossed the room, still clutching the copy of George Abraham's *British Mountain Climbs,* and sat down next to her aunt.

#

Emily let the gap to their parents widen. After the last twenty-four hours, the evening at The Grand had proved a welcome respite. *Land of Promise,* advertised as 'the successful Canadian play', had led her to wonder what an unsuccessful Canadian play might be like, but she'd have sat through the most dirge-like of performances to spend time close to Robert.

She'd told him, a long time ago, how much a career on the stage appealed to her. He'd laughed and said was this to be before or after she became a famous author? The two weren't exclusive, she'd replied. She hadn't been wholly serious, especially as she'd had hopes then of going to university, but it was still an engaging idea. Any suggestion she would not be wildly successful annoyed her, and Robert rarely missed a suitable opportunity to tease her. The verbal sparring was highly enjoyable. At the interval he had wasted little time.

"Does Miss Evelyn Ormonda deserve the benefit of the doubt for Act Two? Or should you step into the breach as Miss Norah Mash?" He stepped back and looked her up and down. "Yes you would be magnificent." His tone of voice suggested the opposite.

"I'd bring greater depth and life to the character, but I can't see myself in such a trivial play."

"How can you ever forgive me, Emily? I'd quite forgotten you were going to be a Great Shakespearean Actress."

"Who steps straight into the shoes of a Sarah Bernhardt or an Ellen Terry," she finished.

"How clever of you," he said, laughing. "Neither are in the first flush of youth, but the age gap isn't that great."

She gave him a piercing look. "They're in their sixties if they're a day, but I'll treat it as a compliment."

"And with your thespian skills, there'll be no wait for some rich patron to pluck you from the obscurity of the chorus line: the name of the incomparable Miss Emily Walker will soon be up in lights."

"You've recognised my abilities at last, Robert." She smiled. "But what role might I be best suited for?"

"Only the weightiest of Shakespearean roles for the latest Grand Dame of the Theatre, so someone mature. Hamlet's mother?"

"What, Gertrude? I'd hoped for a Miranda, but one must do justice to whatever one's given."

She thought, then drank from her glass, before holding it out before her.

"The drink, the drink, I am poison'd," she declaimed, before clutching at her throat.

"Emily."

She became aware of her father's voice.

"Emily! Are you unwell?"

"Oh! I didn't see you, Father."

"Patently not."

He had been standing with his back to her, deep in conversation with Robert's father.

"I'm fine, Father. Honestly."

His expression combined bemusement and anger in equal measure.

"I didn't mean to startle you," she faltered, struggling to explain her re-enactment of the death of the Queen of Denmark.

"Whatever amateur dramatics you *were* indulging in, Emily, I would be grateful if you restricted them to the confines of the back garden, rather than making them available to a wider public and mentioning..."

Before he could list any other perceived misdemeanours, Robert came to her rescue. "Are you enjoying the play, Mr Walker?"

"Yes. Robert. Excellent," his tone of voice lightening. "Very well done. Most amusing, most amusing."

Emily had heard his braying laugh several times in the first Act, and was unsurprised that their views differed. He added little further opinion about the play, and turned to more familiar territory. "Damnable business last night, Robert. Fiendish, unleashing bombs on those least able to defend themselves." Colour moved up his cheeks. "But the grit and pluck of our Tommies will soon deal the Hun a fatal blow. I'm sure you can't wait to get out there and teach him a lesson too."

"Yes, sir. There's little point in all the training unless one can put it to good use."

"Mind you, it's a great shame you aren't in the infantry. Armies on the ground, that's how wars are won. Always have been and always will."

Emily sighed as he continued.

"I can't see the point of this flying business. It's a bit of a dead end. You flyers might be of some use to proper soldiers, but deuced difficult to think how. Presumably they do something out there? Taking messages if other communications break down? But it'll never amount to much on the battlefield. Could you transfer?" He looked at Robert. "No? Thought not. Too late I suppose, but never mind, just hope you don't regret it. Missing out on the real war. The chance to be a real soldier."

Emily was horrified. He might have been repeating what the sceptical majority of his contemporaries believed, but to be so tactless as to address Robert in this way! To her relief, Robert was diplomatic.

"I'm sure I'll be of some use out there," he said. "Everyone will play their part, and who knows how things will develop. Who'd have thought a year ago that this city would be bombed from the air." Emily heard the subtle emphasis on the word 'air', but was sure her father missed it. "Emily was telling me," Robert continued, "of the devastation she and Mrs Walker saw today. And the aftermath on the way home."

"As long as she's painted an accurate picture, Robert. There was much destruction in the town, but being of a more emotional bent, the female of the species is liable to flights of fancy. Experience has taught me that they're not always the most reliable of witnesses. This so-called riot may turn out to be nothing more than a storm in a teacup."

Emily seethed. Why did he have this infuriating tendency to talk about her as if she weren't there? This time it was too much. "Father, I know what I saw!"

Her father looked at her somewhat askance, "Doubtless you're sincere," he said, "but I'm sure your description will prove an exaggeration."

"But Aunt Eleanor..."

Bringing her aunt forward in her defence would be like pouring oil on burning waters and not likely to make matters better. Fortunately, before she could continue Robert intervened. "Have you read this evening's paper, Mr Walker?" he asked.

"I have indeed, Robert."

Emily had been frustrated by the paper's complete absence of news about the raid or the riots. The only comment had been the editor's defence of his lack of coverage. She had agreed with his point that 'our sensible readers do not want to play the enemy's game by giving details of their marksmanship', but it did not stop her feeling infuriated and disappointed.

"Then I'm sure that, if given the chance, Emily would produce some fine copy for the paper, as the report she gave me was informative and level-headed."

To Emily's surprise, her father did not seem displeased by his defence of her and actually smiled. "Well Robert, perhaps it's no bad thing that Emily has you championing her cause. I will concede she has a capacity for writing – that's what that school of hers would have us believe – so perhaps," he said, addressing her, "perhaps I have been doing you a disservice." Emily was stunned by his change in attitude.

He addressed Robert again. "I'm ignoring your father, Robert. Please excuse me." He smiled, nodded and turned away.

"Well that's a first, Emily," Robert said. "You're actually lost for words. And as for your face!" She managed a rueful smile. "But your father must approve of me, despite his neanderthal views on the Royal Flying Corp. Or rather, he approves of us."

Emily was surprised for the second time in as many minutes. 'Us.' She savoured the word as the bell rang to announce Miss Ormonda's return and they made their way back into the auditorium.

Now, an hour and a half later, as they neared home, Emily was becoming more and more conscious of the lack of time. Discovering on the homeward tram that he was leaving at half past five the next morning had been a shock, but she'd determined to keep the mood as light as possible. Robert had returned to their interrupted interval conversation.

"A pity your performance was cut off in full flow, Emily. I'd have liked to see your full panoply of characters."

"That whole conversation with father was so strange. I didn't know what to think. But it could have been worse. It could have been Ophelia. I do do madness especially well!"

"Why am I not surprised?" replied Robert, laughing. "What I would like to see," he said, as he turned to her, "is your Juliet."

She walked on for a few steps, considering her response. "I've no practice as any form of lover, let alone a star-crossed one." She looked at him and smiled, "but with the right encouragement I might attempt the role."

"I had hopes of gaining Miss Evelyn Ormonda's affections," Robert said, "but I'll settle for a Miss Sarah Bernhardt instead." He feigned to move away, as if anticipating a blow, before slipping his arm around her waist. "Remind me, Emily, am I a Montague or a Capulet?"

"Neither. I'll happily settle for a Buckley... even one as annoying as you!"

They reached her front garden gate. Their parents were nowhere to be seen. Emily turned towards Robert...

June 8th, 1915
Westbourne Avenue

The early morning light filtered into Emily's room. Desperate not to over-sleep, she had already woken several times, then dozed fitfully. She shivered as she got out of bed. She pulled her dressing gown around her, then opened her bedroom door. The squeak of the hinges echoed around the landing. She held her breath. Silence? No, not complete silence. The regular sound of snoring came from her parents' room. So far, so good. She realised she was still holding her breath, and let it out in a rush.

In another half an hour, Alice would be bustling about, but for now she had the house to herself. She checked in the pocket of her dressing gown. Yes, it was still there. She tiptoed down the stairs to the hall, where the shock from the cold tiles made her realise that she was bare-footed. The on-ly footwear around was a pair of her father's old galoshes under the hat-stand. It was too late to go back upstairs, so she pulled them on.

She was never the first person to unlock the front door and she struggled with the reluctant top bolt. She panicked – how dreadful to be stuck here on her own doormat whilst Robert walked away down the Avenue! After what seemed ages, it came free. The key turned in the lock, and, remembering to push the snib up – it would never do to be stranded outside – she opened the door, just in time to hear Robert's door closing. He'd said his farewells to his parents the previous night, so she knew he would be alone.

She stepped outside. He was already passing her garden gate. "Robert!" she said in a strangled stage whisper.

He turned and smiled at her before dropping his kit-bag on the pavement. "You woke up in time! I must admit I had my doubts."

She ran towards him, tripped and fell headlong into his arms.

"There was no need to throw yourself at me," he said. "I'd have waited a few more seconds." His grip tightened around her and he pulled her closer.

"These stupid galoshes! They're... Oh, never mind... I was afraid I'd miss you. I'd have hated myself if I had. And who knows what might happen if..." She stopped, not wishing to tempt fate.

"Emily, I hate to say it but I must be going. I can't afford to miss my train."

She unlinked his arms from around her waist and pushed herself away from him.

"At least I'm getting a preview of what the most fashionable young ladies will be wearing this season!"

She examined herself. What a sight! But it couldn't be helped. "One minute, Robert. Please. You've got one more minute, haven't you?" She rummaged in her pocket. "I made this." She took out the small folded length of charred red ribbon, onto which she had fitted a pin and clasp the previous evening. "You'll think I'm silly, but it survived being bombed and then the fire that destroyed Edwin Davis's. And I thought..." She looked at him. "I don't believe in good luck charms or anything like that. Superstitious nonsense, Aunt Eleanor would say. But I'd like you to have it."

He took her hand. "Do you want to pin it on?" She gave him a grateful smile and reaching up, pinned it on his lapel.

"And it's not silly. I'll have it with me every time I'm up in the air."

"I'm so glad."

He leant forward and kissed her on the forehead.

"You must go, Robert, I don't want you to miss your train."

He picked up his kit bag and started to walk away. After a few steps, he stopped and turned. "Emily, I promise that when this is all over... when I come back, I'll be wearing it." He turned again, and this time finally set off.

She watched his blue-uniformed figure recede into the distance. "You'll come back, won't you?" But he was too far away to hear. "You will come back! You must!"

She walked back into the house. Had anyone witnessed their encounter? She looked up to see Alice coming down the stairs. As they passed each other, Alice gave her a conspiratorial smile and pointed at Emily's feet. Emily looked down and laughed. She still had the galoshes on. She took them off and went up again. She paused on the landing. Her father had stopped snoring. She opened her door, this time unaware of its squeaking hinges, crossed the room and dropped onto her bed, not expecting to sleep. Her mind was in a whirl. Parting is such sweet sorrow, she thought, such sweet sorrow, such sweet sorrow.

April 28th, 1916
Bridlington

The postcard had been short and mystifying. 'Be at the far south end Brid beach, 2.30 p.m. Friday. R.'

Emily knew Robert was returning from France, and that he would be based somewhere in Yorkshire, but apart from that she was none the wiser. Now, here she was, five minutes before the appointed time, at 'the far south end Brid beach'. Far enough south, at least, for an excellent view back towards the town.

The day had not started well. Her mother had been against the idea. 'I can't come. I have a Mother Humber fund-raising meeting at three. And you can hardly go by yourself – and anyway, what if he doesn't turn up? He's generally reliable, but if he's delayed, then what? ' She addressed Emily's father. "What do you think, dear?"

Her father had restricted himself thus far to a series of aggressive sighs and grunts aimed at his *Eastern Morning News*. "What do I think?" he replied, lowering his paper. "It's unacceptable." Emily's heart sank. "Two shillings and sixpence! Two shillings and sixpence, twelve and a half per cent of every pound I earn through hard, honest work, going to pay the Secretary of State for Ireland," he paused, "who... it's here somewhere... is paid four thousand pounds a year. Four thousand pounds a year for the serial incompetence that's led us to these scandalous acts of murder and sedition! Mr Asquith says everything is under control, but, and this is my point..."

Her father had expounded at length over recent days about the Budget's iniquities. He was unhappy about what he saw as disgraceful increases in Income Tax and proposed taxing dog owners more instead. He had mixed feelings about some other changes. She had heard him opining. "There is every reason for this halfpenny tax on amusements applying to people who waste their time watching men chase a ball aimlessly around a field. Activities that enhance the cultural life of the country, however, should be exempt."

He had now moved onto the rebellion in Ireland. " ... a wounded Irish officer insulted by a Dublin mob, and what was done? Nothing!" He took a bite of toast, providing a brief respite, before he continued, "As Lord Middleton says, a village idiot could have seen this coming. And this is unbelievable... groups arming, revolutionary posters put up and what was done? Nothing! But it's a great comfort that that Welsh windbag of a Chancellor enjoyed some good trout fishing near Criccieth over Easter. Ha!" After insulting his least favourite Liberal politician, he appeared to be running out of steam, but she realised a moment later that he was refilling his cup.

Ireland had interested her ever since reading *Castle Blair* years ago, with its story involving despicable Land Agents and the plight of the Irish peasants. She was no Fenian, but had some sympathy for the Irish Nationalists. It might be unwise to disagree with her father, as he might respond by vetoing her trip, but she pressed ahead. "Father, don't the Irish have some legitimate grievances? Isn't some form of Home Rule justified?"

"Emily, how can you begin to express such sentiments? That someone under this roof actually sympathises with these fanatics. I am shocked!"

"But Father, that's not what I meant, I don't agree with the dreadful events in Dublin. They were wrong... but shouldn't we try to understand why it's happened? Hasn't the way we've treated some of them over the last how many years had some effect? You were just blaming the government."

He gave her a piercing look. "Your views may be the result of the misplaced idealism of youth, but you will grow out of them. I criticised the government for its leniency, for not cracking the whip hard and thus preventing all this in the first place." He warmed to his theme. "We must act with the utmost ruthlessness. These extremists nurtured by hell hags of the Dublin slums and seduced by German guile and gold must pay the ultimate price for their dastardly deeds. It is the only way." He paused and drank the rest of his coffee. "And now I must go." He rose and addressed Emily's mother. "Isn't your sister free on Fridays? She might welcome a breathe of sea air this afternoon." Emily breathed a surprised sigh of relief.

#

With Robert nowhere in sight, Emily was feeling a little anxious. A smattering of people – one of whom was her aunt – were enjoying the spring sunshine. Her pocket watch said twenty-eight minutes past two. She glanced towards her aunt. She wouldn't mind being dragged on a wild goose chase. There was no way he'd be here on time. It was silly to have come without a proper explanation. She was about to give up, when a couple nearby started gesticulating.

She heard a low buzzing drone before she saw it. A plane was flying towards her about a hundred feet above the waves. As it came closer it waggled its wings – first to the left, then to the right. She clutched her hat as the plane roared overhead. She turned and waved enthusiastically, as it banked to the left over the promenade. There were two people in it. The one behind had his left arm raised as if in salute. She realised that she was laughing, laughing with tears running down her cheeks. "Robert," she shouted. Why she was shouting? He could not hear her. What did that matter? She waved again, dislodging her hat in the process. She shouted his name. Others on the beach were waving too. As the plane circled over the sea, her aunt approached. Aunt, do you see?" she said, "It's Robert!"

"My dear Emily, somehow I managed to work that out," Eleanor answered. "He's coming in again!" The plane was approaching even lower, at forty or fifty feet above the beach, and Emily could see someone leaning out of the cockpit holding what might have been a small bag. As the plane roared overhead, he tipped its contents out. Confetti fell through the air like colourful rain. No, not confetti, flower petals. She tried to catch them and some became entangled in her hair. She was making a spectacle of herself, but could hardly care less. The plane was now flying parallel to the waves, southwards along the beach. Her heart leapt into her mouth. He was intending to land on the expanse of newly washed sand. She need not have worried about this, as the plane made the gentlest of landings. It came to a halt, turned and taxied back along the beach, stopping close to Emily.

A small crowd gathered, but Emily's focus was on the figure jumping down onto the sand. She ran forward, careless of the looks people were giving her, and a moment later was being picked up and swung around. When he'd let her go and she'd regained her breath, she gasped, "Robert! Robert! Arriving like that! What if I hadn't come? What if the beach were full? What if... what if you hadn't come?" She held him tight. "But you did... and the flowers." She opened her hand. A dozen or so delicate petals nestled there. She looked around for Aunt Eleanor. "Aunt, do you have a bag or a book? I mustn't lose these."

"Yes, I'll look after them, and I've your hat too." Her aunt walked a little way off. Some people had drifted away and those that remained were more interested in the plane and in the other young pilot standing beside it than in Emily and Robert.

"I expected you, but never like that. And how did you find your way? And getting back? And when did you arrive from France? That postcard..."

"Emily! Aren't you going to give me a chance to speak? Not that I mind listening to you, but..."

"You haven't told me..."

"Emily!" Robert grabbed hold of her, pulled her towards him and put his hand over her mouth. "I will answer one question – how we found it. We Bradshawed here." Seeing her confused look, he added, "The railway guide."

"You followed the railway lines? How clever."

"And don't worry, it was an hour here, so we've got two hours plus flying time left. I can give you the full spec if you want, fifty-nine mph..." He looked at her in an amused fashion. "No. I thought not."

"How do you know I'm not interested? I might be fascinated by flying backwards or upside down."

"Emily. Listen! We haven't long, but you've got a choice... a short stroll arm-in-arm along the prom. Dip our toes in the sea. Find an ice, if someone's selling them. All of that would be delightful... or choose the surprise instead." He grinned. "But you're not allowed to ask any questions before you decide."

"But that's ridiculous – and so unfair." She felt both exasperated and fascinated. "And you talk about surprises! What about your arriving here like this?... Not even the tiniest of hints?"

He shook his head. "Cruel, I know, but..."

"You must know," she was biting her lip in serious concentration, "what I'd choose. You do? I'd never forgive myself... or you... let's do it... whatever *it* is."

Robert took her arm. "Come on, before you change your mind. Let me introduce you." He marched her towards the young man leaning against the plane.

"Emily, this is Archie." She shook his hand. "Rather too much Archie in France, but this one's a good sport and has the makings of a decent pilot. Don't you, Archie? Couple of hours dual, first solo tomorrow, then get your ticket and you'll soon have your fourteen in."

"Why should there be too many of you in France?" Emily asked, addressing the novice pilot. "And your fourteen?"

"The Lieutenant's little joke," Archie replied. "Archie is what pilots call ack ack, the anti-aircraft fire up over enemy lines. And fourteen is the minimum hours solo before I get out to France."

"Let's hope you get twenty," Robert added. "But get your ticket and with enough luck you'll learn enough at Gosport to outwit the Boche. They may even hold you back for a month or two to teach a bunch of raw recruits. But if it's a choice between a Fokker on your tail and handing over control to a novice for the first time, then," he laughed, "then it's no contest. But we can't stand here chatting. Now Archie has something for you. I hope they fit."

Emily unwrapped the brown paper parcel she was given, to find a leather helmet and jacket.

"Go on," Robert urged her, "try them on."

The helmet was an excellent, snug fit; the jacket a little less so, but it would do. Her aunt was some way away and Emily couldn't decide whether she was looking excited or alarmed. Emily waved and was reassured by the wave she received in return. What a good job Mother hadn't come, she thought.

"Robert, is this allowed?"

"Allowed? That's an interesting one. It's not expressly forbidden," he paused. "A chap in our squadron landed last summer on a beach down south to meet his girl, and some other chaps have given rides, so let's say we are combining those two interesting circumstances." He grinned. "But at least you didn't ask whether it was safe. Would you like a parachute?"

Her hand went to her mouth. "Why, do I need one?" she asked.

"I'm sorry, I couldn't resist it. The powers that be don't approve, as they think too many of us might funk it when things get a little tight. But don't worry, a parachute isn't necessary. You most definitely won't need one." He smiled. "Honestly."

"If I am going to trust anyone," she took a deep breath, "it's got to be you. So what are we waiting for?" Emily laughed. "I shall try to climb in with some decorum, even in this skirt! At least I'm wearing sensible shoes. Come on, give me your hand." As he leant forward, his jacket came open, and she saw the red ribbon pinned to his lapel.

"Never without it, not up in the air." He sounded more serious. "My lucky talisman. My guardian angel, if you like." He took her arm. "Now let's get you up."

Climbing up onto the wing wasn't as difficult as she'd feared and she was soon strapped into her seat. Around and behind her was a veritable maze of wires holding the wings together, sitting as she was in front of the engine and the propeller. Robert gave Archie his instructions and clambered up behind her.

"Don't worry, I won't be handing you the controls." Hearing him without seeing him was disconcerting. "Not this time anyway. You'll just have to wait to join the ranks of Miss Bacon and other women flyers." He patted her on the shoulder. "It'll be noisy once we start, the engine will rattle a bit.

Are you sure you are okay? Last chance to change your mind. No? Ready then?"

She nodded her head, lifted both hands up and gave a thumbs up sign.

"Don't fret, Maurice Farman's Longhorn looks a bit clumsy and odd and I wouldn't want to be over the lines in it, but we can rely on it not to harm a single hair of your lovely head over Bridlington Bay. And I'll tap your shoulder when we're going to land. We'll just..." but the rest of his words were lost in the roar of the engine.

The next few minutes passed in a blur of overwhelming sensations. They'd hardly started moving before they were airborne. Looking down, Emily understood a little of the appeal that flight held for Robert. It was a different world, in which everyday objects such as the beach, the Spa or the people waving were transformed in scale and seen from a very unusual angle. Then there was the strange sensation of her head being pushed back hard against the seat when Robert put the machine into a sharply banked turn; not being able to lift her feet off the floor on another; the world whizzing below her eyes. She had no idea how long they'd been airborne when Robert tapped her shoulder. She concentrated hard. As the aircraft lost speed, the beach came closer, until the wheels and the skid touched down together and it was over.

She was shaking when she climbed down. Not from fright, but from sheer joy. "Oh, it was unbelievable." She tried to catch her breath. "I'd never have imagined. Everything looked... it was... I can't think how to describe it... not at the moment... but thank you. I loved it."

"It was worth coming, then?"

"Was it worth it? It was glorious. In fact, perhaps I should replace Archie on your return trip." She took off the jacket and handed it to him. "I know I'm being greedy, especially after this afternoon, but is there any chance of you getting leave? Mary Pickford's on at the Tower next week. Madam Butterfly, I think."

"Mary Pickford? She's the nation's sweetheart, but she doesn't hold a candle to the one I'm interested in." He called out to Archie. "Time to go."

"Do you have to go so soon?" She could not keep the disappointment out of her voice. "And what about leave?"

"This was always going to be a flying visit." He took her arm. "Sorry."

"For the pun or for your short stay?"

"Both, I might get a day or so before I go back, but nothing's guaranteed. I might be sent to Gosport – the Advanced Flying School – to do some instructing there. Archie will be heading there for his final training, but the sooner I return to Vert Galant the better."

Emily's felt a complex combination of anxiety and pride. She took off the leather helmet and offered it to Robert.

"No, you keep it. It's far too small. I'm not even sure that it's been used. Just too many big-heads in the RFC."

Emily hesitated. "Are you sure?"

"Definitely. But we need to go." He hugged her and gave her the briefest kiss on the cheek. "Ready, Archie?"

"You'll be careful, Robert. Promise?" she said, as he climbed into the plane, but the noise of the engine and the propeller took her words away. The plane moved away, lifted off the beach, and turned westwards before it was lost from view.

She walked over to her aunt, who took her arm. "Are you quite all right, Emily?"

"Don't worry, Aunt. And don't look so worried. I am perfectly all right."

"I would be less than truthful if I didn't admit to feeling a little anxious at times, while you were up in that flying machine – but we won't be short of something to talk about on the train home."

The mention of home made Emily's heart flutter a little. "Mother..." she began.

"Don't worry about your mother. We can say how Robert arrived, and she is hardly likely to ask whether you went up in his plane. So neither of us will need to lie, will we?"

Emily smiled at her aunt. "It's funny – when I was deciding, something you once said went through my mind, about how people who didn't take risks risked missing out."

"It was in the bookshop, when you promised not to be a stick-in-the-mud. You were so serious. So solemn... and so funny. But don't worry, I've never had the slightest doubt about you, my dear."

"Nor me about you, Aunt."

Emily examined the hat and leather helmet she was holding.

"Perhaps the hat is the more appropriate headgear?" Eleanor said, handing her a pin. "It's such a lovely afternoon. Let's stroll back and find somewhere nice for afternoon tea – assuming your exploits haven't taken your appetite away!"

"Quite the opposite, Aunt. Flying always makes us non-stick-in-the-muds quite famished!" Emily slipped her arm through her aunt's, and they set off along the beach towards the town.

July 17th, 1916
Westbourne Avenue

Emily had left Alice and her mother deep in a dull conversation about the merits or otherwise of Owbridges Lung Tonic when she heard the doorbell.

"I'll answer it," she called. As she reached for the doorknob the bell rang again. Opening the door she saw a boy of about fifteen in a high-collared blue uniform. Emily looked at his diagonal-cross belt and polished badge. She looked at his bright red bicycle leaning against the gate. With a feeling of dread, her eyes were drawn to the yellow envelope in his left hand.

"Telegram for Walker, Miss," he said. "Telegram, Miss." He thrust it towards her. "Miss!"

"Sorry. Yes. Sorry. Walker."

Adrenaline surged through her body as she held out a shaking hand. She closed the door. The short walk back down the hall seemed endless. "Mother!" She tried to keep the hysteria out of her voice. "Mother, there's a telegram."

Her mother was kneading dough at the kitchen table. She'd started doing this to help an over-stretched Alice, but had found she enjoyed it. They were discussing the casserole Alice was making.

"You can't get any for love or money," her mother was saying. "Emily, I thought you'd gone upstairs." She hadn't heard.

"Mother, there's a telegram." The words came out strained and cracked. "It might be nothing," she added, unconvinced by her own words.

"Get my reading glasses, will you, dear, while I get this flour off my hands? They're over there on the window sill somewhere," adding with an air of normality that Emily found disconcerting, "and the letter knife as well, please."

Her mother put her glasses on and without hesitation slit the envelope open, before reading its contents. Her face was impassive.

"Mother, what is it? What does it say?" A sick feeling rose in Emily's stomach. She breathed in, trying to control her panic. "Mother, what's happened?"

Her mother stared at her. Silence.

"Mother!"

"Alice, we must contact Mr Walker. Can you do that? He needs to come home as soon as possible." She let the telegram slip from her fingers, and left the room. Emily was unsure whether to follow. No. Not yet.

She knelt down and picked up the telegram.

#

She pushed her food around her plate. "You need to eat something," Alice had said. Emily had managed the odd mouthful but it was cold now anyway. Alice was right. She should be 'keeping her strength up', but a deep, empty, gnawing feeling lay in the pit of her stomach and not just because she hadn't eaten since breakfast. She had never felt less like eating. As a nine-year-old, she had once refused to eat some broad beans. The following day an empty plate had been put in front of her and she had watched as everyone else ate a meal consisting of all her favourite foods. Today her parents made no effort to make her eat. She stared at the congealing food.

Her mother seemed to be in a state of denial. Throughout the long afternoon she had immersed herself in the minutiae of household affairs. An hour after the news, Emily heard her complaining about the butcher's boy and his delivery that morning. She had then spent half an hour looking for a particular button to replace one missing on one of Emily's blouses. There had been no frustrated cry when she couldn't find the right one, just a silent grim determination as she turned to the next mundane task. Emily found this glacial calm unnerving and hard to bear. Her father had behaved in a strange way too.

He had returned not much earlier than usual, unable to postpone a difficult meeting with important clients, he'd said. She'd wanted to scream. What was more important than this? It might have been shock, but he'd made little effort to communicate with or show affection to her mother.

The lengthy silence at the dinner table was finally broken by her father. With icy decorum he'd said, "He's done his duty for God, King and Country and we should all be proud of that. Sacrifices will always be needed and must be accepted in an appropriate manner. Showing respect does not mean soliciting public sympathy through emotional displays." He looked at a red-eyed Emily, who was struggling to hold back the tears. "Giving in to hysterical neuroses is a natural, but unwelcome, part of the female condition. God's way of assuring us of the weakness of women."

"Father," Emily started, "being upset..."

Her father interrupted her. "Emily! That is enough! I will brook no discussion on this." He rose and meticulously folded his napkin. "I shall be in my study and I do not wish to be disturbed." And with that he left the room.

"Mother," Emily exclaimed, "he can't talk like that. Please say he can't. Why is everyone behaving like this? I don't know what's happening to us!"

"Your father has everyone's best interests at heart, Emily," her mother replied, a flatness in her voice that Emily had never heard before. "It's only fair that we respect that and try and follow his wishes." She also rose from the table. "I must see what Alice is doing. I shall send her in to clear the things."

Emily stared across the table, before letting out a small cry as she felt a pain in her hand. She saw that she was clenching her left fist, her nails digging into her palm. With great difficulty she unclenched it. As she did so, she felt hands on her shoulders and then arms drawing her closer.

"Now then, dear, you come here." It was the sympathy she had been longing for all afternoon. She enveloped herself in Alice's arms. "There, there, dear," Alice said. "Don't you worry about crying," as the sobs wracked Emily's body.

"What's wrong with them? They don't care. I know Father is... but he's always like that – but Mother, what on earth is wrong with her?" Her voice rose. "He's right, I am getting hysterical. But why won't she cry? Why won't she hold me? You are. Aunt Eleanor would," she said, adding, with venom, "I hate them."

"Emily, you poor thing." Alice pulled her closer. "You know you don't mean that. I know your mother well enough to see that she's hurting too. She just hasn't been able to show it yet. I don't know why, but she will, I promise." She hugged Emily. "There's nothing... absolutely nothing wrong with you being so upset."

"Are you sure? I feel so terrible."

"You come with me. Your mother has gone for a lie-down, so you can sit in the kitchen while I do the pots. And you can give me a hand with drying them, if you want." She gave her another bone-crushing hug. "Now bring that plate through with you. And don't worry about that food. I'll make you a little something later, if you can manage it."

#

Emily was unable to get to sleep. Her spirits had risen a little with Alice, but the briefest of good-nights from her mother had been followed by the solitude of her bedroom. She loved her room, but not tonight. She put her light on and tried to read, but that short unforgiving message would not go away: 'Deeply regret to inform you that Lieut. E.J Walker Lancashire Fusiliers killed in action July 13th. Lord Kitchener expresses his sympathy. Secretary War Office.'

It was no good. She got out of bed, put on her dressing gown, and went out onto the landing, where she was surprised to find her mother.

"Emily, what are you doing? Can't you sleep either? I saw your light was on." She paused. "I wasn't sure whether to come in or not." For the first time since the telegram, Emily detected something in her mother's voice – some warmth, some humanity. She felt the first faint stirrings of hope – hope that she might find some comfort from her mother. "Would you like some cocoa, Emily? I was just going down to make some. And then we can try and get you back to bed."

"Yes please, Mother. Cocoa would be nice." She paused. "He was so pleased, wasn't he?"

"Yes, dear. Edward was often so pleased with lots of things."

"I know he was, but that's not what I meant. I met him here on the landing, the night that war was declared. He'd been into town with David and was so excited and delighted with it all. He so wanted not to miss out on an adventure. He was worried it'd all be over too soon." She sighed, took a deep breath, pushing her fingers upwards into her hair until her hands were clasped behind her neck. She let her head fall backwards and, with eyes shut, said in a slow tortured whisper, "Oh, Mother... I just wish he was here... being annoying, teasing me, playing one of his stupid, stupid, stupid tricks on me."

"I know, Emily. I know," her mother replied, opening her arms to her, "We are all going to miss him so dreadfully, dreadfully so."

July 20th, 1916
Westbourne Avenue

Dear Robert,

I'm sorry, but I have the most dreadful news. Edward has been killed. I can't believe I have written those four simple words. I should have written when that awful telegram arrived, but I have been in the most confusing daze. A letter came from his CO this morning and that has given me the impetus to put pen to paper. Your letters take four or five days, but his, which I have copied out below, arrived much faster.

Dear Mr and Mrs Walker,

It is with the greatest regret that I am writing to you to inform you of the death of your son, Edward. He was someone who was respected both by his fellow officers and by those under his command. His unfailing sense of humour, ready wit, ability to think quickly and undoubted courage meant that he was an invaluable asset to the battalion in the often trying times that we have been through. I hope you will be reassured by the fact that he not only gave his life in the service of his country but also in an effort to protect the lives of the men under his command. On the morning of the thirteen-thhe led his platoon in an attempt to recapture a section of trench lost in recent heavy fighting. During the attack they came under sustained enemy fire from an entrenched and heavily fortified machine gun position. With little thought for his own personal safety, Edward, with typical courage and determination, led an assault that was ultimately successful in nullifying this enemy strongpoint. Regrettably, in doing so he was grievously wounded and subsequently died from his injuries. I would like you to know that those with him before he died said that he bore his injuries with admirable forbearance.

His body was brought back to the lines and has been buried with full honours. Current military regulations do not allow me to disclose the exact location, but it is in a quiet spot, in a neat and well-kept cemetery. There is a wooden cross with his name on it. If you should wish to visit after the war is over, then, with the help of the War Office, it will be simple for you to find his final resting place.

Your son is to be Mentioned in Dispatches as a consequence of his gallantry. I hope this news will be of some comfort to you even if it does, at the moment, seem scant recompense for your sacrifice. The Battalion Commander has asked me to say that had Edward survived, he would have recommended him for a higher honour.

Do feel free to write to me if you wish to. I think that you are likely to receive further letters from his comrades. His personal effects will be forwarded to you shortly.

with deepest commiserations
Michael Kearns. Capt.

I have had so many thoughts going round in my head since we heard. The Captain's letter has helped a little. Mother was relieved that he had a proper burial. I feel sorry for all those people whose loved ones go missing and are never found. Have you any idea where the cemetery could be? He may have been near somewhere called Guillemot. I might be completely wrong, but he said they were based close to a black and white sea bird that you can see on the cliffs at Bempton. Typical of Edward. I had to look it up. Don't worry if you can't find out, but perhaps you could try? David might know, but it seems much easier to ask you. Father has written to David, but I don't know what he said.

Father has been difficult, though he was pleased about the dispatches. We have to get a copy of the London Gazette, but it could be some time before it's in. Mother is fretting about getting one. I have never seen it around here. It is a little unfair that the only medal you can be awarded posthumously is the Victoria Cross. Not that is going to make any difference to Edward.

The Captain's letter came in the first post, but then in the afternoon we had a shock when a postcard and a letter arrived, both from Edward. The Field Service card was sent on the 12th and the two options he hadn't crossed out were 'I am quite well' and 'Letter follows at first opportunity'. I found it so upsetting. He isn't well, is he? A letter won't be following, will it? The one that has arrived for my parents (nothing for me) is postmarked the 9th. Mother has refused to open it. She rarely stands up to Father, but there has been no persuading her. It is downstairs now sitting on the mantelpiece against the clock. The envelope is quite bulky so it must be quite a long letter. I am desperate to know what it says and am tempted to steam it open when everyone is in bed, but of course I won't. Perhaps she will read it tomorrow, or perhaps never.

Please promise to look after yourself and please don't do anything dangerous. I know that is the silliest thing I could have written as I know it is always dangerous. I should have said reckless instead. I can't bear the thought of your mother knocking on our door... no, I don't want to even think about it, but do please be careful. I shouldn't go on, but now especially. Promise!!

I am making up a parcel for you. We had one ready for Edward. I suppose that will go to David, but I will check and see. Have you got enough cigarettes? I am so glad that you liked the cake. I am getting better – thanks to Alice's help, rather than to any natural culinary talent on my part. At least you weren't rude like Edward was. I don't think I told you what he said, did I? It was in his last letter. He said if only I could be mobilised for the war effort then my cakes could be fired at or dropped on the Germans, and then the war would soon be over! It seems wrong to be mentioning one of his jokes – but perhaps it is the right thing to do.

I am managing and I'm glad I am not at home all day now. I am unsure how useful I am being, but helping at the stall on Paragon station is better than nothing.

Your Emily

xxxxxxx

August 28th, 1916
Westbourne Avenue

"What, I might ask, is the meaning of this, Emily?" Her father was standing next to the hall table reading a letter.

"Father?"

"This!" He gestured with the letter, before peering at it once more. "From Newnham College! I was tempted to put it straight in the bin." He thrust it towards her. "Are we to expect similar written communications from other institutions? Can you explain why you have deceived me by writing to these people without my permission?"

She tried to read the letter.

"Father! I haven't deceived you! I made some enquiries of Women's Colleges, that's all. What is wrong with that? I was just trying to find out about the possibilities. It's not as if I've taken any secret entrance examinations, is it?" She held up the letter. "But as you've been reading my private correspondence, you should know..."

He interrupted her. "That will do, Emily! You will not talk to me like that. I will not have you use that tone of voice! I have every right to know the contents of your letters, especially when they are postmarked Cambridge, are written in a strange hand and concern matters such as this. You are not yet twenty-one. Nowhere near, in fact. You live in this house and you will do as you are told. And how you can be even thinking of such things so soon... so soon after... and what is your mother to think? No, my mind is made up. I may have given you the impression that when you finished at the Convent it might be possible for you to pursue further studies. You will not be doing so. If anything, that!" he pointed at the letter, "that has convinced me. That and your going behind my back." He stalked off down the hall, before stopping and turning round to face her again. "I suggest you think of how others, unlike you, are being so selfless. You will not, I repeat not, reply to the suggestion in that letter! That is the end of the matter."

#

Dear Aunt Eleanor,

I wish you were home so I could come and talk about this with you. Mother said she thought you were back at the weekend? I feel so angry. So disappointed. I am so stupid! Stupid for being disappointed! Stupid for getting my hopes up!

Father has opened one of the replies to the letters I sent. He was in the hall when I came downstairs. If only I had got there before him! I cannot believe that he would do such a thing. He has no right. I would never dream of opening anything addressed to him. Never!

It's the first time he's spoken more than two words to me since Edward's death. The worst thing is that the letter was everything that I was hoping for. My other replies were encouraging, but this one says I should visit. No, it says 'We would love you to visit and look forward to talking to you'. The letter says I sound interesting! You'd think Father would be pleased with that, wouldn't you? Someone at Newnham College thinks I sound interesting! But, no, of course he isn't! Far better if people think I am contented, that I meekly accept my lot. Far better if people tell me what a great help I am to my mother. What are they going put on my tombstone? 'Emily Walker lies here, she was always a great help to her mother.' Is that all there is to look forward to? There must be more!

I know these aren't normal times, but I want to be able to make decisions about my own life. Why should Father decide everything? I know I have responsibilities but I want some freedom too! He said I'd gone behind his back. Perhaps I did? But even if I did, I was only seeking information. I can hardly go without his help and approval. I haven't the foggiest how much it would cost. A hundred pounds a year? Two? If I thought that I could discuss these things with him it would be different.

I know that what I'm suggesting might only lead to more heartache, especially if he finds out, but I would just like the chance to know, to see what I might attain. Father is away for a few days in a couple of weeks – could we go on a trip? I'm sure we could do it in a day. This is my idea. I don't want you getting into trouble with Father. I can say I would have gone unchaperoned if you had not accompanied me. Please think about it, dear Aunt. You must have a friend that we could 'visit'.

I have been giving some thought to other things, if my dreams of academe come to nothing. They are looking for VADs for some of the local hospitals. I am not old enough, but a slip of the pen might see me accepted. It's a possibility anyway - less suffocating! And Father could hardly object to that, could he?

Much love,
Emily

September 6th, 1916
Cambridge

"See, we've even made the earlier train. Your mother will hardly know you've been gone." Eleanor sat down opposite her niece. "It was worth it then? Not a wasted journey?" Eleanor smiled. "To see my friend near Huddersfield?"

"Was it worth it? Newnham? I loved it there. The place, the people. What you can do there. She was so nice. So understanding. Even if I never go... it's something. Shows me what might have been. I just wish..."

Eleanor reached across and clasped Emily's hand.

"You must have impressed her."

Emily took out the short letter she'd been given and re-read it.

"Perhaps I should give it to Father when he returns?" She laughed. "There again, perhaps not. He's never going to be persuaded, not by this and certainly not by me. He'd have to start by listening first."

"Please don't give up entirely Emily... read me that last line again."

"I don't need to read it. I know it already... 'If circumstances ever become more propitious then rest assured that any application that you make to the College will be looked on most favourably'. There you are, Aunt. Nil desperandum. I will keep hoping."

December 16th, 1916
Westbourne Avenue

Emily shivered and closed the door. It was cold outside, and only a little better in the hall, which rarely became warm at this time of year. She put down her bag and a few remnant snowflakes fell onto the wet tiles as she removed her hat and coat. As she hung them on the hall-stand she could hear raised voices coming from across the hallway. Her father and aunt were arguing. Where was her mother? The drawing room door was ajar and her father's angry words were quite clear.

"As to your false peace agitating, if you were not my sister-in-law I would ask you to go. On reflection, I shall take my leave instead, before anything else is said that we may have cause to regret." Emily could not quite hear her aunt's reply. A short silence was followed by the sound of approaching footsteps, which stopped at the door. Her father spoke again. "No. You keep it. Let's call it an early Christmas present. After all, Eleanor, it is almost the season of goodwill. I shall bid you good afternoon." The door then opened.

Emily rearranged her coat on its peg, trying hard not to show she'd overheard. She needn't have worried. Shutting the door, he gave her the briefest of grimaces and strode off down the hall. She was about to sigh in relief when he stopped and returned.

"I'm sorry, Emily. It was most impolite to ignore you like that." His voice had a hard edge. "I see that you've only just come in." He looked uneasy. "You may be aware that your aunt and I don't always see eye-to-eye." He cleared his throat. "You and she have always been close. Now, you may be unwilling to heed my advice, but I have your best interests in mind. You are spending more time with your aunt than current circumstances warrant." There was bitterness in his voice. "When you are together, you should not let yourself be swayed by her immoderate and extremist views. Views that have in the past brought the disgrace of appearances in court and worse on this family! And now she is peddling opinions that are nothing but a betrayal of your brother's sacrifice! While she persists with these persuasions she will visit us less often in future, and not when I am in the house."

Emily was aghast. He hadn't raised his voice, but she could feel the suppressed rage behind his words.

"Over the years I have made allowances, and though tolerant and fair-minded, I lack the patience of Job."

"But Father..."

"Your mother believes your aunt being widowed so early is significant. I am less convinced. It's a pity she never remarried, something that I have pointed out to her. Perhaps it's unsurprising given that..." He left the sentence unfinished. "Unfortunately, becoming a widow of comfortable means..." Emily looked at the drawing room door. Could her aunt hear? "...when still quite young left her too much time and freedom to indulge her fancies. That has proved a lamentable state of affairs. I am not, at present, forbidding you from seeing her, but I am suggesting you consider the adverse effects of her influence on you."

He seemed to have finished. Should she say anything? This was all quite shocking. She felt too taken aback and upset to think rationally or respond immediately. She opened her mouth, but then stopped. Her father, perhaps realising how uncomfortable she was, moved the conversation onto safer ground.

"I see you have just come in. Is it still snowing?"

What she wanted to ask was: *What has happened between you? What court appearance? Do you mean what you have just said?*, but instead found herself saying, "It was just stopping. It was settling, though." She tried to re-arrange her thoughts, not to let her feelings show, to stay calm. She continued, trying hard to keep her voice normal. "Mr Barber said this morning it's been heavy out in the Wolds and there was thirteen degrees of frost in Pearson Park." *What was Aunt Eleanor doing now?* "He said he's glad he's completed the autumn digging." *What had they been arguing about?* "And he's pleased the North Eastern Railway is providing free land for allotments." *And what about her mother? Where was she?* "He'd put someone of a more practical bent in charge, though, rather than someone more versed in the laying out of golf courses."

"And did Mr Barber have any other pearls of wisdom, other than suggesting that perhaps he should be the City Allotment Supervisor?"

Was he attempting to be jovial? The contrast with earlier could not have been sharper. He seemed calmer. "Each allotment should produce a ton of spuds." Hearing her father's sharp intake of breath, she corrected herself. Quoting verbatim had been unwise. "I meant a ton of potatoes. But it's too late to collect all the seed potatoes that are needed." *How had her aunt been affected by early widowhood? There was so much she didn't know.* "He won't be digging up the lawn though." *Had she ever thought of remarrying?* "The wire-worms will just wreak havoc."

Was that a reassuring smile he was giving her?

"What a relief that Mr Barber is preserving a small green oasis of tranquillity for us to enjoy when more clement weather returns next year. You must thank him for protecting us from the scourge of wire-worms when you next have one of your conversations with him." The door at the end of the hall opened. "That is probably your mother. Thank you for the horticultural advice, Emily, which I shall heed, and in return I very much hope you will take careful note of mine." Before leaving the hall, he spoke to her mother. Emily stood still, unsure what to do. She could not hear them, but as she approached her mother's expression confirmed her fears. To her surprise, her first words were completely unconnected.

"Did you get the jar of Bovril?"

"Yes, Mother, I didn't forget. It's in my bag. But what did..."

"Then can you take it to Alice, please. She's been pestering me for it and you know what she's like. And help her bring the tea tray through once the kettle has boiled, please. She's just put it on. I shall be with your aunt." Whether or not this was a device to remove her, it had that effect. Giving Emily no time to respond or protest, her mother went into the drawing room, shutting the door behind her.

With equal measures of annoyance and frustration, Emily picked up her bag, took out Alice's offending jar of Bovril and glared at it. Being dismissed like that! She wasn't a child. What was being said? She ought to be there. She was going to be the most affected. And now she was being sent to the kitchen. She sighed. Alice had developed a wearying obsession with putting Bovril into what seemed like almost everything. It was pointless arguing. Since she had seen the advertisement's headline – 'Do you get your shilling's worth of food?' – it had been Alice's mission to see they did, and she now used it with the enthusiasm of a converted zealot. Emily entered the kitchen determined not to let Alice see how upset she was.

"It'll never boil, Alice."

"Emily, you made me jump. I was miles away. What did you say?"

"A watched pot never boils – that's what you always told me."

"Quite right. I should be doing something else. I've got behind with your mother talking so."

"I've got your Bovril." She tried to think of something light-hearted to say. "Didn't you use up the last jar on all the Christmas puddings?"

"Christmas puddings. The idea! You know very well I don't put any in. If you are that worried, you don't have to eat it on Christmas Day. And you're welcome to check those that are being given away too."

"I wasn't serious, Alice. I'm sure it will be delicious. Mother said I was to help bring the tea tray in. Is there anything to eat?"

"Of course there's something to eat. These may be difficult times, but what do you take me for? There's a cake I baked this morning on the side.

You can put it on a plate. It's only an Economy." She poured the water into the teapot.

"Alice, don't be silly. Why do you insist on calling them that? Look how it's risen. That's no ordinary Victoria sponge – it's good enough for the highest of high tables. Quick to make, quick to bake, quick to eat, isn't that what you said?" The smile Emily received showed her that her flattery had had the desired effect. She moved the cake onto a plate. Should she say anything? Little happened in the Walker household that passed Alice by.

"Alice? I'm not sure if I should ask, but... Father and Aunt Eleanor were... I don't know exactly what's happened, but Father said something about a court appearance. He was very cross, though I don't think that was what was annoying him most – but I wondered... do you know anything?"

For once Alice was a disappointment.

"Your aunt has been a worry to your mother, but I shouldn't say any more... perhaps your aunt is the person to ask. And don't look so worried, dear, there's no need. And whatever it was, it happened years ago... No, Emily, I've said quite enough. Now, are you going to just stand there with that cake? This tea will be so stewed that..." Alice searched for a strong enough comparison, but failed to find a suitable ending.

"...we might as well be drinking Bovril instead," Emily said, opening the door as she did so.

"Thank you, Emily."

Emily followed Alice out of the kitchen, feeling confused and apprehensive about what she might discover at afternoon tea.

#

My dear Robert,

Thank you for your letter. How do you find the time? I'm so glad you did. It's quite late, so I won't write too much. This will be the last one to definitely reach you by Christmas, but I will write again in a few days so there will be one for New Year. I hope you like the card. I deserve top marks for creativity, don't you agree? A parcel is on its way too. Your mother has sent one, and I am sure hers contains more than my meagre offerings. I haven't included any cigarettes because your mother has seen an offer where they are sent directly to you. Do you prefer Gold Flake or Navy Cut? One was 5/- for 280, the other was 8/6d for 500, but I can't remember which was which, or which she chose. I've sent one or two small things that are definitely not useful and I hope you like those, especially the book – I loved it – but everything else is practical. The soap makes you 'pure as the driven snow', but looking out of the window it's snowing hard, and I am not sure that is a good thing. But you will be pleased that 'the quickest and most pleasant route from the Black Sea of dirt to the White Sea of cleanliness is via Sunlight Soap'. So there you are! You need never be dirty again! The new advertisement shows a Tommy giving some to a burly Cossack wearing a large furry hat. I wish I could send you one of those instead - the hat, not the Cossack!

We actually had some butter yesterday, and I thought of sending you my share, but I was worried whether it would arrive in good shape. I hope you won't begrudge my eating it. It was bliss. Back to marg next week! Still there must be lots of lovely French cows and milkmaids near your airfield, and I am sure you can charm beaucoup de beurre from them! But please don't be too charming, Robert.

It sounds as if you are being well fed. I know you face dreadful dangers, but it must be a relief to eat in a civilised fashion, unlike the poor souls in the trenches. Some of the nuns at school talked about missing French food. Sister Marie was always trying to make bouillabaisse, which sounds so much more exotic than fish soup. She said that it was easy to get the fish but it never turned out quite right. I thought of her recently when I heard loud cries of 'Fish all alive!' from a man in the street. He had a large barrow of cod-heads. Disgusting-looking things, but he was doing a brisk trade. I asked a woman what she was going to do with them – fish soup, she said. I hope hers turned out well. I might visit Sister Marie. She was so encouraging – that's why my French is so much better than yours. She made me talk French to her. She was the only nun from the south, which explains my unmistakable Provencal accent. Perhaps that's why you sometimes don't understand my French! Elle dit que j'ai un talent pour la langue, mais malheureusement. Sorry, I shouldn't do that, mon pauvre Robert. I loved studying French as well as English. If only – no, it's pointless going down that path. I mustn't start thinking about that bitter disappointment again.

Have you had bad weather too? I start at Brooklands next week so I hope the snow will have gone by then. Getting to the Naval Hospital in Argyll Street would have been easier, but at least I don't have to go to Reckitts. Mother is still unhappy about me becoming a VAD. I know I am not actually old enough, but I know other girls who have done the same thing. I told her yesterday that I could go down to Rose Downs and work there, as they wouldn't be bothered about my age. She was horrified. I'm not sure whether it was the idea of my filling shells or wearing dungarees that upset her more.

She wants me to help at Peel House - 'Always parcels to pack and never enough hands' but she's also worried that some of the women there will disapprove of my telling a white lie about my age. Most of them mean well and work hard (like Mother), but there are some frightful interfering busybodies who are sticklers for the smallest detail and regulation. My birthday is still the tenth of July, I didn't change that. I told her she should be glad I couldn't pass for twenty-three, otherwise I might be heading for foreign parts. I shall let you know how I get on. It should be a nice change from the canteen stall. More useful! I have a month's probation, so I might yet be back serving tea and currant buns.

I haven't given next week much thought as there has been a dreadful row between Father and Aunt Eleanor. They have had disagreements before, but this was more serious. It's to do with the war, but it's maddening as I don't know exactly what they were quarrelling about. It was awful! I thought he was going to stop me contacting her.

Did you know she was once arrested and charged? I didn't! I'm a bit annoyed. Not about her being arrested, but because she never told me. It must have been some form of political protest, not something like stealing. I had so many questions to ask, but by the time I saw her, mother was there and had obviously spoken to her. There was a distinct atmosphere, but it was clear we were to have tea in a civilised manner. The one topic not mentioned was the quarrel. Aunt Eleanor was quieter than usual, or perhaps it was just that mother talked so much and wouldn't let the conversation flag or drift into difficult areas. I found it hard to concentrate and started thinking of Edward. It's hard not to, especially in the drawing room. He looks so smart in his uniform there on the mantelpiece. The unopened letter is still there.

Afternoon tea did end on a bright note, as I have arranged to meet Aunt Eleanor next week, without Mother! And I shall see her again on Boxing Day. She has tickets for the first night of Aladdin at The Grand, assuming Father – but it doesn't bear thinking about.

It is strange about Father. He can be so infuriating – and not just today – but at the same time he is still my father. We haven't talked much recently, and our paths will cross even less now I will be working more. It's easy to poke fun at him for it, but he is writing to the paper again. He stopped completely after Edward was killed – and now he's sending them letters once more. It must be a good sign, I suppose. One was entitled 'Orange Peel Nuisance'! He was incensed last week because he slipped on some orange peel and almost fell through a shop window. It could have been nasty, so I shouldn't be too hard on him, but his letter was couched in the same grave tones as if reporting some terrible disaster at Gallipoli. He hadn't seen the orange peel in the dark because he was avoiding people on the wrong side of the footpath. He wants the police and military to enforce the correct procedures. Walking more than two abreast should be made a criminal offence! And a speed limit of eight mph in the hours of darkness too! So be warned about your behaviour when you are next home on leave, Robert!

Leave? When might that be???? I hope that it will not be too long. The best Christmas present would be to hear about leave. Is there any chance of you being sent home to do more instructing? It would be even better to find you on the doorstep on Christmas Eve, wrapped up as a Christmas parcel! I have been thinking about Christmas and I don't know what to think. Things will be quite subdued here. Oxtobys' Grand Christmas Show of Game and Poultry has already started and we will still get a bird, but a smaller one. Edward always liked to choose ours. He said that as he was the only one who knew anything about ornithology, he was the best qualified. Of course it was ridiculous, but if you challenged him, you got a lecture in response. Meleagris galloparvo. I always remember that – the wild turkey bird. He must have said it to you too – Happy Meleagris Galloparvo Day. He always said it as I was about to eat my first piece of turkey on Christmas

Day and he'd add something incomprehensible about poor former colonial cousins and their thanksgiving dinners. Cranberries always got a mention - 'Mother', he would say, 'Isn't it about time that we tried some?' And she would reply - 'We will when we can get them on Princes Avenue.' And he would say with absolute certainty, 'Well, that will be next Christmas then.' And everyone would laugh.

I was looking through the decorations. It's hard to know what to put up. I came across some paper festoons we made that first Christmas here. They are a bit battered, but I'd hate them to be thrown away. Some of the ornaments are looking rather tired, but the glass ones are fine, unlike the silver embossed cardboard ones. It's a shame, as I chose them. Most are German, so we won't be replacing them soon. Doubtless some people will say it's unpatriotic to put them up. The gilded walnuts are my favourites, though. I will definitely make some more with Alice. I always enjoy brushing the egg-white on, then rolling them in the gold-leaf. We have a little left. It's the Day itself which will be hard. The cinemas are open, so mother may let us go. At least I won't be performing my awful party piece on Christmas Eve. And don't tell me you don't remember. Clement Moore has much to answer for. I will only subject you to one verse. A private recital!

He was chubby and plump, a right jolly old elf,
And I laughed when I saw him in spite of myself,
A wink of his eye and a twist of his head,
Soon gave me to know I had nothing to dread.

Twas the night before Christmas indeed. I hate it! Hate it! Hate it! Mother adores it. And no Dumb Crambo and no Snap-Dragon! I remember you once playing it with Edward and David and my pleading for a turn. They'd always refused before. Perhaps your being there changed their minds or perhaps they thought I was old enough at last. I can still feel my burnt fingers. Snatching raisins from burning brandy is not the most sensible way to get them! It was exciting. I'm glad Edward insisted on turning the lights out so we could see the eerie blue flames. You were so good at it – I remember being jealous. When this dreadful war is over, the first Christmas Eve afterwards I challenge you to a game of Snap-Dragon. But whatever we do do, I shall be thinking of you on Christmas Day. That's not to say that I don't on every other day!!

Have you heard about these possible peace talks? There was lots in the papers, but no-one seems sure about it. I'm not. Perhaps having a new Prime Minister will make a difference.

Mother has just been in. She saw my light. I hadn't realised the time. I ought to finish and I can catch the first post. I have written more than I intended! I hope you don't mind. Will I be able to think of something for my next letter? You may have to settle for a postcard. Mother is knocking again. I must stop.

Remember to be careful and do come back to me,
Votre amour Emily qui pense à toi tout le temps
xxxxx

P.S. I had to put my light on and re-read your last letter. You say some of the nicest things, which I don't deserve.

Bonne nuit, mon chéri
Un baiser supplémentaire

A real one
xxx

It's morning, but early, and I have just got back into bed to write this. I feel as if you are very near, but I don't want you to say anything, because what I am trying to remember might disappear. It's fading even now. I was dreaming – don't pull a face! – dreaming I was climbing a towering peak, high on a sheer rock face, impossibly steep. I moved effortlessly upwards. Around me were other mountain tops protruding from a sea of billowing white clouds that lay far beneath me. They looked so inviting that I let go and started falling towards them. I wasn't worried, even as I fell faster and faster. Then I plummeted right through the clouds and landed in the cockpit of your plane. You weren't at all surprised, just calm and reassuring. Did I want to go up or down? You'd take me anywhere. We moved towards the clouds and that's where it ended. I woke up wondering what would have happened next. I felt so peaceful and happy. With no glowing embers from the fire, it was quite dark in my room but it seemed quite bright outside. I was so warm and comfortable that I almost stayed in bed, but something about the light made me curious, so I got out, pulled a shawl round my shoulders and drew the curtains. It was breathtaking! It was beautiful. The snow had stopped and the sky was completely clear. The gardens were transformed. Everything was perfect and pristine. I never realised white could be such a vivid startling colour! All the trees and bushes had new identities, laden down as they were with snow. I was tempted to go outside, but the sensible me got the better of the impulsive me!

My eyes were drawn to the setting moon, whose light was strong enough to cast moon shadows. The branches of your apple tree reached out towards me, with long, black arms etched against the snow. Everything was silent. As I stood there, a bird started singing most exquisitely. In the day, there's always other sounds intruding, but against the silence it was magical. I heard a bird singing at night years ago, and I told Edward I'd heard a nightingale. He was scornful. We don't get them this far north, he said. No, it was a humble robin, who will sing at night even in winter. As I tried to see where my bird was singing, the eastern sky showed the first signs of change. I don't know how long I stood there under the song's spell, but as I listened the dream started to slip away. You remember that old scarecrow you and Edward made? Edward insisted that Mr Barber use it to protect the vegetable patch. It's still there – no-one can bear to move it. It has never looked very realistic but under its thick snowy mantle it was totally changed. It is absurd, but I imagined that as dawn broke, it would stir into life, pull out a pipe and accompany the bird's bewitching song. But sadly, the song ended and the Piper became again a scarecrow covered in snow.

And then the first rays of the sun touched the tops of the roofs over in Marlborough Avenue and I realised I was cold and my feet were freezing – but this was the strangest thing, I felt at ease, not agitated and upset as I was yesterday.

I wasn't sure whether to write this, but I am glad I have, though I dare say you are wishing I'd slept the sleep of the just, untroubled by dreams, no matter how soothing!

You felt so close, Robert,

E

xxxxx

I've just looked outside again. It's lovely, but changed. My last day of free-dom today. As soon as I'm up, I will venture out to post this.

December 21st, 1916
Field's Café

If only she could reach down, slip off her shoes and rub her poor aching feet! Emily looked around her. Sitting on the balcony running around Field's Octagon Cafe was hardly the place to do that. Stifling a yawn, she admitted to herself that setting off at six-thirty every morning was proving harder to get used to than she had expected. Perhaps meeting her aunt after a hard day's labour wasn't such a good idea after all. No, she chided herself, it was always a treat to eat at Field's.

A conversational buzz mingled with the gentle rattle of crockery. Waitresses in their smart black and white uniforms bustled around. Below her, surrounded by a jungle of potted plants, six immaculately dressed and groomed young ladies were assembling in the centre of the room. Miss Kate Erl's Orchestra of Ladies was about to begin its programme of varied light music. Behind them Emily caught sight of her aunt and waved.

"I am sorry to be late," Eleanor said, sitting down a few moments later, "We were delayed by a fare dodger. Pathetic-looking young thing, who I doubt has the forty shillings today's journey will have cost her." She sighed. "But to pleasanter things." She smiled at Emily. "Have you ordered? No? Then I suggest a full selection of cakes, a plate of toasted muffins and tea." After ordering Eleanor continued, "Are you all right, Emily? You look a little pale."

"I'm just a little tired."

"I should have thought!" Eleanor said. "Here I am, making you come into town, when all you want is a rest at home!"

"No, Aunt. I don't mind at all, and I am glad to see you." She laughed, "I haven't come just for the cakes, delicious as I'm sure they will be."

"Well I'm delighted that you have come, Emily. I saw your mother earlier and said I hoped you'd return with me after tea as I have something to show you. I won't keep you late – and I shall order a cab to take you home." She looked beyond Emily. "Ah, our cakes. Don't they look splendid?"

Choosing was difficult, but Emily settled on a pastry.

"I might start with one of those too. Here's our tea. Shall I pour?" Eleanor said. "I'm sure there are things you want to ask me and I will answer your questions later – but first, how have you been getting on?"

Emily sipped her tea and thought of the last few days. "It's quite difficult, but I'm sure things will improve. I don't mean it's bad. It's not. It's just I had too high expectations... of what I'd be doing. I've been more of a scullery drudge than a ministering angel. I always took it for granted... what people like Ivy and others do. Even Alice. It's hard work, but at least I can come afterwards to places like this and eat lovely things with you." She held out her hands. "Take a good look and say goodbye. Everyone says you get factory hands after a while. But it's not much of a sacrifice, is it?" She examined her skin again. "I meant to get some Icilma cream. The nurses swear by it. But Aunt," exclaimed Emily, pointing at the cake-stand, "you're still on your first!"

"Don't worry. I lunched quite late with your mother, so I won't starve. We went to the Industrial School's Christmas celebration. The girls were delighted with their three new pennies and their presents from former pupils. But do continue, Emily. Tell me more about Brooklands."

"Most people have been friendly, though I was warned not to get on the wrong side of a couple of the nurses, who look down on anyone in light blue. They've done three years' training, but some VADs have done a lot of first aid, even if I haven't." She sighed. "I suppose I could have continued as I've been doing these last months."

"Things are bound to feel strange to begin with, but someone with your ability shouldn't worry. And I'm not saying that because I'm your aunt."

"It's like being back at school, but blue everywhere – even the walking patients, but at least they have red ties. And blue doesn't particularly suit me."

"Emily! I never thought of you being... vain! Blue not suiting you indeed! What a thing to complain about."

"Oh, Aunt. I'm not that bothered. And I haven't any plans to force the entire nursing profession into browns, oranges or greens, just because they suit me better. No, I'll just take over the hospital, as red would be best of all. But that's enough about me, Aunt."

After much thought, earlier, she had decided on a direct approach. She took a deep breath. "What's happened between you and Father? I've been so worried. What he said confused me. No... confused is the wrong word... baffled, bewildered, disturbed – all of those and more. You know he doesn't want me to see you so often? Mother must have said something when I was in the kitchen. And then the things I didn't know... all those things you haven't told me." She couldn't help it coming out as an accusation.

"Emily, the last thing I wanted was to upset or hurt you, and truly there is nothing for you to be so worried about."

Emily found this hard to believe.

"Please don't look like that. I meant to reassure you, not alarm you. Your father and I have never seen things the same way. On Saturday we had a more vehement exchange of views than we should have done. Your father tends to over-react, something I've been guilty of exploiting in the past. And yes, on Saturday I was perhaps..." Emily had rarely seen her aunt looking contrite before, "...a little over-enthusiastic in advancing my views." She waited for the waitress to deposit some toasted muffins on the table. "And may we have some more hot water please? Have you had enough cake, Emily?" Emily nodded. "And you may take the cake stand. Thank you," Eleanor said, before turning back to her niece. "Your father may be upset, but I've never known him hold a long-term grudge against me before."

Emily thought that grudges had to start somewhere.

"And don't fret. It will blow over." Emily bit into her hot muffin, considering her response. If her aunt was right, then she had been worrying too much, but her aunt hadn't heard everything he'd said or the way he'd said it.

"But what was the argument about? And the things you haven't told me. Being arrested?"

"It's best if I tell you about Saturday and your father now, and answer your other questions when we get home."

She was nervous, thought Emily.

"I was waiting for your mother and..."

December 16th, 1916
Westbourne Avenue

Ten to three! Whatever was keeping her sister? Eleanor looked at the clock again. Edward's letter was still there, still unread. Perhaps she should try again to persuade Clara to open it in the New Year? Poor Edward! Such a terrible waste, like so much in this blessed war!

She sighed. And what about Emily? Becoming a VAD was all very well, but to be denied her chance by that father of hers! Eleanor looked at the fire. "I wish I'd burnt his letter!" she said out loud.

Dear Eleanor,

Thank you for your letter of the fourteenth. I assume that your offer is genuine. It will come as no surprise that I will not be availing myself of it. It confirms that you labour under the misapprehension that you know best where Emily's future is concerned. I am afraid you do not.

You presumably believe monetary considerations played a part in my decision to forbid her to pursue her undergraduate ambitions. Nothing could be further from the truth. In the current grave situation, we should not be encouraging young women to fritter away their time pursuing pointless academic qualifications. There is an essential contradiction between a matrimonial estate, something which I hope Emily aspires to, and working as a woman in a professional capacity. Presumably you think Emily should consider becoming a teacher, an occupation that women quite rightly have to give up on entering marriage. Aren't these women guilty of wasting the resources invested in training them? Women who work in jobs where intellectual ability is a requirement should forego marriage. I hope that Emily will find something more practical and useful to occupy her time. It was disappointing for her, but in time she will come to terms with it and realise that, given the circumstances, I was right to deny her her wishes.

You might consider your wish to subsidise Emily through university a worthy one. Perhaps you do not understand how insulting your proposition is? I resent the implication that I have been so fiscally imprudent that I do not have the resources to pay for my own daughter. I can imagine no feasible scenario where I could not meet the monetary needs of any member of this family. As to your suggestion that we keep this proposed transaction confidential – I would have thought clandestine a more appropriate term – I have no intention of mentioning it to Emily. I do recognise that when I previously requested a cooperative silence on your part, you complied with my wishes, albeit reluctantly. Rest assured, Emily's prospects will not be adversely affected by my rejection of your proposal.

Reading your letter has reminded me of your own fiscal situation. You may recollect that when you found yourself unexpectedly owning a number of properties, as well as having a complicated financial portfolio to administer, I offered to help you. You preferred to handle matters yourself. It would be ungenerous of me not to admit that you have made a reasonable, if inconsistent, success of this, but I remain willing to advise you on your business affairs. I say this now because Clara has told me that you have spent considerable sums of money on improvements to your properties. Whilst this may improve their value as capital assets, apparently you have no intention of increasing your rents commensurately to take account of your sizeable investment. Your tenants may be delighted by this unexpected and unwarranted generosity – largesse even – but it seems perilously short-sighted to a man of business like myself. What you do with your money is entirely up to you. Some of your donations have been admirably Christian, but I worry that you are in danger of crossing the fine line between the charitable and the profligate. I would hate to think of you squandering your inheritance through an inability or unwillingness to maximise its potential. Your late husband would be dismayed if there was the slightest chance of his sterling achievements being put at risk through well-meaning ignorance. If you wish, I would be happy to discuss these points further with you either here or at the bank,

yours
Alfred

The rejection of her proposal had been unsurprising, but even now her blood boiled at the sheer effrontery of the man. Lecturing her about her finances! Not for the first time, she thought what a shame it was that you could choose your friends but not your brother-in-law.

A journal lying on the occasional table at the end of the sofa caught her attention. Perhaps that might prove a welcome distraction. Seeing the title, she hesitated, but picked it up anyway and sat down and opened it.

"You've finally found something worthwhile to read then?" She hadn't heard her brother-in-law come in. "*The Imperialist* – I see you've got my latest copy, Eleanor." He half-smiled at her. "The first issue was only in October. You were so engrossed that I almost hated disturbing you. The other copies are in my study, if you'd like to borrow them, pass them on even... I am sure some of your more eccentric acquaintances might learn something from them."

"Learn something?" If Eleanor hadn't so recently been thinking of his letter, she might have continued in more measured tones, been more diplomatic. "Learn something from this?" She shook it vigorously. "What could I learn from this squalid apology for a newspaper? Apart from the fact that this Pemberton-Billing, MP, fills pages of print with ill-informed, speculative bile. Listen to this, Alfred! 'Undesirable aliens are nested amongst us as vermin incubate in walls of old houses'. By that I assume he means the decent local men and women who've been hounded out of their businesses and homes. Or this. 'The right of asylum has been given to the worst sort – due to the influence of the shekel, an example of the vast and waxing power of the Jewish race'. I despise Asquith, but not because he might belong to this supposed conspiracy of thirty-eight Jewish MPs. What's more worrying is that there are people stupid enough to waste eight shillings a year subscribing to it." Had she gone too far? Might as well be hung for a sheep as a lamb, she thought. "And what do you mean by my eccentric acquaintances? Oh, you mean people who actually care what is happening to this country! People alarmed at the way that our liberties, our free speech, our traditional values are being eaten away, and all in the name of this cursed war. Last month when I was in Cardiff..."

"Yes," he interrupted her, "Clara told me, and it was mentioned in the paper. A wild goose chase half way across the country and for what?" He paused. "To attend a thwarted meeting of the National Council Against Conscription! I am sorry Eleanor, I'm wrong, aren't I? They weren't happy being called that. Aren't they the National Council of Civil Liberties, or have they changed again? It gets most confusing. Was it the Union of Democratic Control you were so fashionably involved with, or is that a different group of dissenters? And the No Conscription Fellowship – where does that fit in? You must give me a lesson some time. Don't look so doubtful! I mean it, know thy enemy." He could not keep the sneer out of his voice as he continued, "And are you still a paid up member of the Independent Labour Party, a political group who spend their time arguing amongst themselves, splitting here, there and everywhere?"

She knew what Alfred said was true. Far more anger and vitriol was directed at dissenters by so-called patriotic miners than was ever directed at the mine owners. As to the local ILP, the level of sheer hatred that existed between its two factions had resulted in the attack she'd witnessed at Cory Hall.

"It's why you and your sort will never get anywhere, Eleanor. Your failed campaigning for the vote should have taught you that. And as to the need for a National Council for Civil Liberties," he paused, "I have never heard anything quite so preposterous. The people putting our liberties at risk are those fighting for the Kaiser and those giving succour to the enemy by their actions. I and millions of others," he gestured at the paper Eleanor was still holding, "prefer to put our faith in John Bull to protect our liberties rather than in... do tell me, Eleanor, might I have heard of somebody on this National Council of yours? Which nonentity did you fail to hear speak?"

Her annual trip to South Wales had been to fulfil obligations she still felt to her late husband's family, or, if she were honest, to still her sense of guilt, but she had timed it to attend the meeting.

"So many questions, Alfred." Why was she sitting looking up at him? She stood up, pleased at how this simple action unsettled him. "Yes, I am still in the ILP. And the Union of Democratic Control – which is, and I hate to disappoint you," she brandished the crumpled copy of *The Imperialist*, "not the pro-German conspiracy your disreputable friends paint it as. Reason must overcome the insanity gripping us and much of the world." He's looking at me as if I were some well-meaning simpleton, she thought. "If I didn't believe that, I would have given in to despair, but I've no intention of doing that. As to the speakers, Ramsay MacDonald..."

"Ramsay MacDonald! Ramsay MacDonald!" Previously patronising and disapproving, he was now angry. "James MacDonald Ramsay is his name. He'd have spoken under false colours, as when he spouts his treason in Parliament. And ashamed he should be, that illegitimate son of a Scotch servant girl!" His malevolence took Eleanor by surprise.

"But Alfred..."

"That duplicitous, deceitful creature does more to denigrate this country, besmirch its standing in the world and help an enemy state than all the rest of his ragamuffin band. It would not surprise me if he were drawing his pay from the Kaiser's pockets."

"Don't be..."

"Don't be what, Eleanor? Loyal? A nationalist? A patriot? Your sort speak as if you're making clever points at some Cambridge debating society. I hate to disillusion you, but we are not. We are at war, Eleanor, at war! Ramsay MacDonald, and those other disgraceful reprobates in his pro-German conclave... that one sacked from Oxford for writing that subversive pamphlet, Bentham somebody..."

"For goodness sake, Alfred! When you slander people, at least get their names right. Presumably you meant Bertrand Russell – who was at Cambridge, not Oxford."

"It doesn't matter what their names are. Your Scottish friend should be justifying his remarks before a court martial. Patriots in Cardiff stopped him from abusing this country's freedoms, promulgating his sedition to misguided, preposterous..."

"Oh, don't be so utterly ridiculous. I wish you could hear yourself," she said. "You actually believe that arrant nonsense? We need to defend liberties from people like you. And you've the nerve to say we're preposterous." She laughed. "The only preposterous thing in this room is you! You've the gall to insult a man of high principle. Do you even know what principles are? A man resigning as party leader to oppose this war. Being against this war does not make someone pro-German. And you have the temerity to lecture me about abusing freedom? Have you *any* idea what it was like to be there? I'm sorry, Alfred, the only people abusing freedom in Cardiff were in that thuggish mob. And what was so sickening was that the rabble-rouser inciting them to violence was a sitting Labour MP." She hesitated, memories flooding back...

The baying crowd outside singing 'God save the King' and 'Rule Britannia' with ferocious menace. The police preventing them from locking the doors and letting the assault proceed unopposed. The rousing rendition of 'The Red Flag' whilst they attempted to keep the attackers out. The cries of 'To hell with the Kaiser', 'Get into khaki', 'Traitors to the flag', and 'Clear the Germans out'. The mob surging in and setting about the men inside. The police leading away the dissenters' leaders to be pelted with mud and tomatoes by the hundreds outside. As a woman, she had been spared physical assault, but it had been a miracle that no-one had been seriously injured or killed at Cory Hall.

"Eleanor, you are so naïve." Alfred said. "You, from your comfortable background. You, with your blinkered view of the British working man. You, believing that the labouring class will follow these dissenters like sheep. Your proletariat... Oh, Eleanor! Your expression! If only you could see yourself in a mirror."

"Alfred, I don't know what you're talking about."

"I've never told you before, but that look of annoying righteous superiority you are prone to does become wearing. Perhaps it's all the time you've spent marooned on the moral high ground. Thank God it's not hereditary! Clara could hardly be more different."

Where was her sister? She'd regret it when she heard about their argument. She attempted a conciliatory gesture. "Alfred," she said managing a weak smile. "Can't we refrain from needless insults and keep this conversation on a more civilised level?"

"We can always try. Clara would wish us to, and I hadn't realised I was being either uncivilised or insulting. Perhaps we should both sit down and proceed in a more measured manner. It would be more comfortable than standing here like..." he searched for a light-hearted phrase, "a pair of pugnacious verbal pugilists." He gestured for her to sit. "What has happened to your tea? That *is* why you're here?" She waited for him to sit. "Very good, Eleanor." It was an uneasy truce rather than a cessation of hostilities. "But if you feel outwitted, Eleanor, you are welcome to retire from the fray."

"Why should I? You confuse arguing powerfully with having a powerful argument." She kept her voice even and moderate. "I shall not give you the satisfaction of seeing me back away."

"I'd be surprised if you did. But there's no need to be shocked by my using the word proletariat. Yes, the proletariat must be a massive disappointment to you. Mercifully, the vast majority of ordinary men will have no truck with ill-assorted pasty-faced pacifists and peace cranks, being nationalists who love their King and their Country." He paused. "Were you about to come out with one of your clever responses?"

"I was, but please do carry on until you've hung yourself with your own specious arguments."

"You may be in for a long wait, though not as long as waiting for your socialist rabble to seize the means of production and lay waste to everything down Whitefriargate. But please help me on one point," he continued. "What about banks and their managers in your new utopia? And the petite bourgeoisie? Excellent! I've surprised you again. You'll have conflicting interests, you know. Your family or your beliefs? You'd have to betray one or the other."

"Do you expect me to answer that, Alfred? You'd expect me to be a tricoteuse?"

"A twentieth century Madame Desfarge? How delightful! As the tumbrils roll you finally find gainful employment. How is your knitting?"

"Excellent, but I haven't knitted your name into anything. I'm struggling to see you as some modern Sidney Carton laying down his life to protect the interest rates of small investors."

"A pointless gesture, Eleanor. The markets always decide. But a far better thing if the Bastille isn't stormed in the first place. Remember what happened to Madame Desfarge! Your friends will have their Robespierre too. But you underestimate me, Eleanor. You always have done. Those who disagree with you are not imbecilic. You've never understood why people with a modicum of intelligence don't always come to the same conclusions as you."

"I've never doubted your intelligence, Alfred. Don't accuse me of that. I simply..."

"I can read you like a book, Eleanor... It may come as a surprise to you, but I've read more than Dickens – a little politics, even. Not that I could match your sheer breadth of literary compass. Give me a good John Buchan any day. All those tales of derring-do! Have you read *The Thirty-nine Steps*? No? You should. All those spies running around the Scottish borders, and Richard Hannay, the quintessential hero who puts his country's interests first. And the denouement? Brilliant. Quite political, quite relevant, but not in the same league as your serious writers." A harshness crept back into his voice. "Your Great Political Thinkers. Aren't they all foreigners? But with your gift for languages, you doubtless read them in the original. German for example. *Eins, zwei, drei* won't take you far, not even in a bank." He laughed at his little joke. "German sounds such a harsh language. Do you pick up the nuances? The hidden meanings? The duplicity? Knowing if someone is being honest is hard enough in English. At least, I say what I mean and mean what I say. Don't you agree?" Alfred looked at Eleanor, waiting for an answer.

"I can agree with you there, Alfred. You'd be happy for 'A plain talking Yorkshireman and proud of it' to be your epitaph. No, it's what you say and what you mean that I have a problem with."

"Very good, Eleanor," he said, not appearing to take offence. "But returning to German, that rousing call to arms – 'Workers of the world unite, you have nothing to lose but your chains'. Complete balderdash, but it has a certain ring to it. What would that be in its original German?"

She decided to humour him. "You'll have to make allowance for my accent, and whatever you may think, I am distinctly rusty. As far as I remember, it's something like... *Proletarier aller Länder vereinigt Euch!*"

"Quite impressive, and fewer words than I'd imagined. It sounds very guttural. If only our local pork butcher was still in business, I could have greeted him with that." He had surprised her.

"Yes, it is shorter. The last line of the original Communist Manifesto translates as 'Working Men of All Countries, Unite!' You quoted the popularised version. But I'm impressed! You sell yourself short in those letters to the *Mail* and the *Morning News*; you should tackle more interesting subjects. No, more thought-provoking, I should say. That one about bona-fide street retailers' livelihoods being threatened by chocolate being sold in large offices was... fascinating," she smiled, "though hardly the weightiest topic to put pen to paper about. If you lack confidence, *I* could assist you. For example, short and pithy can be more effective than the long and verbose. I'd be happy to lend you some reading matter to extend your range. You might become a doyen of the letters page of the *Times*. You could even borrow Engels' *Die Lage der Arbeitenden Klasse in England – The Condition of the Working Class in England*. It's most informative. Please feel free to seek my literary advice, either here or at my home, any time, any time at all."

When he didn't answer and the silence lengthened, she knew she had gone too far. His letters were tedious and banal, but should she have derided them, especially after her earlier conciliatory appeal? It had been satisfying, but she should have resisted the impulse. Deep down she knew why she hadn't – she had never cared for him, and remembering his letter had encouraged her to make her spurious offer. However, it was too late. Attacking his views was one thing, mocking his letters was another matter entirely.

"A magnanimous offer," he finally said, his voice distant and abrasive, "but one I must decline." His demeanour had changed: his lips were pursed, his brow furrowed and there was a sour expression on his face. The tension was palpable. "Reading the work of a German, even a dead one, hardly seems appropriate. And how an unreadable diatribe might prove a subject for a letter is beyond me. Presumably you lectured on it during those infernal Lake District trips when you were promoting International Friendship with your foreign friends. You and your comrades thinking you'd avert a war by sitting round a camp-fire singing in German. Pathetic. You've stayed in touch with your..." he paused, loading his last two words with invective, "continental confidants?"

"I'm still in touch with some, but with others it's too difficult. And the language around a camp-fire is irrelevant, Alfred. We often sang 'La Marseillaise'. A decent tune to sing along with is important, understanding the words isn't."

"Thank God, there aren't many people singing along to your tune, let alone listening to your measly words. Your cause is nothing more than an exercise in complete futility!"

"Typical. You seem to believe that the majority is always right. I'm pragmatic enough to know that some of my views are unpopular..."

"Some?" he snorted.

"Far better to be a voice in the wilderness than like you: comfortable, self-satisfied and complacent. I almost said smug. Yes, smug! Mesmerised by the platitudinous lies this government and our newspapers feed us. Aren't these peace offers making you think? No, better to be prejudiced, ill-informed and unwilling to learn anything. Isn't there the tiniest chink in that armour of unquestioning acceptance? You say I underestimate you. Show me I'm wrong. Write about something important. Write to Lloyd George, even. No, I forgot. You detest the man, but only for putting a penny on income tax, not for condemning thousands more families to the heartache that this family has gone through. And you accuse me of an exercise in futility. What was more futile than Edward's death? What do you want?" She pointed at the mantelpiece. "Another letter Clara won't open?" She hesitated, before adding in a voice which was softer, barely audible, almost pleading and breaking with emotion, "Isn't one good enough for you?" Her words ebbed away into silence. She felt drained.

"How dare you! How dare you! Don't you think a day hasn't passed when I haven't thought of Edward and questioned whether his dying was worth it? You won't understand that his death would only be pointless if we're taken in by the hypocritical humbug and lies coming out of Berlin. Lies you've completely fallen for. If more sacrifices are needed to prevent the greater disaster of peace with an arrogant, unrepentant Germany, then I am willing to pay that price." He looked at her with glacial intensity. "Lecturing me about the war," he waited, then added, "and interfering in my family. But we know why that is, don't we?"

"I can't think what you mean," she said, but her hesitancy betrayed her.

"*I* have had a family, which, for all my perceived faults," he glared at her again, "I have raised and supported. You have done neither. Yes, it was a personal tragedy, being left a widow at such a young age, before you had children of your own. I cannot blame you for what happened, and it was shameful when some people suggested otherwise. If Thomas's relations are content for you to visit, then what right has anyone to say anything about it? But the weight of responsibility, even one so unfairly attributed, must be a wearisome thing to bear. I have always admired the way you've done that. You may not have reached the celestial city, but your sojourn in the slough of despond is behind you." His weak smile and feigned sympathy were infuriating. He was waiting to see if his barbs were having the desired effect.

"It could have happened to anyone, Eleanor. Accidents do happen, so you mustn't still blame yourself. It was a long time ago."

She mustn't let him see how upset she was. "What has... what has what happened to Thomas to do with what we've been arguing about? Your children have been a tremendous boon and comfort to me."

"You're right, Eleanor. No, it was unforgivable and ungentlemanly, mentioning such a difficult topic, and I apologise," his voice oozed insincerity. "Please don't look so hurt, it doesn't suit you. It just makes you look... pitiable."

Annoyed she'd let him see the wounding effect of his comments, she made no effort to disguise her emotions, and gave him a look of the purest venom.

"Bravo, that's so much better. It suits you so much more. I do believe you've found your natural expression."

With difficulty she ignored the comment.

"I may not have had children, but what I do know is that yours turned out so well despite rather than because of you. And I hope, pray even, that Emily overcomes the obstacles that you've strewn in her path. She's so bright, has so much potential, and if she fails to fulfil it... but I'm just wasting my breath."

"Yes, you are. And as you mention Emily, you have had, and are having, far too much influence over the girl, something that needs my serious consideration. I wish I could describe it as a benign influence! But I can't. As to your false peace agitating, if you were not my sister-in-law I would ask you to go. On reflection, I shall take my leave instead, before anything else is said that we may have cause to regret." He started to move towards the door.

"Don't you want to take this drivel with you?" She held the *Imperialist* out towards him.

He paused, before taking a few more steps, and stopped with his hand on the handle. He half turned to face her.

"No, you keep it. Let's call it an early Christmas present. After all, Eleanor, it is almost the season of goodwill. I shall bid you good afternoon." With that he opened the door and strode out of the room, pulling the door shut behind him.

She stared at the door, and sighed. It had been the most ferocious argument they'd ever had. She felt light headed, almost dizzy. A strange mixture of exultancy and deep regret coursed through her. The argument had been invigorating, but his last comments had left her uneasy. And this veiled threat about her and Emily! Part of her wanted to laugh. He was criticising her for having too much influence, when that was the last thing she wanted. Emily was of an independent mind and thought for herself. How little he knew his daughter! Arguments before had blown over in days, but this might be different.

She was still clenching the copy of the *Imperialist* and deposited it with relish in the waste-paper basket. If only she could wash, and cleanse her hands of its filth. She was at a loss as to whether to stay or go and find her sister. Voices were coming from the hall. If it were Emily, what should she say? No, it would be better to wait here. She noticed that the fire needed making up. The temperature in the room had dropped in more ways than one, she thought. She returned to the basket, removed the offending journal, tore off its front cover, screwed it up and threw it on the fire. It was satisfying seeing it burst into flames. She was tempted to burn the whole thing, but that would damp down the fire, so she picked up some tongs and added a couple of pieces of coal instead. She heard the door open behind her.

"You could have waited for Alice to do that when she brings the tea things in." Eleanor turned and saw her sister. "But why worry about the fire? *That* can easily be made up," Clara continued, giving her a look of utter exasperation. "I blame myself, as I'd almost forgotten you were here. I came back from next door only to be waylaid by Alice bending my ear about her workload and how she wants us to take on a tweenie. Then I come into the hall to be confronted by Alfred in a foul temper. What on earth happened? I've never known him so furious. He's considering not letting Emily see you again. I'll do my best to persuade him otherwise, but whatever you've said, you've gone too far. You've always had a selfish streak, Eleanor, even when you were little. You happily go your own way, not bothering about the consequences of your actions. Have you ever thought what it's like being the one in the middle between you and Alfred? No, of course you haven't. Why should you? You actually enjoy arguing with him. I suppose it was about the war. You know how he feels. But no, you couldn't resist it, could you? It was too good an opportunity to miss. I dread to think how much time I've spent over the years mending fences between you, but this time they might be beyond repair."

Clara moved to an armchair and slumped into it. "Oh, do sit down, Eleanor," she finished, irritated beyond measure, "Don't just stand there holding the tongs."

Eleanor generally thought Clara too meek and mild-mannered for her own good, but being subjected to this withering attack took her back to her childhood, when her sister had habitually ordered her about. She sat down. "I'm sorry, Clara, but you should have heard what he was saying."

"It's too late for apologies, Eleanor," her sister said. "The damage is done. He doesn't want you here in the house when he's at home... for the foreseeable future, whatever that means. And Emily will be here in a few minutes. Oh dear, I'd almost forgotten about her. The tea was nearly ready when I left Alice, so..." she took a deep breath and let out a long sigh. "I sometimes wonder whether the Lord sent you as some sort of trial for me. Punishing me for something, perhaps."

For once, Eleanor stayed silent. Her sister gave her a warning look.

"When Emily brings the tea in, don't make any sort of remark. It would be better if you didn't say anything at all, but you will not say anything about this afternoon's events either. Is that clear?"

"Yes, but..."

"No buts! You know what Emily thinks of you. She had the misfortune to be in the hall when Alfred came out and he has already spoken to her. I don't know exactly what he said, but I have a very good idea. He mentioned your relationship with her. She was looking extremely worried when I sent her to the kitchen, so be careful what you say. I will do my best, and so will you, to keep this a normal afternoon tea."

"Clara, she's bound to ask at some point about what's happened, especially if Alfred has been blackening my name. If she asks me I'll have to answer."

"That will not happen this afternoon, Eleanor, I assure you. If the topic comes up later, you will give her an edited version of events. One that paints neither of you in too black a light. I won't ask you to lie, but you will omit the more unpleasant details. Oh, I can hear them coming. Do you promise, Eleanor? Eleanor! Do you promise?"

"Very well. I promise," she said, adding under her breath as the door opened, "to do whatever is in Emily's best interest."

December 21st, 1916
Field's Café

"But there must have been more to it than that? Why should he be so angry, if it were just about the peace proposals? And would he have said some of the things he did... about you, unless there was something else?"

Eleanor took a long time to reply. "Your father has been looking rather weary recently, and when people are tired they say things they don't really mean. I've been guilty of that in the past. But if he has a good rest at Christmas, his spirits will improve, and who knows what will happen?"

"You could both make New Year's resolutions," Emily said, "to make allowances and try to get on better."

"Your father's never been keen on New Year's resolutions. And I tend to agree. Mine have never lasted beyond the ninth or tenth of January."

The tenth. Robert's birthday, Emily thought.

"Let's see what happens, Emily." Eleanor reached across and squeezed Emily's hand. It was evident that was the end of the matter. "Now, any more tea, dear?" she continued. "There's a little hot water left. And the last muffin. You aren't letting it go to waste?"

"They're delicious, but I couldn't eat another thing." Emily was reasonably, if not totally, reassured by her aunt's words. "And I've had enough tea, thank you. It was all lovely."

"Then, if you can attract that waitress's attention, I'll pay, and if you're not too tired, we'll head off home, where I promise I'll tell you about my escapades with his Majesty's Constabulary."

Emily gave her aunt a questioning look.

"Emily, I promise. You may ask me anything you like."

Pank! Pank! Pank!

"This was my favourite," said Emily, laughing and holding up a card. "I'd quite forgotten! Here they are... the two ladies, one in green, the other in purple, brandishing their umbrellas at three large policemen. I always wondered what happened next." She placed the card face up on the table and started sorting through the rest. "It was a bit like rummy, wasn't it? I always felt sorry for the lady being offered food in prison. Gaol! Gaol! Gaol! you had to shout if you collected all of those. I sometimes used to put all the cards face down and try to pick matching pairs and then arrange them in sets." She smiled at the memory. "Have you got the box? Yes, here it is." She studied the cover, then read, "PANKO or Votes for Women. The Great Card Game. Suffragists v Anti-suffragists." She smiled. "We should have another game sometime."

"Yes, we must, though it's a long time since we've played, and when we did I always avoided talking about the Cause, because your father held strong views. Now he's said what he has, things have changed. Why don't you pick a card, then finish sorting them into their sets? They might help me tell my story."

"Pank first, I think," Emily said, choosing a card showing a determined-looking, middle-aged woman, standing with her arms folded, a purple head-scarf drawn round her head.

"The Pankhursts? It's difficult knowing where to start. An extraordinary family! But as you've got Mrs Pankhurst, we'll begin with her. For a time, I admired her more than almost anyone else alive, and like many others I believed she'd change things almost single-handedly." She sighed. "Mrs Pankhurst was, in many ways, a remarkable lady, but my opinion, as on many other things, changed." Eleanor looked uncomfortable. "Nevertheless, I wish you could have seen her. She was a brilliant speaker. I heard her many times, but that first time, when she spoke on Hessle Road in the 1907 by-election, I remember as if it were yesterday. You were far too young to come, and your mother wouldn't, even though it was only on the corner of the Boulevard. When I arrived, there was a fair sprinkling of women, but most were ordinary working men, there out of curiosity, I imagine. She would have been a bit of a novelty. She spoke for over an hour and was so impressive, but anyone indulging in public speaking on Hessle Road, especially in a broad Lancashire accent, is likely to get some ribbing." She smiled and took a deep breath, "'Come and join uzz!'" Eleanor laughed. "She was fond of saying it, but not quite like that."

"No, Aunt," said Emily, laughing. "You're wrong, that was magnificent. But do carry on about Mrs Pankhurst."

"She was especially good at coping with heckling. It was good-natured back then, unlike later, when abuse was the least you had to worry about. Her deep voice carried without resorting to shouting, whether in Hyde Park or the less grand stage of Hessle Road. A friend said she delivered 'iced but brilliant discourses', which is a trifle unfair. She was an impassioned, fanatical torch-bearer for the Cause, and she was *never* a dull speaker. I was unsure about militant suffragists then," she smiled, noticing Emily's doubtful look. "I know, everyone, even the Pankhursts, uses the term suffragettes now, but anything that starts as a term of abuse invented by one of Lord Northcliffe's minions at *The Daily Mail* leaves me feeling a little uneasy. I know I am being particular, but put it down to my strange, idiosyncratic nature. And the NUWSS was always much, much stronger here."

"The NUWSS?"

"Emily! I'm shocked! We ended up with a plethora of organisations, but I'm surprised... The National Union of Women's Suffrage Societies. You must have heard of Millicent Fawcett?"

Emily made a confident guess. "Its leader?"

"Yes, an extraordinary lady. A great friend of Murdie's, and Murdie was the reason the NUWSS was the dominant force in suffragism around here."

"Murdie? Your friend, the doctor, who died earlier this year?"

"Yes, in March." Eleanor sighed. "Such a dreadful waste. But it was typical of her, going out on a emergency visit in the middle of an awful night and ending up wading knee deep through the snow." She shook her head. "And then she ended up with pneumonia. She'd already had pleurisy that winter. Her system just couldn't cope." Eleanor stood up, picked up the decanter on the sideboard and poured herself a glass of sherry. "When I first changed my allegiances, I felt guilty, that I was betraying Murdie. All those weekly committee meetings at her house, and the rest, but the WSPU..." she glanced at Emily.

"The Women's Social and Political Union. I *do* know that one."

"...seemed more dynamic, invigorating, able to breathe new life into the Cause. Murdie was sympathetic, as was the local branch, and her refusal to condemn militant actions eventually led her to resign and join the WSPU herself." She gave Emily a rueful smile. "It was shortly before I deserted them. Not the best timing on my part, but it never affected our friendship. Nothing ever did." She reached forward and took the card from Emily. "Mind you, she never had time for Mrs Pankhurst; too autocratic and controlling, she said." She studied the card. "It's not a bad likeness, but she was frailer when I last saw her: all those hunger and thirst strikes took their toll. I dread to think what the outcome would have been if anyone had force-fed her. Someone once said to me that Emmeline had tragic, smouldering eyes, which was rather a good description. I also heard it said that she displayed a wearied contempt for people, but that's a little harsh, though she could be aloof. She was much better at communicating with crowds than individuals. But woe betide you if you crossed her or Christabel."

Eleanor regarded her glass. "Would you like a drink? I should have asked. There's some cordial if you are thirsty."

"I'm not, thank you," Emily said.

Eleanor replenished her glass. "I do remember you writing to me at Clement's Inn, when I lived in London."

"I recall writing to you a lot in London, and other places too. Clement's Inn? Yes, I think so. It always sounded like some Shakespearean tavern."

"It wasn't the Boar's Head tavern, with or without a Prince Hal. No, it was a former Inn of Chancery, though some of the barristers who passed through it were a pretty dissolute lot." She smiled and took a sip of her sherry. "Mentioning disagreeing with Mrs Pankhurst reminded me of it. Clement's Inn, the WSPU's headquarters thanks to the unlimited largesse of Frederick and Emmeline Pethick-Lawrence. People said they put a thousand pounds a year into the coffers and provided the money for the Pankhursts to move to London, as well as starting the *Votes for Women* newspaper. They worked tirelessly for years. They did so much and they both suffered, physically and financially." Emily could tell her aunt was enthused about them. "But when Emmeline, or Peth as everyone called her, expressed her disquiet about the way the campaign was going, she found herself expelled. Ironically, the Pethicks were sued and ended up paying more than six thousand pounds in compensation for militant actions they'd actually opposed."

"Six thousand pounds!" Emily couldn't help but show her astonishment at such a huge sum.

"A number of us attended the auction at the Mascot and bought some of their possessions in order to return them, but she told me that only made three hundred pounds. It was a good job they had deep enough pockets to cover it all, but they came close to bankruptcy. But, and this is what was so annoying but also typical, since her expulsion she's never heard from or seen Mrs Pankhurst again."

"Do you still see her, Aunt?"

"Peth or Mrs Pankhurst?"

"Peth."

"I don't spend as much time in London as I once did, but I do see her now and then. She's always charming. We share common interests, belong to the same groups. She's active in the Women's International League for Peace, and she hasn't abandoned the Cause because of the war." Eleanor paused in her account. "Are you hungry, Emily? It's Sarah's evening off, but

I can rustle up something simple for us. There's some vegetable soup we could have, and there's neither parsnip nor swede in it."

"I'm still not hungry after our lovely tea, but soup, in a while, would be nice."

Eleanor looked again at the card of Mrs Pankhurst, before giving it back to Emily and continuing. "Like Murdie, I came to believe that Emmeline and Christabel were campaigning for democracy, while running their own hollow, authoritarian form of it. Military discipline, that was what they wanted! They were fighting a war, albeit a civil one. That wasn't the straw that finally broke this camel's back, but I did find it hard to accept. There again, military discipline didn't mean always being in control. According to Peth, the Pankhursts thought Emily Davison was a loose cannon. Always acting off her own bat, whether barricading herself in her Strangeways cell and being almost drowned when the fire hoses were turned on her, or throwing herself down an iron staircase at Holloway – and of course there was the tragic event at Epsom. But whatever the Pankhursts thought of her, they exploited her death unbelievably well for its propaganda value. No, perhaps I'm being unkind. I'm sure they were aghast too."

"Did you ever meet her, Aunt?"

"Meet? Emily Davison? Yes, I did. She was working full-time for the WSPU before I left, though we were never close. She made a striking figure about the place; slim and tall with a shock of red hair. I was always taken with her green eyes. She had such long arms. It's a strange thing to remember about someone. Very long arms."

"Were you able to watch the funeral procession?"

"Yes. So many women, some in white carrying laurel leaves, some in purple carrying red peonies, and the rest in black with their purple irises. It was magnificent. Where I was standing, the crowd was silent, and people were clearly moved by the spectacle. Regardless of what else I felt, it was impossible not to be affected by it. She was a martyr to the Cause."

Emily thought for a moment. "Father wouldn't have been affected. He wasn't at all sympathetic when he read about it. I remember him being angry and contemptuous. He described her as 'a deranged, mentally unbalanced woman whose actions put the King's horse and jockey at risk of serious injury' or something like that." She placed Mrs Pankhurst face down on the table. "What about the other Pankhursts? The daughters? You mentioned Christabel."

"Christabel? She had a cool analytical mind and would have made a brilliant barrister, if only she hadn't been refused entry by Lincoln's Inn. She had a law degree from Manchester, but what she didn't possess was the one qualification she could never acquire. She wasn't a man." Eleanor paused to let her words sink in. "She did make an attractive figure on a public platform, and when she spoke there was a clear, almost musical quality to her voice. But as to her character, there opinions start to differ. I reread Constance Lytton's autobiography recently. Please could you pass it to me? Second shelf towards the right. *Prisons and Prisoners.*"

Emily fetched the book.

"Thank you. I've marked a few things... Yes, here it is... Constance said of Christabel, 'She was the sunrise of the woman's movement, I cannot describe her in any other way. The glow of her great vitality and the joy of her being took hold of the movement and made it gladness. Yet, her nature being so essentially a woman's, there was a vein of tenderness throughout her speech, and her strength lay in her steadfast, resourceful and brilliant intellect.' She shut the book. "I'd agree with some of that, but she could also be cynical, and ruthless, even cold-hearted. I never found her an easy person to deal with and I found myself increasingly at odds with some of her views." Eleanor shrugged her shoulders, "Now that she and her mother have abandoned the Cause and spend all their time pontificating about their pro-war views from their jingoistic soapboxes, you won't be surprised that I have even less sympathy with them. I always much preferred the other daughters. Sylvia, for example."

"The eldest one?" asked Emily.

"No, the middle daughter. Unlike Christabel, Sylvia was always concerned about the plight of poor working class women. She believed all women should be enfranchised and not just the well-to-do and comfortably off. I was once asked what it was like to be a member of the Society Women's Political Union."

It took Emily a moment to understand the joke.

"At the time I laughed it off," Eleanor continued, "but the most effective jest, especially a barbed one, is one with an element of truth to it. Many of the WSPU's supporters were society women, but one could *never* accuse Sylvia of being a mere lady of fashion, resplendent in her silks and satins. No, she had no airs and graces. She was typically English, a little like you, quite slender, even girlish, with blue eyes and hair like yours. And politically, I had a good deal of sympathy with her, and not because she fell out with her elder sister and mother. She's been so active. The No Conscription campaign, the Labour..." her aunt gave her a penetrating look. "I know you're unsure, Emily, about my views on the war. But perhaps we should put those aside for now, though I apologise if they seep in from time to time."

"That's all right, Aunt, " Emily said, "do go on."

"I'm still in touch with Sylvia, but not as often as I once was. I liked Adela too, the youngest sister. She was only five foot, but was the most impassioned open-air orator of them all. She spoke here in the city several times and many times across Yorkshire. She was the best I've ever heard at dealing with hecklers. In Bradford, a man shouted out, 'If you were my wife, I'd give you a dose of poison.' Quick as a flash she replied, 'And if I were your wife I'd drink it.'"

Emily laughed out loud. "I could never do that, Aunt. I'd always think of something clever or witty afterwards, when it was too late. But I can't imagine speaking to a crowd either.'"

"You never know what you're capable of until you try, and I'm sure Adela didn't either. She was delightful, and I'll always remember her with affection. She was once in the iron grip of a hulking brute of a policeman who told her she should be at her wash-tub rather than disrupting Mr Churchill's speeches. She became so annoyed that she slapped him on his enormous hand. Seven days in Strangeways for assault! Such a slender slip of a girl! But Adela, like Sylvia, ended up having doubts, and now she's no longer with us. No, Emily, I didn't mean that she's died ... she's gone to Australia. There were rumours that she was encouraged to emigrate after arguing with her mother about the increasing violence."

"I can see why you have mixed feelings about the Pankhurst family, Aunt, but they do sound extraordinary."

"They were certainly that," said Eleanor, "but we've finished with Pank for now, so please pass me another card."

Toot! Toot! Toot!

Emily thought hard, then picked up the card depicting a bagpipe player dressed in green tartan. "I always liked the little dagger tucked into the top of her purple stocking," she said.

"The Trumpeter." Eleanor answered. "Such an odd name. I never heard the bagpipes being played, but there's nothing better than a march led by a fine silver band. Of course, the Salvation Army knew the value of a good rousing tune and we borrowed 'Onward Christian Soldiers' from them." A mischievous expression passed across her face. "I think I can still remember all the words –

'Forward sister women! Onward ever more,
Bondage is behind you, Freedom is before,
Raise the standard boldly, In the morning sun;
'Gainst a great injustice, See the fight begun!
Forward, forward sisters! Onward ever more!
Bondage is behind you, Freedom is before'.

There!" she said, looking embarrassed. "I didn't hit all the right notes, but it wasn't too bad for someone so rusty."

"But that was lovely, Aunt! You have a beautiful singing voice."

"You're kind to say so. I once hoped you might have joined our children's choir."

"I do remember it being mentioned, but I don't think I would have been much of an asset." Emily smiled. "What else did you sing?"

"Let me think. There were lots of songs. The best were those where people already knew the tunes, such as 'The Women's Battle Song' set to 'Onward Christian Soldiers'. I enjoyed 'Shoulder to Shoulder', that was to the tune of 'Men of Harlech', and 'Rise Up Women!' to 'John Brown's Body' as well," she said, before adding, "I was so optimistic then. We all were on those early marches." Eleanor pointed to a large brown paper bundle. "Emily, why don't you unwrap that parcel?"

Emily picked it up from a side table and untied the string around the package.

"Be careful, some of them are delicate," advised Eleanor.

"But they're beautiful, Aunt," said Emily, unfolding the pieces of material inside. "Did you make them yourself?"

"I can't say they're all my own work, but a good deal is. All those hours I was made to do needlework finally came in useful. It wasn't that hard, once we agreed on the designs," Eleanor laughed. "That always took a lot more time!"

Emily laughed too. "I can imagine." She studied one of the banners: three golden crowns set below the city's name against a backdrop of three vertical, blue wavy stripes. She let the finely tasselled fringe slip through her fingers.

Eleanor continued, "That was my first effort – some of my others are better. Mind you, you should see what some people made. That first London march was such a sight, there on the Embankment with all the banners waving. Unbelievable! The silver bands were all playing and when we set off we marched six abreast. It stretched for miles! We waited a whole hour before we moved off. You should have seen some of the banners! The most beautiful one was close to us, carried by a contingent from Huddersfield. I can picture it now as clearly as that first time I saw it. In the foreground were some canal-side mills with smoke rising from their chimneys, and behind them was the most beautiful of heather-clad hillsides. 'Votes for Women' was embroidered across the top, and at the bottom was a fine ram's head. And the colours! The purples, the greens, the oranges. Breathtaking! I was so impressed that I had a long conversation with the woman carrying it and we ended up exchanging addresses, then letters, then visits. I now know that it's the view down the Colne Valley from Milnsbridge and I've stood on the spot where Florence made her original sketches."

"I wish I could have seen it."

"It's as fine a work of art as you could ever see. I've been meaning to write to Florence, so I could ask if we could visit. Perhaps you don't have the time now, do you? Or if Florence came here she could bring it with her. We'll see. Things haven't been easy for her these last two years. She holds the same views as I do, and her husband's family, the Lockwoods, are the bedrock of Colne Valley Liberalism. That means they are as staunchly pro-war as it's possible to be. I've only had your father to contend with, whereas she's had her husband and all the Lockwoods too. She's had to fight many of her own personal battles."

Emily suspected her aunt's worried frown suggested there was more to this than she was saying.

"Thinking of Florence reminds me of Murdie," continued Eleanor. "She was very good at putting on a spectacular show too. I wish you could have ridden in her carriage during the election, bedecked in the colours and pulled by two fine chestnut horses. She even dressed her dogs in red, white and green ribbons."

"I wish I could have too, it sounds fun. I do remember meeting her once and she seemed quite a forceful lady."

"Yes, she was. There's no denying that. I'd never have become a Poor Law Guardian without her encouragement, when she cajoled ten of us to stand for election. I never understood how she fitted so much into her life. I find it hard enough, and I wasn't a doctor in General Practice and the Senior Physician at the Children's Hospital who launched a crusade against the appalling public health and housing in this city. I'm sorry, Emily. I know it's not Christian to say so, but when you think of some of the worthless people who live to a ripe old age, whereas... quick, pick another card!"

Law! Law! Law!

Emily leant forward and chose a card showing a woman in judge's robes who was holding a scroll with 'Votes for Women' on it. "'Law! Law! Law!'" she read out, "and worth thirty points."

"Worth collecting then, Emily! Unlike Lady Justice on top of the new Old Bailey, she does not turn a blind eye to the injustices that women continue to suffer."

"But, Aunt, surely women receive as fair a trial as men?"

"They may be judged by twelve good men and true. Twelve men, who'd say they would never judge a woman differently to a man. That's not the point! Women are not allowed to serve on juries. Women have to prove two grounds for divorce rather than their husband's one. Women are refused full membership at Oxford and Cambridge. I could list so many more things. Women gaining the vote would force politicians to acknowledge these iniquities and, more importantly, to do something about it."

"Don't you think things are changing, Aunt?"

"There have been improvements in my lifetime. When your grandmother married, she couldn't own property, whereas I could, and though too many men still treat their wives as private possessions, the likelihood of a woman being sold as a mere chattel by a Michael Henchard is now re-mote."

"I know the *Mayor of Casterbridge* is your favourite Thomas Hardy novel, Aunt, and I've never understood why. Henchard is such an unpleasant character." She smiled. "I much prefer *Far from the Madding Crowd*."

"Bathsheba is wonderful. She's such a strong-minded, independent woman. But Henchard is flawed and it's such a tragic end. No sexton called to ring the bell. Who would wish that in their will?"

"I agree, no-one would, but I'm afraid I prefer happier endings."

Eleanor pointed at the card. "I hope all the unsung heroines seeking justice will have happy endings. Some of the newsies I worked with were wonderful, as were those I went vanning with. It's too easy to concentrate on the speech-makers, the writers of the articles and forget... Sorry, Emily, I'm lecturing you, and I was determined not to do that. But those women were inspiring, they stopped me becoming disheartened."

"No Aunt. I don't mind. But you haven't told me about being arrested."

"Patience! I will come to that."

"Very well, I'll try," Emily laughed. "The next time I see you working as a newsy on Monument Bridge, I shall buy a *Mail* from you."

"You might laugh, Emily, but I've sold *Women's Franchise* and *The Common Cause* in town and *Votes for Women* in London. Volunteers were always easier to find down there. Some local NUWSS members were too embarrassed to sell papers in the street. They found it distasteful joining the costermongers and flower sellers in the gutter. They didn't mind helping Murdie deliver bundles to the newsies, but actually selling papers? No, that was what working-class boys and men did. For some, however, it was a first act of faith, standing there with your board, a release from their normal constraints. Others did it almost apologetically." She looked at Emily. "Remember, we have nothing to apologise for."

"I'll try, Aunt." Emily replied. "What I don't understand is why I never saw you? Mother took me into town lots of times."

"I always told her when I would be there as part of our agreement." Emily waited for her to elaborate, and her aunt continued. "You asked about my being arrested. Even being a newsy put you at risk. You had to keep your eyes and wits about you. I soon learned not to stand on the pavement because you'd be arrested for obstruction. You had to hop smartish into the gutter."

Emily found the idea quite shocking. "Were you good at selling papers?"

"Not to begin with. I was hopeless. I thought that everyone was staring at me. But once I got used to accosting people, delaying the scurrying masses, I ended up enjoying the challenge. And standing was always easier than walking the gutters."

"Why would you want to do that?" asked Emily, surprised.

"That was when I was sandwich-boarding. Neither task was easy in London. Some of the younger women were subjected to the filthiest of jests, particularly from elderly men who'd approach under the pretence of wanting a copy. Whereas they treated you as a lady in a drawing room, stand the most respectable of women in the street and they felt able to act in a despicable way. I chased one down the street once. Vile creature!"

"How awful, Aunt."

"New newsies weren't always warned lest they were put off before they'd begun. Once I couldn't understand why some navvies in the Strand were making ribald remarks until I looked at my board, which said 'What shall we do with the wives?'. I always checked my board before going out, after that! At least I sold copies to women who might never have plucked up the courage to buy one from their local stationers. That was pleasing to the soul. And others felt the same freedom of doing something in public for the first time. It was the same going out vanning, nerve-wracking to begin with. I almost had stage fright the first time I spoke at a public meeting. You could feel the hostility from men who thought I should sit in silence while they did all the talking. And that was after I'd spent the afternoon walking around a strange town ringing our hand-bells, and getting backache from stooping to chalk on the pavements. Thankfully no-one let any rats free in that meeting! That would have finished my speaking career before it began. But I survived."

"Rats!" said Emily, horrified.

"That was only once, thank goodness. I'm afraid our opponents relied more on physical disruption than the force of their arguments. As a result we learnt from experience what to do and what not to do. Never ever speak standing on a chair, for example."

"Why not, Aunt?"

"Far too easy to pull away from underneath you! Search out a friendly grocer and get a sturdy soap-box to stand on instead. And a robust raincoat to defy the elements. I always swore by my Omne Tempus. And remember wear a large, wide-brimmed hat." She looked at Emily.

"Shelter from the rain and sun?"

"True, it would help protect from those, but more important is the protection from over-ripe fruit or from even harder missiles. It's vital to continue speaking, it's fatal to be deflected. Keep going. You might forget your point, you might be speaking gibberish, but keep going and you've got a chance of winning them over."

"It all sounds frightful!"

"Some of it was. There's nothing pleasant about being jostled by hooligans who've wrecked your meeting, or someone threatening to push your caravan down a hill. I must say, though, that many of the people we met were delightful. They were warm and friendly. They cooked us meals, entertained us, encouraged us, even took us into their homes. It was better to have a newly-laid egg cooked for you than a rotten one thrown at you."

"I wish you'd told me this before, Aunt... but I'm glad you're telling me now."

"The best trip was one summer bicycling around Cumberland. The weather was kind, so not only did we enjoy the magnificent scenery in my favourite part of England, but we held our outdoor meetings without getting soaked. Our reception was better than anywhere else I'd been, whether it was from iron workers, miners, farmers or seaside visitors on the coast." She smiled. "Not a single rotten egg either!" She glanced towards the fire. "Perhaps you would put some more coal on, Emily, please."

Emily got up, opened the lid of the coal-scuttle and made up the fire.

"But our opponents could also improvise," Eleanor continued. "I was at an anti-suffrage meeting in Whitby and someone was speaking about how women were a privileged class under law. A friend of mine stood up and asked what percentage of men suffered as a result of this terrible injustice, and how did it compare to the number of women who suffered due to the unfair divorce laws? This threw the meeting into confusion. The chairmen said that as it was a mixed gathering and young girls were present the topic couldn't be discussed. Complete rubbish, there wasn't anyone even your age. We tried asking more questions, but they resorted to their final defence... playing the national anthem... so that was that." She examined the card and said to herself. "We still need justice." She smiled, and looked at Emily. "Fetch me the basket from the bottom shelf of the bookcase, there's a dear. I brought it down earlier from my study. There are a few bits and bobs you'd be interested in. And do remind me before you leave that I've got a few cuttings upstairs for you."

Emily smiled to herself. Her aunt had the endearing habit of cutting out pieces from newspapers and journals that she thought Emily would or should be interested in. She extended this service to a wider circle of her friends and acquaintances. Emily believed it was fatal to express an interest in anything in her aunt's hearing. One of the rooms upstairs, which Emily thought was rather inaccurately termed 'my study', was the repository of much of this material, along with much else. Her aunt insisted she knew where everything was and could place her hands on anything in seconds. As far as Emily could see, a system that including mixing lists of things to do, old newspapers that had 'an interesting article I've been meaning to read', theatre programmes, cuttings, the odd recipe and much else besides was not the most efficient way of organising things. Emily had once picked up a couple of these piles to sort into logical categories, but her aunt had been horrified. She had let Emily help on one occasion, but when the sum total of an hour's hard labour was the throwing away of a single receipt for a hat her aunt no longer possessed, Emily had given up. Her aunt had been pleased, however, to find a delicate paper programme from Queen Victoria's funeral. "Your mother and I went down to London to see it, but my over-riding memory, apart from the enormous crowds, is hanging on for dear life to a lamp-post, because I could barely stand thanks to the new boots I'd been stupid enough to wear for the occasion. I am sorry but when anyone mentions the late Queen, all I can think of is my poor squashed toes." Emily had laughed about the boots, and said that she was glad she had finally learnt something useful from her aunt, before suggesting that if they looked long and hard enough they might find a misplaced invitation to the King's coronation that had been sitting there for the last few years.

Emily placed the basket between them and opened its lid. A few things she'd seen before, but others were new. She picked out a box she recognised from her childhood and pressed its catch. She smiled as a Jill, rather than a Jack, sprang out of its container. She fingered its 'Votes for Women' sash. "I used to love this, Aunt, despite always finding her rather frightening. She's quite grotesque."

"A well-worn tactic of our adversaries." Eleanor laughed. "I couldn't resist collecting them, or the cards either. There's a mixture, some for and some against."

Emily picked out a card. "This one's lovely." She showed her aunt a Christmas card with a little drummer girl dressed in purple and green on it. "You could have sent it to me for Christmas... in 1909," she said studying the text. "She's so pretty. But look at these!" She peered at a card showing a sour-faced woman waving an umbrella, backed by a grim-faced group of seated harridans. She picked up another. "This is even worse!"

"My favourite!" said her aunt. "It's grotesque. I am sorry to say that I was sorely tempted to send one to your father, when I came across it."

"I'm glad you didn't." Emily said. The card showed an ugly woman who had her enormous tongue nailed to a table. She read the caption out. 'Peace at last!'

"I shouldn't laugh," Eleanor said, "especially when you think of the women who suffer violence, but it's just *so* perfectly dreadful. And I'm afraid their poetry was little better. Do read that next one out."

"'A perfect woman, nobly planned, to warm and comfort and command'," Emily read. "She's beautiful too, unlike the ones who could have been modelled from gargoyles. I haven't seen this before, either." She picked out a metamorphic puzzle entitled 'The Elusive Christabel' and pulled its tab down. Christabel disappeared, to be replaced by two policemen crashing into one another.

"Those were popular after she fled to Paris. There's several whirl-a-gigs there too and some dolls. There's a wind-up one somewhere. I bought it to remind me of my time as a newsy. See if you can find it." She rose from her chair. "I'll put the soup on."

Emily found the little clockwork doll, and wound her up before putting her down on the table. She watched as the little figure started to wave its *Votes for Women* newspaper and ring its little bell. It was so charming that she wound it up several times.

"Our soup's ready," Eleanor called.

The doll came to a halt. Emily stood up. "Coming!" she said and set off for the kitchen.

Turn 'em Out!

While eating, Emily had confined herself to relating recent news from Robert. Now, back by the fire, she waited for her aunt to pick another card.

Eleanor chose one and held it at arm's length. "The politicians, and a different one on every card! I enjoyed collecting those most. 'Turn 'em out!' you announced when you had the set. It's a sentiment I have a great deal of sympathy with, though I wouldn't tar all politicians with the same brush. Some are decent, honourable men, but..." she let the word linger, "those with real power never let their principles get in the way of short-term political advantage."

"What do you mean, Aunt?" asked Emily.

"Before the war, there were sizeable majorities in favour of women's suffrage, but the government never allowed time for any bill to become law. Those who supported the Cause were divided; many Liberals were against only older women or householder's wives having the vote because they feared they'd vote Conservative, whilst many Conservatives thought if more were enfranchised then the Liberals would gain. At least you knew where you stood with politicians who were opposed in principle. The worst were those who made promises with no intention of keeping them." Eleanor gave the card to Emily. "I once sat in the same room as Asquith."

Emily studied him. He was wearing a frock coat with a red carnation in his lapel. He stood erect, his left arm jutting straight out in front of him. "He looks formidable, Aunt. I can imagine him saying 'No!' to someone."

"Very true, Emily. One reward – or perhaps penalty – for being so involved was being part of a deputation to Downing Street. That experience left me unsure whether to laugh or cry! The way people looked at us! The most poisonous look of all came from Mrs Asquith, who could not disguise her contempt. We might have been lunatics, escaped from an asylum, rather than women seeking their rights. I sat at the back but had a good view of her husband, who was a study in total intransigence. Lloyd George next to him at least gave some impression of being affected by our entreaties, but Asquith? He was completely unmoved by anything we said."

Emily could see the memory was a bitter one.

"Our points withered as fragile blooms do." Eleanor sighed. "When we finished our submissions, he surveyed us, then made a few meaningless polite noises, before announcing that as long as he was Prime Minister, no facilities would ever be granted for discussion of a Bill in Parliament. And that was it. We were dismissed. I was so angry, not with him but with myself, for being so naïve as to believe that logical arguments could change his views. Someone then called out, 'Then you must be moved.'"

"Did he say anything, Aunt?" said Emily. "Did he answer?"

"He stood immobile, his thumbs in his waistcoat. I don't think he knew who'd challenged him, but then he threw his head back and said 'Move me!' There was such a tension in the room. Someone said 'We will!' and everyone repeated it – 'We will!'. It wasn't a Damascene moment, but I was convinced Asquith and his like would never willingly change. They would have to be moved."

"But they haven't, have they, Aunt? Nothing's changed." The frustration was clear in Emily's voice. "Nothing's moved! For all your efforts, nothing's changed!"

"Emily," Eleanor replied, "Please don't sound so disillusioned. I've been discouraged at times, but you're much too young for that."

"What's age got to do with it? Enough things have happened these last few years for anyone to be disenchanted." She shook her head. "But it's complicated, and the events you're describing seem to be from a different world." There was a brief silence before Emily spoke again. "I'm sorry. I didn't mean to sound critical. I agree with what you were campaigning for, but was it all worth it?"

"No, Emily, I should be saying sorry, not you. You've nothing to apologise for. I'm afraid I sometimes still think you're that little girl paddling on Bridlington beach, and I know you're not. And don't worry about questioning me – you're only asking what I've asked myself many times. The last thing I want is for you to always agree with me. Unfortunately, your father can't recognize that. Even though I was away a great deal, he believed I was trying to mould you, and because of that we came to an understanding. Then various events in London led to our relationship became more strained."

"Did you regret it, Aunt?"

"Yes, but circumstances made it inevitable. I did try to influence you, but only by encouraging you to think for yourself. I'm not saying your father wouldn't want that too, but..." she shrugged her shoulders. "As to whether it was worth it: the letters, the demonstrations, the protests? I'm positive everything I was involved with was worth it. I'm not revelling in some idea of glorious failure. Tennyson, if he were alive, wouldn't be putting pen to paper about it, but what was the alternative? Feeble acquiescence? I don't think so. We will gain the vote in your lifetime." She smiled before adding with a twinkle in her eye, "If not in mine."

"Aunt!" said Emily. "You a pessimist? I don't believe you. Never! But don't worry, no matter how old, decrepit and grey you become, I will push you down in your wheelchair to cast your first ballot."

"Why do I find that strangely reassuring, Emily? There I am on my deathbed, deep in conversation with the Grim Reaper, when my delightful Guardian Angel of a niece intervenes, ferries me to the polling station to make my cross and die a happy woman. Who knows, I might be granted long enough to hear the results declared before I shuffle off this mortal coil? Wonderful, Emily. And if, once through the pearly gates, I discover that hell is empty and all the politicians are there in heaven, I shall find Mr Asquith and tell him – yes, we did move you!" She sat back in her chair with an air of immense satisfaction. "But what's this about decrepit? Old and grey I can accept, but decrepit?"

"I take back the decrepit." Emily smiled, "You might be slightly thread-bare instead."

"Threadbare?" Eleanor pretended to give the notion serious consideration. "That I can accept. Just! But I'm not without hope. There are rumours that a Speaker's Conference may be set up. And with a new Prime Minister? Perhaps the co-operation between the NUWSS and others, including the Labour Party, might bear fruit. Many Liberals are looking over their shoulders at the size of their majorities. When change comes, it will be despite the WSPU, not because of it."

Emily was taken aback by the bitterness in her aunt's voice. "Aunt, you sound almost like a woman scorned."

"You may be right, Emily. My life revolved around the WSPU for such a long time. When Christabel announced a 'Women's War' against the Labour Party, it forced many to choose between the Women's Labour League and staying in the WSPU, and I, like many, chose to leave. I was reminded about it the other evening, when George Lansbury was speaking here. I was reminiscing with him about the Bow and Bromley by-election campaign." She looked at Emily. "November 1912. He'd resigned his seat to stand as a 'Women's Suffrage and Socialist' candidate – so you'd have thought he'd have had the wholehearted support of the WSPU, especially as he'd been to Boulogne to see Christabel and her mother beforehand. I'd resigned by then, but I was still friendly with Sylvia. She was the suffrage movement in the East End, but outsiders with little knowledge of the area but armed with instructions from France were sent in to take over her branch. Some canvassers found things difficult and were shocked by the sheer poverty of the area. And many put all their efforts into getting the WSPU into the public eye and selling *The Suffragette*, rather than persuading potential electors to vote. It was incompetent! The pettiness and the nitpicking! There were some in the local ILP at fault too, working men who found it hard to work with middle-class women. But on polling day the WSPU wouldn't let its fleet of cars be used to ferry George Lansbury's supporters to vote. It was unbelievable. And all because it meant taking instructions from a man about when and where to go. I argued about this with one of them and was told that Mrs Pankhurst would never allow the Union to work under the men." She shook her head. "It was depressing and inept, but I'm not sure it was crucial in the end as George lost by over seven hundred votes." Eleanor raised her eyebrows. "The Tory campaigned under the slogan, 'Women do not want Votes!' At least the WSPU's antics convinced me that resigning had been the right thing to do. But despite the massive disappointment of losing, I have happy memories too. If I shut my eyes, an inspiring sight comes to mind: there in the filth of the Bow Road, painted above a baker's doorway, in large, bright, golden letters – 'Votes for Women'. Women from the most desperate of slums, working in the worst of sweated trades, turned up and were dealt with in the most sympathetic way. Sylvia treated everyone as if they mattered. It's too easy to play Lady Bountiful. I hope I behaved in the right manner too."

"I'm certain you would have, Aunt."

"And to think, at her first public meeting there, Sylvia was pelted with fish heads and worse."

Emily shuddered, thinking what 'and worse' might include.

"And mentioning fish, you complain about the smell we sometimes suffer here. It can be bad, but the aromas in that part of the East End were truly pungent and eye-watering – a combination of tanneries and soap-works that penetrated every crack and crevice, no matter how small." Her aunt wrinkled her nose.

"Wasn't it a bit silly? Resigning and losing, if he was already an MP?"

"Sylvia thought so, which may be why she was sidelined during the campaign. But the world would be a less interesting place if we always did the sensible thing."

"I'm glad you did the right thing, leaving."

"Yes, I enjoyed being one of the women campaigners who weren't members. And nothing's happened since to change my mind. What could justify banning WSPU members from appearing on public platforms with men? That sparked Sylvia's final conflict with Christabel, as she later appeared at a meeting with George. How could you refuse an alliance with a labour movement just because it included men? How could you reject men who'd worked indefatigably for the cause, who'd gone to prison, some who'd been on hunger strike? And the arson attacks had started in earnest by then, the bombings too, the escalating violence. People I respected in the Labour Party argued that the militants' antics were childishness masquerading as revolution; 'pettifogging middle-class young damsels with little hammers in their muffs' they called them. The militants attracted people's attention, but not their support. MPs who'd once voted in favour of change abstained or voted against. Anti-suffragists in Parliament were exultant." She paused. "I don't regret my decision. I was right to leave. George and Sylvia then set up the United Suffragists, and that has turned out to be the final resting place for this... decrepit piece of political, suffragist flotsam to wash up at." Eleanor smiled and looked at Emily. "You're not too tired? You've had a long day. I can call your taxi now and I can carry on another time..."

Emily shook her head. "No, it's still quite early, and I'm not at all tired now. In fact, I'm excited by what you've told me!"

"Excellent. Pass the card back to me, dear." Her aunt addressed the figure on the card. "So, Herbert Alfred, that is a fine red carnation in your lapel, and standing there at the dispatch box you ooze arrogance from every pore – but it's not the waging of Mrs Pankhurst's Holy War but the muddle of your leadership in this cursed war that finally brought you down." She placed him, with evident satisfaction, next to Mrs Pankhurst. "You've both been accused of political chicanery by your opponents, so perhaps you do have something in common after all. Another card, Emily, I think."

Help! Help! Help!

"The colourist has made those red flowers on her hat look so striking, and though I've never seen you in one like that, you have to admit she looks like you." Emily laughed. "Not that you wear yours pushed down sideways across your face. But her scarf is just like one of yours. So if I could just hear you shout 'Help! Help! Help!' with your mouth as wide open as hers, then I can be sure."

"I'm sorry, Emily. I'm normally happy to indulge you, but the woman on the card will have to remain a mystery."

Emily smiled. "I didn't think it was you, but you have to admit it could have been."

"And several thousand others. Looking at the policeman, he could be the spitting image of the first officer who arrested me – though if it was him, he's been promoted. I was arrested by a constable; the man leading away your mystery lady, possibly even to Cannon Row Police Station, is a sergeant."

"Cannon Row police station?" said Emily. "Was that were you were taken?"

"Yes, anyone arrested anywhere near Parliament or in most of central London was taken there. It became almost a home-from-home for the more persistent protesters."

"It must have been awful!"

"No. It wasn't that bad. You might think it strange, but I quite enjoyed the experience. I even wrote to your mother from there, though that did lead to some unexpected consequences...

#

Dear Clara,

As you can see from my current address, some (though not all!) of your worst fears have come to pass. I was in two minds whether to write, but as circumstances might make it difficult to do so in a few days' time, I took advantage of the kind offer of an off-duty officer and sent out for writing paper, envelopes and some stamps.

So here I am in the billiard-room of Cannon Row Police Station. A surprising location, you will agree! Not somewhere your average malefactor is ever likely to see the inside of, let alone enjoy the quite decent tea that was sent in for us. But needs must and there are just far too many of us to fit in their cells! I have asked how long we shall be held here and have been told 'How long is a piece of string?' – which means, purportedly, until after the House has risen, whenever that might be. It was well after eleven yesterday evening, and it is now a little after nine. This is the first letter I have ever written whose length may be determined by the wishes of Parliament!

Why I am here? I have been charged with 'disorderly conduct'. Disorderly conduct! I do not consider my behaviour 'disorderly'. People such as my MP Mr Guy Wilson who profess support for women's suffrage yet do nothing to help achieve it are the ones who should be charged. My polite written requests to see him went unheeded, so it seemed reasonable conduct to gain entry to the lobby of Parliament to petition him – something I was quite prepared to do in an orderly fashion. This right was denied to me and as a result I have been summoned to appear at Westminster Police Court this coming Friday morning, where I hope I will be given the chance to put my views to the magistrate.

I can picture you quailing as you read this. Please don't! Mother and I often disagreed, but she was right about one thing, when she said, 'Clara, you worry too much!' So please don't worry now. You will also be concerned about what people might say. If I am not concerned about that, then I don't see why you should be either. Feel free to depict me as a black sheep if that makes it easier for you. When or if you tell Alfred is up to you, but judging from the reporting of previous cases there will be something about it in the *Morning News* or the *Mail*. If it is any consolation, I have not been charged with obstructing a police officer, unlike the charming young woman writing her letter next to me. I made her acquaintance this afternoon when she attempted to rescue me from the clutches of the police. On my first attempt to gain entry to Parliament, I was carried away by two burly policeman who rather reminded me of Tweedledum and Tweedledee. They deposited me back on the side of the road. It was on my third attempt at pushing up against the police lines that I was arrested, whereupon Lavena, the young lady, valiantly grabbed hold of my constable's belt in an attempt to free me. And that, dear sister, under the law of the land constitutes insulting behaviour and obstructing a police officer! So we arrived here together and I have been talking to her throughout our admittedly comfortable incarceration. This has been an immeasurably rewarding experience for me and I have been reflecting on my own situation after meeting this young woman. She left school at the age of ten, yet has ambitions to write about her experiences and is desperate to learn about things that many of her so-called betters would say are completely beyond her experience or understanding. She has great hopes of her new local branch of the WEA. Alfred cannot see the point of providing lectures on economics or philosophy for working people, but I wish he could see this young woman's intelligence and sheer determination. She has even given up her weaving job in Halifax and travelled down here, expecting to go to prison. I shall be in the public gallery tomorrow to hear her state, 'I have nothing to say except that the police resisted me in the execution of my duty'.

She plans to refuse to pay any fine and despite spending fourteen days in Holloway last year, she considers prison a preferable alternative to agreeing to keep the peace. She is entirely admirable! It is strange how a chance meeting can have such an inspiring effect. She is right. I know I told you the other day that I would pay any fine imposed on me, but what sort of sacrifice is that? I have an ample income and would hardly notice it, whatever sum I might have to pay. I have decided to find lodgings here, as well as maintaining my house at home. My previous visits here have been fleeting ones, and though attending large demonstrations is inspiring, I can be of more use if I spend longer here. There is an overwhelming sense of being at the centre of things here. I am almost looking forward to Friday!

The camaraderie this evening has been wonderful. We have had several rounds of singing which everyone, including our captors, enjoyed. When one wag from their ranks joked that we should be invited to perform at their upcoming police concert, someone replied that we would be delighted to do so, but unfortunately some of us might be engaged elsewhere by then.

I have just noticed that people are stirring at the other side of the room, so perhaps our illustrious rulers are even now retiring to their beds – or more likely to their clubs – and we may be about to be released. I shall keep you informed about this Pilgrim's Progress,

finished in haste,
your affectionate sister,
Eleanor

P.S. Please remember Mother's advice!

Clara,

What were you thinking of? If I am being charitable I will assume that you thought that you had my best interests at heart. If I am not, and I have your note in front of me, I would say that you have interfered for purely selfish reasons. I wonder that Alfred did not write himself, rather than allowing you to do his dirty work for him. It would not have 'brought disgrace on the family', if I were to go to prison. What do you think I am, a common criminal?

As to your comments regarding my contact with the children, especially Emily – what am I? Some form of contagious disease from whom she will catch dangerous ideas? When I get home early next week we must come to an understanding about this. I trust that your current melodramatic stance will have been moderated by then.

You will see that I have included a postal order for £1 17s 6d. I have added three extra half crowns. One each for the 'heartache, distress and anguish' that I have caused you.

If nothing else, this episode has taught me an important lesson, and I only have myself to blame. I should have known how you might have reacted. I will never again stand, arguing fruitlessly with a clerk of the court about my refusal to have a fine paid for me. I will achieve this through the simple expedient of not informing you about any subsequent court appearances until after the event. This will also spare you future 'mental torment'.

Thankfully no-one meddled in the affairs of the young woman who helped me. She has started her six week sentence with her integrity intact.

Please give the children my love (assuming this is still acceptable!)

Eleanor

Dear Clara

I am glad that you will try and find it in your heart to forgive me for my 'temperamental outburst'. I am also relieved that Alfred believes that hysteria brought on by the stress and strain of my situation may have been responsible and therefore absolves me of any direct blame.

I am looking forward to discussing things in a 'calm and considered manner', especially as you think I have misinterpreted what you said about the children. I will do everything possible to allay your (or Alfred's?) fears, which I stress are groundless.

I intend to catch the four o'clock train on Wednesday afternoon, so shall call on Thursday, if you let me know a convenient time to do so,

Eleanor

#

"Tell me more about the young lady who tried to free you," asked Emily.

"Lavena? My friend from Fustianopolis," Eleanor replied.

Emily was bemused.

"Fustianopolis, the centre for fustian cloth?" added Eleanor, but Emily was still none the wiser.

Eleanor sighed. "Hebden Bridge. And as to fustian cloth, I will excuse you there, as it's much coarser and heavier than you are ever likely to want to wear, though it does have the advant..."

"The young woman, Aunt?"

"Oh, Lavena? Yes, she blossomed, and showed what people can achieve if only they're given the opportunity. Some of her *Letters from a Tailoress* are in the old W.E.A. magazines I've got upstairs. There's one letter about mothers' suspicions that their daughters might have high notions, wanting more from life than a clean front doorstep or a polished brass fender. I've always remembered what it said." She thought for a moment. 'If girls developed a craving for wider ideas, their mothers feared they would become Socialists or Suffragettes, a Socialist being a person with lax views about other people's watches and purses, and a Suffragette a person whose house is always untidy." She looked at Emily.

Emily laughed. "I'm sure you're not guilty of the first charge, and as to the second, would Sarah appear for the prosecution or for the defence?"

"After years of working so hard to instil better habits in me... a defence witness, without doubt. And if I were convicted, the worst I'd face is the disapproval of my neighbours, rather than incarceration on Hedon Road."

Emily shivered. She rarely had reason to venture eastwards, but had seen the prison, a grim and forbidding sight.

"But you didn't go to prison that time in London?"

"No, not on that occasion," Eleanor said.

"There aren't many people who regret not being gaoled. And my parents paid your fine?"

"Yes. I'd been expecting to be taken to prison when all the cases had been heard, but found myself being released instead. And even ten minutes of insisting I hadn't paid and demanding to serve my sentence was all to no avail."

"But weren't you angry with them?"

"Your parents? Well, yes, I wasn't happy, but for whatever reason they believed they were doing the right thing."

"And was it some time around then that you talked about me?"

"Yes... no... it was complicated. They hadn't approved of my activities for some time. They were worried that you might be unduly influenced by my views, and when my actions involved breaking the law, appearing in court, going to prison even, they became even more alarmed."

"But I wouldn't have minded. I agree with what you were doing and I'm sure I would have done then too, even though I was younger."

Her aunt gave her a pointed look.

"So you came to an arrangement," Emily suggested.

"It wasn't that hard. I was careful. It wasn't as if the Cause was a completely taboo subject. And there were a thousand and one other things to talk about with my delightful young niece."

"And now this recent argument that you've had with father. This agreement between you has broken down. That's why he said what he did to me."

"There seems to be a lack of understanding, yes, but your mother is very good at reconciliations, and your father takes more notice of what she thinks than sometimes might appear." She gave Emily an encouraging smile and indicated the cards. "Only three left."

Fourteen Days!

"They are a disagreeable bunch and it's hardly the most flattering of portraits. If they were modelled on real people, none of them would be commissioning a full painting."

"The magistrate looks very severe," replied Emily, "but those below him, who would they be? Court officials, lawyers? One or two look ape-like, the way they've been drawn. It can't have been like that in court?"

"No, unlike the policeman on the earlier card, there's little resemblance to the people I saw. My second court appearance was at Bow Street before Robert Alfred Bullock Marsham, who, besides his long name, had the longest white sideboards I've ever seen." Eleanor gestured with her hands. "Well below the level of his chin. He'd have made an excellent Father Time, if only he'd grown a full beard to match!"

"I'm surprised you could even think of things like that. Weren't you very anxious?"

"In the dock? No, you would think so, but no. I was more nervous beforehand. Far more so than at Cannon Street. Perhaps it was because more of us were down to appear, whereas before, by the Friday, most cases had been dealt with and there was only a handful of us. But at Bow Street I had to push my way through the considerable crowds milling around outside.

They were supporters, but it was still an unnerving experience. And once inside we were marshalled into an area much like a loose-box. Waiting for my name in the roll-call was the worst moment. We had to present our arrest warrants and I'd folded mine into a tiny square without noticing what I'd been doing. I've still got it if you'd like to see it."

"Yes please," said Emily.

"You'll have to be careful, as it's a bit fragile."

"I see what you mean." Emily said, taking it and peering at it. "Thirty-two squares. It wouldn't have survived if you'd managed sixty-four." She read it to herself and then out loud in a serious tone of voice. "'Take notice that you Eleanor Alsop are bound in the sum of five pounds to appear at Bow Street Police Court at 10 o'clock A.M. on the third day of March...' I can't read the date, as it's worn through... 'to answer the charge of conduct likely to cause a breach of the peace, and unless you then appear there, proceedings will be taken'. And it's been signed in an illegible scrawl." She handed it back carefully. "Goodness, Aunt!"

"After that, it was very queer: we were all paired off with our respective arresting constables and we sat facing each other on either side of a long narrow corridor. Waiting there *was* strange. I looked to the far end and imagined the top couple standing, linking arms and spinning and twirling down between us all, whilst everyone clapped, before I swung arm-in-arm with the policeman as he came back down our line."

"Strip the Willow, Aunt. That's always been my favourite."

"And mine too, that must have been why I thought of it. It would have been difficult to have done a Circassian dance."

Emily laughed, "Forming a grand circle in a corridor might have been a trifle ambitious. You should have asked for a large empty court-room instead!"

"Why didn't I think of that at the time? There were some handsome policemen I could have danced with as we progressed around the room – but sadly, when the lead couple did rise, rather than starting a fine bout of country dancing they merely disappeared into the court room, and we all shuffled along a place. My partner was actually a decent sort, but that didn't stop me becoming anxious as I got nearer the end. But when my name was called, I realised there was no escape," she smiled, "and my worries slipped away as I realised I wasn't frightened at all. Not that it did me much good," she laughed, "as Robert Alfred Bullock Marsham had got out the wrong side of bed that morning. Perhaps even fallen out! Perhaps he'd had some difficult cases before mine, but either way he was cantankerous in the extreme. Yet standing there gripping the rail at the front of the dock was an affecting experience; thinking of all those who'd stood there before me. I wish I could have emulated Christabel Pankhurst and called the Home Secretary and Chancellor of the Exchequer to come to court as defence witnesses, then cross-examining them so brilliantly! I asked my policeman a number of questions, quite pertinent ones, but that was hardly the same. Still, I was convinced I'd made a good case... as far as I was allowed to. Though it was irrelevant because Robert Alfred Bullock Marsham had made his mind up before I even spoke." She shrugged. "I wasn't surprised – nor was I surprised when he said I was to keep the peace for six months, which I politely declined to do. He replied, 'Then you shall serve twenty-eight days instead.'"

"Not fourteen days, then?"

"As on the card? No. I'm afraid not. Possibly if he'd been in a better mood."

"And did my parents know about the trial – and what happened?"

"No, I hadn't told them. Your mother was upset when she did find out, but we both survived my only experience of incarceration."

"And were you sent straight to prison?"

"No. There was a lengthy wait. I was taken down and crammed into a narrow cell with four or five others. But it wasn't long before friends visited me, and besides bringing me the reassurance that I'd acquitted myself well... more importantly, they brought some provisions. I knew where I would eat my next meal, but as to what it might be and when I might eat it, I had no idea. I was famished, so the food was very welcome."

"I'd have been frightened, not hungry," said Emily, "waiting, not knowing what to expect."

"If I'd been some poor, companion-less woman, perhaps. But remember I knew many women who'd been to prison, so it wasn't a total leap in the dark. Even so, when I first stepped up into the Black Maria I would be lying if I didn't admit that my heart was in my mouth."

#

It might have been her over-active imagination or a trick of the light, but moving towards the open door was like being swallowed into the hull of some vast seafaring vessel. The police outside the court, impatient to be rid of their charges, hurried her along. Stepping inside, another image came to mind – this time of entering a hearse which was accepting a consignment of upright coffins. She halted mid-step, struggling to control the sudden panic surging through her, but before it could take control, she felt someone behind her grasp her hand and give it a reassuring squeeze. "Don't worry, you'll be fine," a voice said, "you're not on your own. You'll see."

The woman in front of her bent down and fitted herself, with some difficulty, into one of the tiny separate cells running along each side of the van. Seconds later she was inside her own cubicle and the door was shut. She had never been comfortable with confined spaces and, though her earlier anxieties were subsiding, she felt distinctly uneasy. She forced herself to concentrate on the cacophony filtering in from all around her. As she tried hard to decipher it, she found that by sitting with her knees squeezed up against her chin she could achieve some comfort. She'd been told the journey would last about an hour. While she gathered her thoughts, she became aware of women in the passage outside her cell. She wished she hadn't been amongst the first on board; far better to have the human contact out there. But then there was a knocking on her door and she heard a voice say, "Are you all right in there?"

"Yes. I'm a bit squashed, but I'll survive."

"We're packed like sardines out here, not that we mind too much."

Then a second voice added, "Yes, it's quite cosy. Get ready. They're shutting the outside doors."

A heavy metallic clanging reverberated around her and she found herself cast into a stygian gloom. Even forewarned, it was still a shock. A sudden jolting and bumping threw her against the side of the cell. They were under way. Veterans of Black Marias had told her the motion was very like being in a bathing machine going out to sea. She decided they were right and tried to imagine herself in a suitable costume – one with arrows on it, perhaps. She leant back, her head against the back wall, and laughed. No-one would see her in this darkness and it was much too cold to have a dip in the North Sea anyway.

She lost all sense of time until the sound of cheering brought her back to the present. She looked back at the door, visible in outline now that her eyes were more accustomed to the dark. She pushed her face up to the ventilation grill and called, "Hello? What's happening out there?"

One of the voices from earlier replied. "Someone's pushed a scarf out through the small window in the door, so the purple, white and green are trailing out behind us, and someone heard cheers from outside. That's what we're responding to." Her words were suddenly lost in another round of cheering. This time Eleanor found herself joining in. As it died away, she heard someone break into the first lines of 'Shoulder to Shoulder':

'From the daughters of the nation, bursts a cry of indignation,
breathes a sigh of consecration, in a sacred cause.'

The stirring tune of 'Men of Harlech' always raised her spirits and she sang it with great gusto. There was something strangely atmospheric and moving about singing it in this unusual situation. She wondered if anybody in the streets outside could hear them and what they might be making of it? With the song reaching its final verse, Eleanor put her very heart and soul into it.

'Let no ancient custom bind you, let one bond of suffering bind you,
leave unrighteous laws behind you, soon you shall be free.'

The words died away, and with an irony she couldn't miss, the persistent lurching and bumping ceased.

"We're here," a voice shouted. It was several minutes before the outer doors opened. She was to be disgorged, like Jonah from his whale – but thankfully before three days and nights had passed. She heard a key turning in the lock. She unbent herself and walked out awkwardly. After the darkness of the Black Maria, the fading daylight of the bleak March day seemed bright and welcome. She looked around, wondering what dubious delights His Majesty's Prison Holloway might hold for her.

#

Emily had the 'Gaol, Gaol, Gaol' card ready as her aunt paused.

"I hope you didn't suffer like this woman when you were in Holloway."

Eleanor took the card and gave Emily a reassuring smile before continuing her story.

Gaol! Gaol! Gaol!

Eleanor examined the picture. "I hope you don't think me a coward, but I could never have faced what would happen to her. Luckily I was never under any pressure to go on hunger strike."

"I'd *never* think you were a coward! You had to be brave to do all the things you did do," Emily said. Eleanor gave her a relieved smile.

"What happened after you arrived?"

"Once we were out of the Black Maria? We were marshalled into line by the wardresses. It's odd, I'd never had occasion to think of prison wardresses before. They dressed rather like nurses, with their Holland dresses and their small black bonnets and black velvet bows – though I hope your nurses talk to your patients more considerately than that first wardress spoke to us. I can still picture her – she was quite young, with a good figure and good hair, but as to what she said – she read out a list of rules, in such a rapid incomprehensible monotone that I was none the wiser. The other characteristic the wardresses shared was an inability to look at you when talking to you. I don't know why, but they focused on a point some way behind your head as if you weren't there. Most odd."

"A prison can't be the pleasantest of places to work, Aunt."

"I agree, but it's where a love of filling in ledgers and an intransigent nature will see you progress. My circumstances were recorded in the greatest detail, but my efforts to be classed as a first division offender fell on deaf ears."

The reference to divisions brought Edward to Emily's mind. She smiled to herself.

"Have I said something amusing, dear?"

"No, Aunt. It was your mentioning divisions. It made me think of Edward... and football. It was that teacher at Hymers who was to blame, having played for Corinthians and England... why should that have stuck in my mind? But Edward once insisted on explaining all about cups and leagues, promotions and relegations to me, and why there were two divisions – even though I made it clear I wasn't interested, not that that did any good. When he started on the intricacies of working out goal averages, I told him that I couldn't see why anyone should be the least interested in watching twenty-two men chasing a silly ball around a muddy field, let alone working out whatever their goal averages were." She raised her eyebrows, "Not that that stopped him. He congratulated me on knowing the number of players in a team, before insisting that you never knew when any knowledge, no matter how trivial, might come in useful. So he explained it anyway! I'm sorry, Edward," tears welled up in her eyes, "knowing that you divide goals scored by goals conceded has yet to prove any practical use to me." Her aunt reached out to squeeze her hand.

"I'm sorry, Aunt. You were saying about wanting to be in the first division."

"Yes, I was told to ask to be treated as a political prisoner. But I wasn't surprised when they refused. At least second division was better than the poor souls in third. Then, after a cursory examination by a doctor, my clothes and possessions were taken away. I was given a bundle of old clothes, and told to get into the grubbiest bath it has ever been my misfortune to see, let alone bathe in. Picture one with uneven, blistered grimy paint, and with enough cracks and crevices to hide who knows what, and all the colour of Humber mud, then you have a Holloway bath off to a tee. Perhaps one of their bath sets might make a suitable Christmas present! A large but well-worn scrubbing brush, a small piece of soap smelling of the strongest disinfectant imaginable and the piece de resistance... a few square inches of the coarsest linen masquerading as a towel. An object specifically designed not to absorb water," she laughed, "but at least the water was hot and clean. I forgot, if you've been very good, I'll add the vermin-infested comb."

"Aunt! You've spoilt the surprise," Emily said. "Now what have I got to look forward to on Christmas Day? And I was so hoping for a collection of prison clothes."

Eleanor laughed. "If only I'd known, it would have saved me a good deal of time. I'd have smuggled mine out on my release, whereas now there's barely time to petition the authorities for a set. Perhaps for your birthday." She smiled. "My pawnbroker's collection! That's what I was reminded of. I was like one of those poor women struggling along to the pawnbroker with a bag of old clothes. But at Field's earlier you were saying you couldn't decide which colours suited you. Luckily in prison there's only a choice between green or brown."

"I'll take green," decided Emily.

"That's a relief. Brown was for third class. Your dress will be a dark green serge; a much patched and dubiously clean affair, which you'll find just about acceptable. And for underneath: besides the cotton drawers and two petticoats... again reasonable, I'm afraid the stockings and the stays..." she shook her head, "will prove a major disappointment. The only virtue of the former is that they keep your legs warm, but their coarseness is so irritating that you will itch and itch... just thinking about them makes me want to scratch."

"But if they're for my birthday, it will be warm enough by then and I can do without."

"True, but the stays had no redeeming features, no bones, as stiff as a board and they took forever to lace up." She shuddered at the memory. "Definitely not Paris fashion! And I almost forgot – to cover my hair, a little Dutch cap, which, like much else, gave the outward appearance of cleanliness whilst being stained inside by a long succession of rusty hairpins."

Emily laughed. "I'm sorry, I was imagining my parents' reaction on Christmas morning when I open a large parcel and it contains a set of prison clothes."

"That would be worth seeing!"

"You said Mother was upset when she found out. How did that happen?"

"I was lucky. I was imprisoned during a brief period during which suffrage prisoners were treated a little more leniently, and one benefit was that I was able to freely receive and write letters."

"So you wrote to Mother and told her where you were?"

"No. Much to my surprise, I had a letter from her first."

Dear Eleanor,

I now know why I haven't heard from you for the last week or so. Did you have any intention of informing me about your present circumstances, or did you plan to keep me in blissful ignorance? As ever, your self-centred actions take little account of how other people may be affected by them.

I was in Hammonds this morning when I was accosted by Mrs. Trafford. I cannot abide the woman. She is an insufferable, overbearing bore who takes a disproportionate pleasure in the misfortune of others. So when she caught my eye across the haberdashery department, my heart sank. She approached me with a look of malicious glee on her face, so I knew something was amiss.

"I'm so sorry about your sister," she said to me, her voice dripping with insincerity, and when I gave her a blank look, she continued with unalloyed joy, "You don't know? It was in this morning's paper. Eleanor has been imprisoned for twenty-eight days." I'm not sure whether I was surprised by this news or not. After our previous intervention, and discussions, I had hoped you had put your more extreme, infantile stupidities behind you - it appears you have not. I was still trying to decide what to say when the wretched woman continued. I am going to the trouble of reporting her words so you can appreciate the position that you have placed me in.

"You poor dear," she said, "I feel dreadful being the bearer of such bad tidings. George spotted it at breakfast. There's a decent-sized paragraph on page two. 'Local Suffragist Refuses to Keep Peace' was the headline. Eleanor's been sentenced to 28 days. If only I had a copy with me to show you."

Yes, I was quite sure she wished she had it with her, as she would have liked nothing better than reading it out aloud, there and then. You will doubtless accuse me of over-exaggerating, but it was a mortifying experience. To be told, "How terrible for you to find out like this." Indeed, Eleanor, indeed! She gave me the gist of the report, interspersed with expressions of her deepest sympathies. It was several minutes before I could escape by pretending I was late for an appointment. But before we parted, I actually found myself thanking her for telling me.

I would have thought it was not beyond expectation to have been given some warning, if not directly then from one of your dubious acquaintances. At least I will now be prepared for any future Mrs Traffords that I might meet, but as to what I shall say, I know not. I have a meeting of Bootless Bairns tomorrow and a whist drive on Saturday.

I will intercept Alfred on his return this evening, something I am not looking forward to. He was in a great rush and took the paper with him, but whether he will have had time to read it, I do not know. He always buys a copy of the Mail on the way home, however. One thing is certain – this will never be discussed over the dinner table.

I must finish as Alice is demanding my attention. I would send Emily to the post, but I can hardly let her take this. I assume H.M Prison Holloway, London will be a sufficient postal address. Looking at it on the envelope leaves me lost for words. I trust you are well, and not planning to do anything extreme,

Clara

Dear Clara,

Thank you for your letter. I am sorry you learnt about my present whereabouts courtesy of that interfering busybody. You may be surprised, but not everyone reacts with shock and disapproval. For those that do, please tell them that you are not your sister's keeper.

Apart from that, as you asked, I am quite well, thank you, though some things take getting used to. Bolts being bolted, locks being locked and the constant jangling of keys, for a start. And bells ringing and no-one answering them. That does become tiresome.

The clothing is bearable. The food is somewhat grim – if I'd wanted to eat well I would have chosen tea at Claridges instead. A hand thrusts itself through the hole in the cell door and presents one with something to eat. Yesterday it was cold pressed meat in a dirty tin served with hard little brown loaves. All washed down with a fine Beaujolais! No, all washed down with either a loathsome concoction masquerading as cocoa or some of my pint and a half cold water ration. I swear the tins in which the drinking water stands are cleaned with a mixture of soap and brick dust. And the instruments we are given to eat with are as useless as this prison pen I am writing with. It appears the authorities are worried about a potential suicide risk, but the only way I might risk a charge under the Suicide Act would be if the boredom of being locked up in my cell became too much for me. I have a Bible and a copy of 'Home Beautiful' (I am not sure why), which I can read whilst reclining on my bare wooden bench.

I know I have complained in the past about the lack of good reading matter in the Northern Library. Never again. Holloway Prison Library and the phrase 'tedious and dreary in the extreme' will always now be synonymous. I am unsure how many have forced themselves to read 'A Perfect Home and How to Keep it', or taken its advice. Beverley Road's bookshelves groan with a literary cornucopia by comparison.

Some of my fellow inmates communicate by tapping on the water pipes but I've not mastered it. I should have paid more attention when it was explained to me, but you won't be entirely surprised that I didn't.

You will be relieved to know that many of the rules that govern us are currently being implemented in a rather more relaxed manner. We have Mr Churchill to thank for this, but I do not trust the man. Do you remember he spoke in town once? There was some disruption and heckling at the meeting. He is a shifty individual, but I suppose I should thank him for my being able to write this. Silence is not being enforced as it might be either. We are allowed to talk on exercise, and this is the highlight of my day. The flights of fancy that conversations can reach are delightful. This morning the most fantastical schemes of escape were being plotted. Do you know of anyone who owns a hot-air balloon?

Discussing how to smuggle things in fills an enjoyable ten minutes too. According to Mother, my sponges were always light whereas your fruit cakes were particular heavy, so if you baked one it might be an ideal receptacle for an iron file. And if I were unable to cut through the bars, then in desperation I could always eat the cake.

I am sorry, Clara, I can hear you tutting, as you read that last paragraph. I know you will disapprove of my levity. And your fruit cake is actually quite good.

I would welcome a reply, even if it is filled with criticism and disapproval. Reading does help the time pass. I have also included a short note for Emily with this letter. You will have no need to censor it as there is not the slightest clue to my present predicament. If she does wish to write she can send it via Clements Inn and it will get to me. I will finish now as the light is going.

Give my love to everyone,
your far from penitent (I'm afraid) sister,
Eleanor

P.S. I have no intention of refusing food. I have seen the effects on those brave enough to do so.

#

Emily smiled. "I'm glad you didn't refuse food, Aunt. I'd hate to think of someone forcing you to eat. The woman on the card looks fit and healthy, though."

"Yes, she does. But give her time. I've seen released women looking like famine victims: their skin turned brown, staring at you through half-open, heavy, hollow eyes and speaking in voices reduced to a hoarse whisper. The strangest thing though was the pervading smell, their breath full of the

most foul, offensive odours – a result of being infected by their torturers'
equipment."

Emily was shocked by the acerbic edge to her aunt's voice.

"Constance Lytton's book has many harrowing passages, as you'll find
when you read it – so, though I'd hardly recommend darning filthy socks
as a way of spending one's time, it was nothing compared to being pinned
down on a bed as twenty inches of a two-yard long unsterilised tube was
forced up your nose and down into your stomach." She gave Emily a wan
smile. "To think some people denigrate those women!" She made a deliberate effort to be more cheerful. "Now, my dear, have we finished?"

"Just one left, Aunt, my favourite, the three policeman and the woman
with the umbrella."

Votes for Women!

"There's a newspaper over there, Emily. The *Daily Mirror*. Do examine its front page."

Emily picked up the paper and looked at the date. Saturday 19 November 1910. She studied the large photograph. "That's shocking. Are you saying you had something to do with this?"

"I was close by, but I didn't witness that actual incident, though I knew people who did. But being there on that Friday afternoon was the most terrifying experience of my life."

#

Why was she not surprised? Parliament was to be dissolved in ten days time, with no promise of women being enfranchised. Even a majority of over one hundred for the limited suffrage that would have given her and a million other female householders the vote wasn't enough to persuade that wretched Asquith to grant more time for the Bill! Yet another betrayal, after the heady promises of the last few months.

Eleanor looked around. Yes, she was keeping up with her Yorkshire contingent. She felt a little nervous – justifiably so, if reports of how the police were behaving were true. Mrs Pankhurst's words from the Women's

Parliament in the Caxton Hall resounded in her head – 'You will press forward in quietness and peaceableness. Offending none and blaming none, ready to sacrifice yourselves, even unto death if need be, in the cause of freedom.' She smiled to herself... hopefully, the demand for the ultimate sacrifice would not prove necessary.

She tried to estimate their numbers. Hers had been one of the last small groups to set off, with three to four minute intervals between them. Others were coming from Clement's Inn, so there must be three, four – even five hundred of them. The procession slowed as they reached Parliament Square. Their instructions were to make for the Stranger's Entrance, in order to support the leading deputation. Anything that might be construed as a violent act was to be avoided at all costs. She'd even left her umbrella behind in case it was seen as a potential weapon. She looked at her companions; she'd never seen a less threatening group of individuals. They would not pose a threat to Mr Baden Powell's Boy Scouts, let alone the Metropolitan Police.

She looked into the gathering dusk. The House of Lords was silhouetted against an intense blood-red setting sun. Mist drifting in from the Thames and the soft lemon-yellow glow from recently-lit street lamps gave the whole scene an ethereal effect. Some buildings had taken on an almost bluish tinge. Eleanor took a deep breath. Blue was the predominant colour in front of her. They were completely outnumbered by the largest police contingent she'd ever seen. The pavements around her were overflowing with people, and even the streets were congested, with vehicles. She looked again at the massed police; it would need divine intervention to cross this Dark Blue Sea.

She glanced up at her small purple bannerette. 'Where There's a Bill, There's a Way'. A voice to her right called out, "Try to stick together". Eleanor stepped forward.

A hand reached roughly across her and snatched her bannerette. For a few seconds she struggled with her assailant. A shock of pain shot up her arm. He'd grabbed her by the wrist and was twisting it sharply. She let go. What was happening? A tall shabbily-dressed man was stamping on her bannerette.

"What do you think you are doing?" she shouted.

He looked at her with contempt. "Whatever I want."

There were some policemen a few yards away. Eleanor gestured towards them.

"Don't expect any help from that direction today." His words had a chilling certainty. He leered at her and shoved her towards the police. Eleanor stumbled forwards. A policeman reached out to catch her, then let her sprawl full length on the ground. She lay there winded, before being unceremoniously dragged to her feet.

"I am so sorry Madam took such an unfortunate fall. Is it possible that Madam has been drinking?" A policeman thrust his face towards hers and sniffed. She flinched at his own bad breath. "No, my apologies. It's only nasty cheap perfume that I can smell."

She was regaining control of her senses. Previous experiences in the Square, if not exactly enjoyable, had been interesting, and the police had been polite, almost gentlemanly, throughout.

"Don't speak to me like that, Constable. You must have seen that man assault me. Look, there he is." She could see him less than twenty yards away, harassing another woman. "There he is, you should arrest him."

"I'm sorry, Madam must be mistaken, as I know the gentleman assisting that young lady."

Eleanor's heart sank. He had no intention of helping her. "I will let you in to a little secret. The gentleman is a colleague of mine. Plain-clothes, but his rough appearance is ideal for spotting any ne'er-do-wells hoping to disrupt your peaceful procession. Speaking of which, shouldn't you be on your way? We can't have you loitering... with or without intent. And the man you were accusing... did he push you... like this?" For the second time in a few minutes Eleanor, felt herself being manhandled.

"Take your hands off me." Her words had no effect. He whispered in her ear, "Just be glad my hands didn't wander anywhere else, Madam. You're not my sort, though you might not be so lucky if you meet someone who prefers mutton to lamb. And I wouldn't bother complaining. We can do what we want today, and there's nothing you can do about it." And with that he flung her into the turmoil.

The next hour passed for Eleanor in a kaleidoscopic blur. Police cordons broken, but no-one arrested. A woman thrown down the Strangers'

Entrance steps. A large group of sailors in US navy uniforms lined up out-side Westminster Abbey. A policeman forcing his knee up under a woman's skirt and trying to lift her off the ground. Another young woman being led away with her skirts above her head whilst men shouted obscenities at her. A confusing melee.

Eleanor found herself forced into a side street. She stopped, gasping for breath, glad to recover for a few moments. She screamed as her head was jerked backwards. An arm came around her waist and a hand seized her left breast and pinched it hard. It was excruciating. She screamed again. Tears of pain and rage came to her eyes. She could hardly see.

"Take your hands off her, you scum!" a man's voice said. Suddenly the pain eased. She staggered backwards. She tried to focus on her Good Samaritan. Was that him being dragged away by the police? Another man was shouting something unintelligible in her face. "Whore!" The punch in the stomach forced her to her knees. She wondered whether she was go-ing to be sick. A gap opened in front of her. She staggered to her feet. He seemed to have gone. Or was he just waiting to attack her again? Desperate-ly she made for some nearby railings. Reaching them, she hung on tightly, thankful for the brief respite and sank to the ground.

"Eleanor? Are you all right? Eleanor?" A friendly voice. "Are you all right?"

"I think so. Yes. I think so." She looked up. Did she look as dishevelled as her friend?

"Let me help you up. You're in a bad way."

They clung to the railings together. Eleanor laughed. "Me in a bad way! Have you looked at yourself?"

Her friend's dress was covered in blood and she had the beginnings of a black eye and her nose was red and swollen.

"I'm fine, Eleanor. I've been back to Caxton Hall and they patched me up. They've set up an ambulance station there for the walking wounded." She gestured at her dress and laughed. "It'll be difficult getting the blood out of this." She touched her face and winced. "I'm a little sore. Copper was using his helmet as a weapon. Still, I'm not as bad as some. Do you know Ada Wright? She was knocked down two or three times, and the police were hitting her so hard with their batons whilst she was on the ground that a man intervened, arguing with them, and trying to shield her, but they took no notice. Just carried on belting her. The last I saw of her before that brute attacked me, she was slumped on the ground, possibly unconscious. But what does surprise me is that I've hardly seen anyone arrested."

"I thought the same," Eleanor said. "They're more interested in terrorising and humiliating us than anything else. And some of the bullies in the crowd are police too. I'll be black and blue in the morning, but I've got my breath back now – so if our orders are no retreat, then I think we should give it another go." She gave her friend an encouraging smile before they attempted once more to reach the Strangers' Entrance.

#

Emily was aghast. "It sounds terrible, Aunt. Were you arrested in the end?"

"No, but a hundred or more were, and that was after many hours. Strangely, they were all later released without charge. The only plausible reason was that they didn't want a lot of stories about brutality coming out in court. Some people believed the police were acting under orders from the Home Secretary, Churchill, but there was no way of proving that." She pointed at the paper Emily was still holding. "He supposedly tried to have that copy of the *Mirror,* with the picture of Ada, suppressed. He did call us 'copious fountains of mendacity', and there were plenty willing to believe him. I'm afraid I lost my faith in the Press after that. I can't believe they didn't see what was going on. According to the *Express,* we were shameless women, sexless creatures, and my favourite... demented viragos." She smiled at Emily. "And everyone agreed that the police displayed great good temper and tact in protecting themselves from us. They were the victims and we were the aggressors, with our trivial cause. That was what the *Daily Mail* called it. A trivial cause! We were no better than an inebriated collection of fishwives trying to force their way into a public house."

"Was that the end of it then, Aunt?"

"I suppose it was the end of that, except for the memories of those who were there. Our eyewitness evidence was presented to Parliament to try and force Churchill to hold a public inquiry, but he was obdurate. Events moved on, and many women decided that it was better to get arrested immediately for smashing a window than risk being brutalised by the police."

"But didn't anything happen about the attack on her?" Emily said, pointing to the photograph of the woman being assaulted.

"Ada, according to the police, had sunk to the ground, exhausted from her struggles, and the proof that nothing untoward happened is that you'll see one of the men in the background is smiling. Ridiculous! But no, Ada recovered, even if the police's reputation amongst many women didn't. My goodness! Look at the time. One of us has to get up early in the morning." She stood up. "I'll need to arrange a taxi for you."

Emily fanned out the Panko sets in front of her, before shuffling them back together into a pack. She rose to her feet when her aunt returned. "Would you mind awfully if I borrowed the cards?"

"Of course you can, my dear. Sarah would be only too happy if you relieved me of even more memorabilia and made more space for her duster." She gave Emily an envelope. "One last thing for you. Open it later, when you get home." There was a knock at the door. "One of them always reminded me of you. Hair a little darker, perhaps," she added. "Time to put on your coat."

Emily gave her aunt a kiss. "It's been so interesting. You've given me such a lot to think about. I'll see you again soon, whatever happens." She put on her coat, opened the door and stepped out into the cold. She turned back to see her aunt framed in the doorway. "I almost forgot! It was a delicious tea. Thank you. Do go in now, Aunt. It's freezing cold outside." Emily turned again and went to the taxi.

#

Half an hour later, Emily was sitting on her bed, studying the photo that had been inside the envelope. Three girls had been posed, standing in a row in front of some park railings. Each held a different placard: 'READ OUR PAPER', 'VOTES FOR WOMEN' and 'ONE PENNY WEEKLY'. They all looked serious, but that might have just been from the effort of keeping still. The 'ONE PENNY WEEKLY' girl bore a fleeting resemblance to herself, and must be the one her aunt had meant. She turned the photograph over and read the inscription on the back.

For Emily,
Who might have been one of these.
Take it with you
when you cast your vote,
to remind you of
this sentimental suffragist.
Aunt E

.

Emily smiled, positioned the photograph in pride of place on her bookshelf, then busied herself getting ready for bed.

January 6th, 1917
Westbourne Avenue

My dearest Robert,

I hope this arrives in time. If not, Happy Belated Birthday, but I was/am/will be especially thinking about you on the tenth. I have put something in the your mother's parcel.

I cannot resist telling you about something else I have for you. I wanted to give it to you in person, but then I thought of giving you clues and letting you spend the next few months working it out – but that would be cruel, and you would never guess anyway. So I shall tell you and hope you are pleased. At great expense (the princely sum of one shilling plus postage!) I have bought something for your collection. It is only small, but there is a letter of authentication with it. It's a piece of the airship Lieutenant Leefe Robinson shot down at Cuffley! Are you pleased? I do hope so.

Isn't it strange how someone like Robinson becomes instantly famous? After being decorated by the King, he was mobbed in the street by adulatory crowds. It must be hard to get used to. There has been much publicity recently about a French flyer, Lieutenant Heurteaux, who has fourteen kills. I know you said the RFC doesn't make as much fuss as the French and Germans do about these sort of things, but the newspapers do like to take up individuals and propel them forward, and people do find it cheering.

Thinking of Zeppelins, Big Lizzie hasn't disturbed our slumbers of late, but Mother still dreads Buzzer nights. She has ever since last March, when she was serving in the canteen on Paragon Station only hours before all those poor people were killed, and then the next day seeing its glass roof destroyed. And then a house was damaged in the Avenue in August. At least after Zeppelin Sunday she knows they are not invincible. That mood of anger at how defenceless the city was has gone and it's hard to imagine an RFC officer being attacked now. It's five months since our last raid, and long may that continue.

Mother's interest in spiritualism continues to increase, especially since the empty void that was at the heart of Christmas Day. And with the estrangement between Father and Aunt Eleanor, New Year has hardly been a time of hope. Unfortunately, she has also found a ready audience in Alice. I always thought her more level-headed. Both are convinced by the Angel of Mons and Mother has the Spiritualist magazine that recounts the event in detail. I am unsure whether to pour cold water on her ideas. Aunt Eleanor has Arthur Machen's book about how the snowball of rumour took off after his original short story about phantom Agincourt Bowmen at the Battle was reprinted as fact by various parish magazines. Aunt Eleanor said some people consider it almost treasonable to question the tale, as it does give people comfort and hope, so it is hard to know what to do. Mother has also bought a copy of 'Raymond or Life and Death'. She was telling Alice how Sir Oliver Lodge has contacted his son Raymond through a medium and her spirit companion, Feda. What an odd name. When I told Aunt Eleanor, she said if she wanted to spend half a guinea on tripe she would visit her butcher rather than her bookshop. We shall have to see what happens, but Father is sceptical, though his current preoccupation is the launch of Victory Loans next week. Did you know I could have bought you a birthday present of a hundred pounds worth for only ninety-five? No? Until breakfast, neither did I. If you want some, hurry, there are only a hundred million bonds being issued!

I keep wondering whether you are flying at present? The weather has been pretty grim here but without the dreadful fogs and consequent chaos they've had in London and Birmingham. Perhaps it's better over there? If you are not flying, are you spending more time learning Morse? It seems such a bore, and telling each other stories in it doesn't sound much fun either, even if you do pay forfeits to the beer fund for any mistakes. But in sympathy with you, and at no little effort, I have attempted the following, and I have set aside a penny for every mistake for your beer fund!

    — -.— -.. .- .-. .-.. .- .. -. —. .-. —' -... . .-. -

       .. — .. .. -.— —- ..- ... —-

  .—. .-.. .- .... -.-. —- — . .... —- — . .... .- ..-. . .- —- — .

The hospital has been fine. I am getting used to things and am not as tired as I was. We have to be frightfully on our toes as Matron delivers a terrible wigging to anyone who isn't. There was a sad little incident the other day. A young woman came to visit her fiancé only to discover so had his wife! There was an almighty kerfuffle by his bedside. She left in tears – the former fiancée, that is. Matron had to be called. The patient was due to be discharged, but whether to face his wife or the Germans first I do not know. It gave everyone something to talk about. You had better not be collecting your own French fiancées!

Mother has brought the post, including a Letter From You, which is wonderful. And there is one from David saying he expects leave next month, so that has cheered her immensely. I should write more but I cannot resist opening your letter.

I shall write again tomorrow and tomorrow and tomorrow

ta solitaire petite pauvre

Emilie

xxxxx

February 16th, 1917
Westbourne Avenue

The shouting woke her. She'd been dreaming. A man was calling out, trying to attract her attention. Struggling into wakefulness, she'd realised the cries came from the next bedroom. She waited, her heart pounding. There it was again, clearer this time, but impossible to make out any words.

It was late. The fire in the grate gave off the feeblest of dull orange glows. The room was cold. Silence had returned, but something about the cries prompted Emily to venture out. She put on slippers over her bed socks and wrapped her dressing gown around her. She half expected to meet her mother, but the landing was empty. Light was visible under David's bedroom door. She stood still, unsure whether to risk being seen as interfering. His coughing made up her mind. She tapped on the door. "David? Are you all right?" She waited a few seconds, and as she tapped again the door opened.

"Emily! What are you doing?" he said in a fierce whisper. "You'll wake everyone."

She thought he would shut the door, but instead he said, "Don't just stand there. You'd better come in for a minute."

He let her into the room, before shutting the door. "Here, put the eiderdown round you... Not that it seems that cold to me," he added as he handed it to her and got back into bed. She saw he had been sweating. He gave her a weak smile. "I was sitting up reading until quite late, so the fire's still going and should burn up if you make it up. Did I wake you?"

She nodded.

"Sorry. Was I shouting? I wasn't sure. I must have been asleep, but I may have left the light on." He shook his head. "I'm not... It can take me ages to drop off and I wake up a great deal. Too many dreams. I've forgotten what a proper night's sleep is. If I can make it till six, that's excellent. It's lying awake from four that's hard – so annoying when you have to snatch what you can up the line. Dropping off standing up – I can do that. But in a comfortable bed, I can't."

She gave him a sympathetic smile.

"We've never been that close, have we? You and me? You and Edward always were, but I don't know... I think you think me a bit of a stuffed shirt... rather like Father."

"You've always seemed more serious, David, but Edward was such a joker, so..."

"...by comparison, I'm dull as ditch water."

"I'd never have said..."

"Don't worry, I'm not offended. It's true, anyway. I always assumed I would follow in Father's footsteps, though he hoped I'd become something more than a provincial bank manager." He stopped and shook his head, an irritated expression on his face. "Sorry, I sometimes get an annoying ringing in my ears. No, or something in the City. Justify my public school and Oxbridge education. Make use of all those helpful contacts."

"David..."

"Not very likely now."

"But when the war is..."

"And I've been feeling dog-tired. But you don't want to hear this, do you? And look at the time, haven't you got to be up early?"

"Honestly, I don't mind listening – if you want to talk, that is. I'd like to. And I'm on second shift tomorrow, so don't worry about that."

He looked relieved. "I can't talk to them... not properly, anyway."

"What, to Mother and Father?"

"Did you see her looking at me this evening? Not all the time, just when she thought I wasn't paying attention. That look in her eyes. The desperate, concerned worry that she's trying to mask."

"But she's been so looking forward to you coming home. She's talked of nothing else for days. She so wants you to enjoy your leave."

"I know she does, but... with Edward... it's a responsibility. I saw the letter. How long will that stay there?" He lay back against his pillow. "And as to Father, he just doesn't understand what it's like out there. Not that I blame him. He's not alone in that. Most people back here are like him. Just haven't a clue. I don't know what the officers in that hospital of yours say, but believe me they'll be understating the awfulness. But Father and the rest see it in black and white, so simple. Brown and grey more like. And there's no point trying to tell them. They just believe you're exaggerating. It's not what they want to hear. Even when they see people who've been destroyed by it. The poor so-and-sos who've been gassed or are going to spend the rest of their days as cripples. What do they want us to say? Cheer up! Look on the bright side? The next big push will take us a hundred yards closer to Berlin?"

She was shocked at his bitterness.

"And there's always an act of individual bravery to read about. Make us feel better about what a wonderful job the cheerful Tommies are doing. Father used to send me *Punch*. He meant well, but have you read it?"

"I've glanced at the cartoons, but I've never read it cover to cover. I've heard Father chortling, though."

"Trivial rubbish packed with deceit. They might be writing about the Boer War, for all the relevance it has. And they force their insufferable propaganda down your throat, when all you have to do is put your head outside and see it's all lies. I wrote and told him to stop sending it. I haven't told him its most popular use was as toilet paper. Pass my cigarettes, will you? I wish I'd brought a *Trench* magazine home. They're not produced by professionals, but at least they're worth reading, even if they go a bit overboard on the poetry." He smiled at her. "You're the family member who's so keen on literature. I shall save you one and you can give me your considered opinion. But," he looked more doubtful, "you'd need a glossary of Army slang to understand it properly."

"Perhaps you should teach me a couple of words a day whilst you are here, David, and then I would have a head start. An A to Z. And I know an A... A is for Archie... anti-aircraft fire. And theirs explode with black smoke and ours with white, for some reason that I've forgotten."

David smiled. "Of course, Robert... B is for Baby's Head."

"Baby's Head?"

"The meat pudding that's part of Army field rations."

"That's awful, but go on... a couple more... C is for..."

"Coal Scuttle... a German's steel helmet... they do look rather like them. And D is for Daisy Cutter... a shell that explodes immediately it hits the ground. They're used to try and clear barbed wire... But Emily, shouldn't you be getting back to bed?"

"No, I'm wide awake. And I do want to hear what you have to say. It's sad that you can't talk to Father about it. You were very quiet at supper. They thought you were tired from the journey."

"No, I wasn't, it wasn't that bad – and it's one way of travelling for free, though mentioning that got Father complaining about rail fares going up by half." He paused while he lit a cigarette. It was peculiar hearing him talking to her like this. He was changed, more open with her, more vulnerable.

"Mother seemed quite happy relating all the goings-on of people I do and don't know, and then she was grumbling away about the food, which she shouldn't, as it was a jolly decent spread."

"She and Alice have been saving things up for weeks. But we shouldn't be complaining at all. Though the flour is so poor and bread has lost its nutty flavour – and as for the sugar, when you can get it... sorry... how embarrassing! I sound just like Mother. What was it you said when you wanted the sugar? Pass the sand?"

He laughed. "I had enough sand for a lifetime in Egypt. It got everywhere. It clogged your rifle bolts and the Lewis guns and it seemed to get into every meal, though it was useful for cleaning pots and pans, even your clothes." He smiled. "I can't see anyone here using sugar to do that, no matter how poor it gets."

"Do you wish you could have stayed in Egypt?" she said, unsure how much to ask. "It must be different now."

He shook his head. "That's a hard one to answer. Not much difference in the weather."

She laughed.

"Both France and Egypt have their lice that need chatting. There you are, another C for you." He rolled up his pyjama sleeve, puffed on his cigarette, peered at the inside of his arm and then pretended to stub it on something. "Chatting. A flaming end for the little blighters. You can run a lighted candle along the seam of your clothes too." He grimaced, "But they always come back. I haven't brought any home, though. Mother wouldn't be too happy if I had. And as to Egypt or France? I didn't see much of Johnny Turk in Egypt. You could hear packs of wild dogs out in the desert at night, so you'd be on edge wondering whether there was anything else out there, but there never was – apart from the occasional spy. The greatest danger was disease. I don't suppose there's many on Cottingham Road suffering from Red Water Fever, but if you ever visit the Pyramids, don't drink from the horse troughs."

"I shall remember when on my Grand Middle Eastern Tour," Emily said. "But there's plenty who've had Trench Fever."

"Not something I've had... as yet... And unlike in France there wasn't much call for rubbing whale grease on my feet on the banks of the Suez canal."

"Make sure you do use it. Only the other day someone showed me where he'd had a couple of toes amputated last year."

"So it's pretty grim a lot of the time," he sighed, "I've seen things... I've seen things... but at the same time you have to carry on. I must admit I'm in danger of losing my faith in the Almighty. You see people thanking God it wasn't them. One of our privates had his hair parted by a sniper's bullet which passed clean through his helmet, but he was unscathed and then there are others... who go west..." his voice faltered, "who didn't have God or Lady Luck on their side. It was said we were the lucky Tenth, but nothing ever lasts and that hasn't. Some become fatalistic, saying if it's got your number on it there's nothing you can do about it." He lit another cigarette. "Not that I believe that. And then there's the arrangement between us and the Germans. An eye for an eye, tit for tat. There's a lot of that. They bombard us, we retaliate, we snipe at them, they respond and so on. And I'm only here now because both sides *can* be sporting too."

When it looked as if he wasn't going to tell her more, she said, "Sporting? How?"

He inhaled deeply, leant back and blew smoke up towards the ceiling. "It was only a small incident at Bus-les-Artoises last May. Nothing, really. I was out with a wiring party just before midnight. We'd made an almighty racket getting over the parapet, so there was no way the Germans wouldn't have heard us, but we were out there and had to get on with it, expecting to come under fire any second. And then we heard the Germans. They were out doing the same in their wire. It's what I meant about tit-for-tat, both of us no more than fifty yards apart. They started talking loudly, laughing as they worked, so we did the same. We could have been any two groups of workers labouring away anywhere in the world. And then we realised that things had gone quiet. They'd finished and gone. We carried on, knowing it might get a trifle uncomfortable, but they let us carry on – until eventually they sent up flares over us. We were sitting ducks, as easy to pick off as at the fair, but they didn't fire. It was a signal so we were able to scarper back to our trenches. Then they sent a few bursts of machine gun fire above our heads to show normal service was resumed." He stubbed his cigarette out. "And then a few weeks later a similar situation arose, we were first to leave – but that time their wirers had the pleasure of a full artillery barrage raining down on their heads. Sporting, unsporting... life, death. It's a fine line. That's one thing I've learnt. And not to rely on tit-for-tat."

Emily got off the bed, surprised at how much closer she felt to David than she had before. "You can always talk again," she said, "while you're home. Especially if you can't talk to Mother and Father." She smiled at him. "But only if you want to." She stopped near the door. "Have you any plans for tomorrow?"

"There are a couple of people I need to see, and I might call in on Aunt Eleanor. Father was a bit odd when I mentioned her."

"It's complicated. I had hoped... No, it's too late. Tomorrow perhaps." She laughed. "Actually it's tomorrow already. I hope you manage to get some sleep. Goodnight."

"Goodnight, Emily

She opened David's door and, careful not to disturb her parents, returned to her room.

May 2nd, 1917
Vert Galant, France

My dear Emily,

You can thank the Almighty for the early arrival of this letter. I was on last night's list for action, but at four o'clock I was woken by the delightful music of rain drumming on the hut roof. I pulled the bedclothes back over my head and before I knew it, my batman was waking me with coffee and bringing me hot water for my shave. Then I tucked into a late, leisurely breakfast of bacon, eggs, toast and marmalade, at the civilised hour of a quarter to eleven. You would enjoy the futuristic garb some chaps were wearing in the mess. One came in in a long, bright green scarf, striped pyjamas, flying boots and a barely functional greasy flying tunic – the height of sartorial elegance!

I'm already looking forward to dinner. Five courses, white linen tablecloths and a buzz of animated conversation, all of which makes it possible to imagine that we're not at war. I feel guilty about it at times, but what would be the point of refusing or not enjoying anything out of sympathy for those enduring hardship at home or in the trenches? At least we put our lives at risk, unlike the base wallahs who share our privileges.

So no Dawn Patrol and, seeing how filthy the weather is, little chance of flying today. I've got some OR letters to read and censor, which is dreary in the extreme, so I am spending a more enjoyable time writing to you first. One or two of my recent efforts have been a little gloomy, much of April having been pretty grim. I'm heartily glad to see the back of it. Now it's a new month and I'm positive things will improve. I shall pick out a few cheery things to tell you.

We had a jolly time last Friday as guests of the 28th. They plied us with coffee cocktails beforehand and all manner of drinks later. Thankfully, I knew I was not flying the next day! There was lots of ragging. Kelly suggested a bull-fight, with him as the bull. He put on a fur coat and we dug out some old snow boots for his hands and feet. Hart was made into a matador, with a curtain round his middle, a tablecloth over his shoulders, a red cloth and a stick for a sword. Everyone else was draped in various coloured cloths. I was a picador riding piggy-back on one of the other chaps. The ugliest fellow in their squadron, called 'The Beautiful Senorita' for the occasion, conducted ceremonies from the top of a piano. There was a parade with appropriate musical accompaniments and then, to great cheers, the bull was let out of his pen. The matador toyed with him, to which the bull gave a spirited response and then we picadors joined in, which led to a most frightful commotion. The Senorita, who was banging a drum, fell off the piano. Everyone was screeching and with the music at a crescendo for the kill, the door opened and their CO walked in! You could have heard a pin drop. Everyone stopped – except matador and bull, who were so involved in the finale that they continued unawares. Thankfully the CO, rather than putting anyone on a charge, found the whole bizarre spectacle uproariously funny.

'Over the Top' has proved a good turn at our guest nights. Two sides face each other over three sofas placed across the middle of the room. At a signal the artillery barrage starts – a most infernal din of banging saucepans and tin drums, blowing horns and whistles, which ceases at zero hour. Then the first wave surges forward over the sofas to capture a defender and carry him back to their lines. Last time, after a fierce fight, I was collared and ended up with a sofa upended on top of me. We had a great time.

I have a couple of days' leave due, but not enough to return home. A Major from a new squadron is coming before then. Rumour has it he's after a couple of pilots to complete their complement of eighteen. The minimum requirement is five kills, and I have seven confirmed. One or two fellows can shoot-a-line when claiming but generally there's someone around to put them in their place. The great attraction is that they will be flying the new SE5a. The mechanics can supercharge the engine to get it to 20,000 feet, which means we can finally compete with the Hun's Albatros on equal terms. It can get a bit nippy when you are flying that high. Imagine me in my outfit of leather clothing, long sheepskin boots, fur-lined helmet and gloves with silk underneath. Even then it will be cold. They are meant to be incredibly stable in a fast dive – sorry, I get carried away at the thought of flying one. Unfortunately they will be decked out in drab regulation colours. I wish the powers-that-be, just once, would let us paint our buses like the Huns do. There were some Fokkers the other day with green and yellow striped wings and bright red noses and tails. I would not be surprised to come across one painted all the colours of the rainbow. The only thing about us being drab is it makes distinguishing friend from foe easier when it's a bit hectic. Perhaps I should become another Albert Ball – he's got away with sticking an aluminium bowl, painted bright red, onto the propeller hub of his Nieuport.

I have been outside and the rain has eased but the clouds are low and threatening. A definite dud day, so I might do a bit in the garden later. Do thank Mr Barber for the seeds. I never thought of myself as a gardener, but when the chap who started the venture bought it over Amiens, just letting all his hard work go to wrack and ruin seemed wrong. If I do move on, then someone else can eat the benefits of my labours! Mr Barber would doubtless have me start a few marrows and beans off in pots, but turning up somewhere new with those might get me a few strange looks. Once you're accepted it's different. A fellow called Archibald James returned from leave with four pairs of hounds he'd bought at his local Sussex harriers. It caused a bit of a stir, but he hunts hares around Armentierres now. I can't say that appeals to me. It's a pity these new buses aren't going to the 41st and that they aren't recruiting people to fly them there. Their CO commandeered an un-used Red Cross hut, had it dismantled and transported back to their airfield in his officers' cars and then reassembled as a theatre that seats 250 people! Your aunt will be amused to hear that they put on a couple of Shaw's plays. Not everyone's cup of tea these days, even if still hers, I imagine. Can you see me in greasepaint? As Androcles or the Lion? Or perhaps a solo turn? I could recite some Lewis Carroll.

Twas brillig and the Slithy Quirk
Did drone and burble in the blue,
All floppy were his wing controls
(And his observer too).

'Beware the wicked Albatros',
The O.C. Quirks had told him flat,
'Beware the Hun-Hun bird and shun
The frumious Halberstadt.'

But while through uffish bumps he ploughed,
The Albatros, with tail on high,
Came diving out the tulgey cloud
And let his bullets fly.

One, two; one, two, and through and through,
The Lewis gun went tick-a-tack,
The Hun was floored, the Quirk had scored,
And came galumphing back.

Oh hast though slain the Albatros?

Split one, with me, my beamish boy,
Our RAF-ish scout has found them out,
The C.O. Wept for joy.

Not my own work, but a pretty good twist on the original. It was written by a chap in the 40th called William Bond. And a word of explanation – a Quirk is a BE2c – it's what he flies. The Huns called earlier versions of them 'kaltes Fleisch' – dead meat – which tells you everything you need to know. And you don't see many Halberstadts now – vastly inferior to the Albatrosses. I shall learn the verse and recite it when we next meet, whenever that may be.

Thinking of poetry, another chap always takes his William Blake in his flying jacket – says at least he'll have something decent to read if he ever comes down in Hunland. I shove the latest incoherent ramblings of someone who writes to me into mine.

I'm not counting my chickens about a possible move. If it does go ahead it will be hard leaving here, as all in all they are a decent lot, both on terra firma and in the thick of it. This Major will not be our first interesting visitor. Recently General Castlenau awarded a Croix de Guerre to one of our chaps. With great pomp and ceremony he pinned on the medal, then kissed him on both cheeks, much to the recipient's disgust and our merriment. What was so delightful was that the General was five foot tall and his 'victim' was the tallest member of the squadron. If only it could have been photographed! There was plenty of ribbing in the mess that night.

Have you heard from David recently? From what you said he is not far from here. You asked about Americans. Plenty of Canadian flyers here, but no Yankees yet. Everyone jokes that they will declare war on us too, just to prove they are impartial.

Someone's just said Major Blomfield is on his way here from Liettres, so I'd better finish. He's had some musicians drafted under the Military Service Bill and sent out to form a squadron orchestra. It's a pity I didn't keep up my music lessons. I'll just hope my flying record stands me in good enough stead.

Do write asap. Will let you know how things turn out, thinking of and missing you

R

xxxxxxx

There are a few sweet pea seeds in Mr Barber's collection. I shall dedicate myself to producing the perfect bloom, which I shall christen – Sweet Emily.

June 18th, 1917
Cottingham Road

The sun shone from a cloudless sky. Emily looked across at the gates of the new St. John VAD Hospital. Everyone not confined to bed had come outdoors from Brooklands to see. The less mobile waited directly outside, whilst others, like Emily, had made their way to what they hoped was a prime position. The size of the crowds had surprised her. She glanced at her watch. Almost two o'clock. She should be finishing about now – but not today.

"Emily!" called a familiar voice.

She turned and smiled. "I was wondering if you'd get here in time."

"It's only a flying visit," Eleanor said. "I'm getting the early train to London tomorrow. Thankfully not all the rolling stock has crossed the Channel and I should get a seat. I'm a little late because I couldn't resist stopping outside Newland Orphanage. They're having an afternoon of sports, a cricket match and then tea. A large group of children was waiting to play in their band and their faces were a delight. They're hoping the motorcade might stop outside. I was tempted to stay, but I didn't want to risk missing you."

"I'm glad, I..." Loud cheering to her right interrupted her. A number of cars were approaching. The local units drawn up around the hospital gates came to attention. As the first vehicle came closer, Emily felt the surge of excitement. Everyone was waving flags. She strained upwards on tiptoes. A bearded, distinguished-looking man in khaki uniform and a woman in sapphire blue, with a hat garlanded with pale-pink roses, passed in and out of view as the car swept through the gates. Her momentary sense of anti-climax was tinged with envy; Brooklands wasn't receiving a visit.

"I was expecting it to take longer than that. It's a bit unfair. General French opened the hospital in April and now there's this visit. The nurses there have all been practising for ages. Forty of them in a long line, with Lady Nunburnholme and the Matron on the steps. They're bound to get a good view."

Her aunt's look suggested she wasn't overly disappointed for Emily. "It must be strange for the nurses there, with it having been built as a school rather than a hospital."

"Yes, the gym's now a dining room, the botany room is for billiards and they're taking baths in the handwork room and the library, where they can presumably read a good book at the same time." Emily laughed. "The kitchens are on the playground and Old Girls and staff from Central Secondary are helping out there. And the dining room, assembly hall and classrooms are all wards. I don't know what the King and Queen will make of the dark green tiles everywhere. Someone said they're depressing."

"I'm sure their Majesties will cope, Emily."

"And the Queen laid the foundation stone on their last visit."

"That I did know."

"I'd always imagined her busy at the school with a mortar and trowel but I was told that it was far more ingenious than that. The Queen was two miles away in the City Hall. She put a silver plug into a socket to complete a circuit, so that the stone fell into place when the rags around it burnt through." Emily smiled. "We had a better view of them that day, as they were in an open-topped carriage. Do you remember the crowds?"

"The crowds were unbelievable! That was on a hot June day too." Eleanor's voice dropped a little. "Less than forty-eight hours before that other royal visit to Sarajevo." She grimaced. "Do you want to stay any longer?" People were starting to disperse. "We can wait until they leave."

"No, I ought to get back. I've a few things to do. But we can take our time. Everyone isn't expected back straight away." She took her aunt's arm. "It was strange seeing all those cars, wasn't it?" She laughed. "They could hardly not find some petrol for the King! Did you notice whether he was wearing a purple ribbon? Alice was keen to know. She's planning to wait near the Polar Bear, as she thinks the car will slow down as it turns towards the Naval hospital."

"And will Alice be wearing a purple ribbon?" asked Eleanor.

"She's in two minds. She thinks it's admirable for the King to exhort us to eat less, but she's proud of how inventive she's been in making a little go a long way. She's worried about economising even further. And these new baking regulations have upset her. When she's scrimped and saved enough ingredients to bake with, she hates being told what she can use them for. She's dreading answering the door to find the Food Controller there, who'll accuse her of not only baking a cake but of using sixteen per cent sugar in it, and of then being whisked off to prison for that extra one percent. I told her she'd need a special licence if she ever bakes a wedding cake. Not that she needs to bake one!" she added.

"What a ghastly thought," her aunt replied. "I'm sorry. That came out all wrong and there's no need to look alarmed. I didn't mean the cake, or Alice being incarcerated, but to have that creature turn up on your doorstep. I doubt he makes the sacrifices he demands of others. As Ben Tillett once shouted on Tower Hill, 'May God strike Lord Devonport dead!' A sentiment it's impossible to disagree with." She looked at Emily's face. "I've shocked you."

"No, Aunt, but you became quite vehement without warning. So you aren't an admirer?"

"Admire that inveterate strike breaker? 'Lord Underweight of Margarine', as Hillaire Belloc described him. No, I am not." She smiled. "But I agree it's criminal to waste food and I am eating less bread."

"I wouldn't imagine you doing anything else, Aunt."

"And I've seen that statistic that's everywhere. If every person saved one teaspoon of breadcrumbs a day, that's forty thousand tons a year. A statement your brother would have liked."

"I can see Edward now, measuring out and weighing a teaspoon of breadcrumbs. He'd do flat and heaped as it doesn't say which it is. I almost feel I should work it out myself for him."

She spoke in a passable imitation of his voice. "'Sixteen times one hundred and twelve, times twenty, times forty thousand gives you the ounces of breadcrumbs they think would be saved, and if you multiply the ounces in a teaspoon of crumbs by three hundred and sixty-five and then by the number of people in the country then they should be the same'". Emily laughed, as she ran out of breath. "Come on, I thought you were good at mental arithmetic. Haven't you worked it out yet?"

"There's more chance of the King driving along Cottingham Road with the Kaiser than there is of my doing that in my head, but I'll await your answer with interest."

"I shall give it my full attention, Aunt," she said laughing. She slowed, as they neared Brooklands. "It's a pity you weren't here last week. A bi-plane flew over, circled a few times and, after some acrobatics, dropped a large brown package in that field over there." She pointed. "You'd never guess what it contained – pyjamas!"

Eleanor laughed as Emily continued.

"I'd been in the ward on Monday as an RFC officer was leaving, and I heard his fellow officer call to him that he was short of pyjamas, but I didn't expect them to arrive like that. He didn't land and offer any of the nurses a spin, though." She smiled. "It's over a year now. I still get goosebumps when I think about it."

Her aunt squeezed her arm. "How is Robert?"

"Excited about this new squadron and getting a chance to fly some new plane, which is better than a couple of months ago when he seemed quite melancholic."

"Yes, you told me in one of your letters."

"Yes. About examining the mirror for that haunted look he'd seen on other faces. He once mentioned how some pilots changed, how they became stale – tired and irritable on the ground and erratic in the air, taking unnecessary risks." She sighed. "So I couldn't help worrying. All the losses they were taking affected him. Bloody April, he called it. Coming back to too many empty chairs. But then he got news of the transfer and had some leave and he adores his new CO, so... so he's fine."

Eleanor smiled. "I thought I'd take you out for a treat this evening. I've reserved seats for The Great Carmo at the Tivoli. I've seen him in London. You will love him. How does seeing a full-grown lion disappear from his cage appeal to you? The Zylbastrians are on the bill as well. I hope your mother will come."

They entered the hospital grounds and Emily motioned her aunt towards an empty bench. "Let's sit down. I've still got a few minutes. I'd love to go to the Tivoli. A disappearing lion sounds wonderful! And the Great Zylbastrian Band are such fun with all their instruments. I always feel sorry for the man left banging the big bass drum when the other seven play that giant xylophone. Is he the only family member who can't play it? Or perhaps the xylophone was designed for four men and three women. And they're so fast." Emily smiled. "I shall tell Mother. You're right, they're one of her favourites." She hesitated. "Father's, too."

"Your father is very welcome to come, but I imagine he'll have some pressing engagement."

"I have tried, Aunt."

"I know you have," she patted Emily's hand. "How is your mother?"

"She's at the station rest canteen and hoping for at least a glimpse of the Royal Train."

"No. I meant how is she feeling now?"

"About David? After that dreadful business on his way back? It was awful. But she's much better than she was. It's been over a month now, and David's still at the Southern General near Bristol. I wish they'd move him nearer home or at least to a hospital closer to London. He's recovering physically, but as to the rest?" She shook her head. "Mother's talking as if he'll be well enough have a Medical Board and join the Humber Garrison." Emily looked at her aunt. "That won't happen... but she's still hoping it might. Anyway, looking forward to today's royal visit has cheered her up."

"I'm glad she's brighter, and a lot of people need a reason to celebrate. It was so dispiriting after the terrible losses at Oppy Wood." Her aunt rose.

"But if we're going out this evening I must get back. I've a few things to pack. And I'll have an even better reason for celebration tomorrow. If you're coming to the theatre, I'll see you later. Shall we say quarter past seven on the corner of Paragon Street and South Street?"

Emily nodded. "Mother will come, at least." She stood and kissed her aunt on the cheek. "And if we're lucky we'll see the lion going in through the stage door – before it disappears, that is!"

As she watched her aunt walk away, a group of patients came towards her. "Enjoy that, Nurse?" one said to her.

"Yes, it was lovely. Did you get a good view?" She stood up and joined them, and they made their way into Brooklands together.

June 7th, 1917
London

My dear Emily,

I feel far too excited, ecstatic even, and the last thing on my mind is sleep. I have been talking and talking, but as I promised am putting pen to paper at this very late hour to tell you about today's events.

My mind is still in a whirr. The Ayes to the right – 385 – the Noes to the left – 55. The figures are so magnificent I shall write them out in full. Three hundred and eighty-five to fifty-five. A majority of three hundred and thirty accepting the Women's Suffrage Clause of the Representation of the People Bill!

After March's vote everyone seemed confident, but little nagging doubts still lurked in the back of my mind. All our recent hard work has paid off, and even that dinosaur Curzon in the Lords can't obstruct it now. I don't even care if E.P and S.P try to claim all the credit despite their conspicuous absence over these final few months.

There were times this afternoon and evening when it all seemed unreal. Our supporters were in that little cage of a Ladies' Gallery, high up, almost in the ceiling, behind the Speaker's Chair. The unfortunate occupants of the Sultan's Harem in the Topkapi Palace gazed down at their master through a golden grille, whereas we surveyed the tops of the heads of those who'd frustrated us through years of struggle from behind a heavy brass one! And such an irritating one! It was impossible to focus both eyes through the same hole, and that and the hot stuffy atmosphere were a recipe for a bad headache for several of those penned in there. But not a single one of us would have missed it!

Though part of me feels we have betrayed the Cause by settling for too little, it is a vital first step. As the Honourable Member for Handsworth put it, as he clung to his anti-suffrage rock against the onrushing tide, 'If you grant the franchise at all, it will only be a short time before you have to give it to them on the same terms as men.' How true, Mr Ernest Claude Meysey-Thompson, how very true! Hopefully that will be of some consolation to the teacher living with her parents or the factory hand in rented accommodation, when they realise they are amongst the one-fifth of women over thirty who cannot vote. And if anyone tells you that women are being rewarded for all their work in this war, tell them to stand outside Rose Downs' factory gates and ask how many of the women streaming out when the hooter blows are old enough to vote.

Only six months ago I was so pessimistic, but now the Royal Assent will be signed early next year, and this wretched war must be over before too long. Then there will be an election so, barring a sudden loss of the use of my legs, I will not need to avail myself of your kind offer to push me to the polling station! But please accompany me anyway, and at the following election in 22 or 23, when all women will surely vote on an equal basis to men, then I shall accompany you!

I am staying on in London for a couple of weeks, but will see you on my return in early July. I did enjoy the Theatre! Was that only yesterday evening? Has your father recovered from his indigestion? I hope today's news does not make him more dyspeptic!

Your very happy, soon to be enfranchised Aunt!

July 7th, 1917
London

The crippled pavement artist had caught the Zeppelin in the searchlights especially well, thought Eleanor, She leant forward and dropped a few coppers in his mug. Now, what should she do with her last day in London?

The windows of a dress shop and the milliner's next to it caught her eye. A new hat, perhaps?

Nothing immediately appealed when she looked in, though there was one... perhaps she'd come back later, she decided. She walked on, looking for a gap in the traffic, to cross the road. As a fishmonger's horse and cart stopped in front of her, she glanced up at the increasingly hazy sky.

Afterwards she would find it hard to remember what caught her attention. A large low-flying flock of swallows or swifts was approaching. No, perhaps they were rooks. She gave up counting when she reached twenty. Why was she feeling uneasy? It was the dull drone, a drone that slowly asserted itself over the general hubbub in the street. She stared at them. There had been no air raid warning. Enemy planes would hardly arrive unannounced and unchallenged, in broad daylight, over central London. But then it was only weeks since the horrors around Liverpool Street station. She hesitated. A sinister, deadly parliament of rooks.

"They're not ours," a woman shouted.

People around her started running. A hundred yards away was an underground station. Even from a distance she could see the crush of people around the entrance. Memories of a newspaper photograph came to her – an orderly queue outside an air-raid shelter – children, then women and finally men. This could not be more different. Ripples of panic radiated out towards her. Suddenly her arm was grabbed and she was pulled into a shop. "Get behind them!" A man gestured towards some large rolls of material.

Eleanor did as she was told and sat with her back against a cloth stack and waited. If she stretched, she could touch the far wall with her feet, but instead she pulled her knees up, clasped them and shut her eyes. She had an urge to laugh. As if closing her eyes would deflect a German bomb! "I shall be all right," she told herself.

A blinding flash penetrated her closed eyelids. A deafening crash followed. Her ears hurt and felt strange. She opened her eyes. She sensed chaos and breaking glass. Had the building swayed? Had the plate glass window fallen in? She was unsure what to do. She felt the roll of cloth. It was reassuringly real. She waited for another explosion. She looked up; at least the ceiling was still in place. The man who'd dragged her in said something indistinct, distant, distorted to her. She shook her head and made an effort to concentrate. To hear him. To make sense of things. Gradually his words became clearer.

"I said, I think it's over." His voice lacked confidence. "I've looked outside. They've gone. Are you all right? You're not injured?"

She pushed herself up and swayed on her feet.

"Madam? Are you sure you're all right? Do you want to stay? It might be..."

"No, no," she said and started to push past him. She stopped. "I'm sorry. I'm fine... I think."

Yes, she was steadier. She should ask him who he was. "And I must thank you, Mr..."

"Lightbourne."

"Thank you, Mr. Lightbourne, for pulling me in here. I dread to think what might have happened." She shook her head. "You say there's no sign of the German planes?"

"Nothing. But there's some unpleasantness out there. Please stay longer if you wish."

"No, I must go. And thank you again!" She walked towards the front of the shop. The window was still intact but had been punctured by innumerable marble-sized holes. She turned, and shuddered. The rolls of cloth were pockmarked as if by a fusillade of shots. The door hung off its hinges. She pushed gingerly past it and went out into the street. Even forewarned, the shock was overwhelming. There was so much to take in, so much that was wrong.

Horses lay twisted and mangled in front of her, their skins covered in a greenish powdery residue. To Eleanor's eyes, the eeriest thing was that each animal's mouth was drawn into a vicious snarl, as if in great pain even after death. The fishmonger's horse, however, was still alive. It screamed and writhed until a fireman walked up and dispatched it with his axe.

Outside the underground station bodies were heaped up on the pavement. She turned and retraced her earlier steps. Debris fell sporadically from a building's remaining single wall, before the whole edifice crumbled into the street, sending a large plume of dust arching out towards her. She stepped back and collided with a man who held up a bloodied hand towards her. Three fingers were missing from it. He stared at her briefly but said nothing.

A little further on, she stopped, shocked at the sight of the carnage before her. To her immense relief, the misshapen and grotesque mass of bodies turned into a collection of dismembered mannequins. She realised they had been blown out of the windows of the dress shop and the milliner's. The desire to laugh hysterically was almost irresistible until she thought of what might have happened to the shop's human inhabitants. She could hear a pitiful mewing coming from the milliner's. She looked inside. A small cat whose fur had been blown away sat amongst the wreckage. Hats were everywhere. There was the one she'd considered buying earlier. She'd meant to return. Not like this. Not now, she thought. Her gaze returned to the mannequins.

One was far more life-like than the rest. Life-like was the wrong word. A woman in her twenties, her head thrown back at an unnatural angle, lay there. A thin line of congealing blood ran from the single shard of glass that had penetrated her neck. It was pointless but she had to do it. Eleanor knelt down and picked up the young woman's hand. She held it, almost caressing it. A minute or more passed. "I'm sorry, I'm going to have to let go." She squeezed the woman's hand and laid it to rest on the ground.

She stood up. There was the pavement artist, in the same position, leaning against his wall. He would not have been able to run, just watch everyone else doing so instead. She walked over to him, expecting him to be dead too. Yellow deposits of TNT clung to his clothes and hair, but to her amazement he was very much alive.

He smiled. "Excuse my language, Ma'am, but the bastards will have to do more than that to get rid of me." His mug was on its side and Eleanor leant down and stood it upright again. She looked in her purse. She'd given him her copper earlier, but she had some silver left. She emptied the contents of her purse into his mug.

"Thank you, Ma'am. Very kind indeed." He seemed overwhelmed, whether by the air raid or her generosity she could not tell.

"Where were you?" she asked.

"Battle of Loos. An Old Contemptible. Boche tried his damnedest then, and now he's had another go, but I'm still here." He broke off in a fit of coughing. "Mouth full of..." he spat on the ground, "brick dust. Pardon my manners again, Ma'am. No, make no mistake. My old mother always said I was a lucky so and so." He took a swig from a bottle. "Can I do you a drawing? Don't worry, you won't need to lug a pavement slab away with you. I've got some paper."

"No, there's no need."

"Please. I'd like to. It won't take me long." He picked up his crayons.

She looked around. Her mind had cleared. Her train wasn't till seven. Should she catch it? Was life in other parts of London continuing as normal? She had heard that during the first daylight raid people had interrupted their shopping to come out of greengrocers and butchers to watch the German bombers. Would she have felt the same if she'd observed this second one from some detached vantage point instead of from its epicentre? She didn't know. She looked down at her clothes. She was filthy. She must get cleaned up. It was not often that she needed a stiff drink. She was tempted to ask the artist what he was drinking.

"Bit of a rush, but here you are, Ma'am." He handed the drawing to her. "And it's not bad, even if I say so myself. Not my normal work. Let's call it my short-lived realistic period."

She studied it before looking down at the now obscured picture of the Zeppelin.

"Thank you. I'm not sure if you'd sell many of these now. It's too... brutal... too honest... but who knows – in the future? It's excellent. I can't imagine anyone else capturing it so well. Thank you."

"Don't worry, Ma'am. I know what brings in the pennies, and drawing what people would rather forget isn't one of them. Let's be honest, you're hardly likely to stick that on your drawing room wall. Generally those who like that one most," he indicated the drawing of the Zeppelin, "haven't seen one. Have you?"

"Yes."

"There you are, then – the exception that proves the rule. I thought there was something about you earlier. You look after yourself now, Ma'am."

"And you too."

"I will. Take more than a few bombs to get me to move on. Not before five anyway."

She looked at him.

"That's when my mate turns up to help me. Not that there'd have been much left to help if that one had gone off." He gestured across the road. "And God knows what he's doing with it."

A policeman was lifting a heavy metal object into a sack before raising it cautiously onto his shoulder.

"Copper's from Tower Hill station. Must be taking it in for questioning. Rather him than me. Anyway thanks again, Ma'am... and goodbye."

She gave him a last smile. A pair of grey ambulances came towards her. She walked away in search of some semblance of normality.

September 3rd, 1917
Liettres France

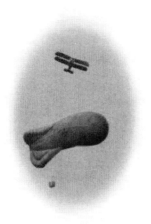

Robert walked across the grass of the aerodrome, wound his scarf around his neck and strapped on his helmet. A few faint pink daubs brushed the grey canvas of the eastern sky, but away to the north and west brighter stars were still visible. He found the Pole Star and wished on it... a little over three hundred miles on a heading 2.7 degrees due west of it would see him home. His SE5a, with its top speed of a 120 mph and its endurance of two and half hours would get him close. He smiled to himself; he'd keep enough height to glide across the Humber, so no need to crash land on someone's roof in New Holland. He'd never lost his fascination with balloons and when, a few weeks earlier, he'd been out on evening reconnaissance, that first conversation with Emily had come back to him.

It was twilight when he saw it. He'd been right, there were always one or two about on days of major battles. He smiled. No sun to glint off his wings and give him away. He climbed above the observation balloon, cut his engine, and glided down and fired from close range. The crew must have been alert, he thought, as seconds before their Drachen ignited in a spectacular fireball the two Luftschiffers leapt into space. Their egg-shaped parachutes opened below him. One became momentarily entangled in the balloon's winding cable, before he lost sight of them. Emily's Professor Gaudion came into his mind. He didn't begrudge the Luftschiffers landing as safely as he had in Bridlington Bay. He turned and headed home.

A change of note in the dawn chorus's distant rumbling brought him back to the present. He looked east, the destination of today's show.

"Morning, Penn," he said as he reached the hangar.

"Morning, sir," his flight mechanic responded, adding, as he helped Robert into the cockpit, "She's a silky smooth engine today, sir." He adjusted Robert's safety harnesses, and climbed down.

"Good luck, sir."

Robert was alone. He reached inside his Sidcot suit and touched the red ribbon pinned there.

"Contact."

"Contact," Robert repeated.

Two of his crew pulled down hard on the propeller. As it started to move, a third rotated the magneto handle on the outside starboard cockpit wall. Robert opened the throttle as his Hispano-Suiza engine fired and thundered into life. He checked the oil pressure: fifty psi within thirty seconds, but not more than a hundred and twenty or the oil pump drive might fail. He kept his revolutions per minute well below a thousand as he listened for any suggestion that his engine wasn't running smoothly. Only when convinced that he could coax those crucial extra few ounces of power out of it if necessary did he open up to a thousand RPM and finish warming up. His mechanics held down the tail as he completed his power check, revving up to full throttle against the chocks. The harsh metallic roar mellowed as he throttled down to idling speed. Once the chocks were pulled away he moved out with the five other members of his flight. He turned into the wind and at full throttle skimmed across the grass. Within seconds he reached fifty miles per hour and lifted into the air. It took him ten minutes, climbing at sixty, to reach the rendezvous at ten thousand feet with a formation of DH-4 De Haviland bombers. He thought them formidable machines, more than capable of engaging any German fighters they might encounter. Robert continued to climb. When the bombers reached the operational ceiling of the enemy scouts his escort duty would be over. They would then go on alone to drop their pairs of one hundred and twenty pounders on the railway junction at Ascq, east of Lille. Robert felt comparatively relaxed, as the chances of meeting enemy aircraft this deep in friendly territory were remote. Sporadic flashes of gunfire from the front accompanied them as they flew east.

He'd joined the 56th thinking himself very much the finished article. He had soon discovered otherwise when the squadron reached its full complement of eighteen pilots, with the arrival at Liettres of Captain James McCudden. McCudden was obsessed with the fine detail – if you were to survive and prosper, knowing every facet of your aeroplane was vital. Robert now took especial care with his machine guns, aligning the sights precisely and supervising the loading of ammunition. If his Vickers gun played up, he would be thrown back on his less powerful, highly jammable Lewis gun. He carried two extra drums of ammunition for the Lewis, but holding his control stick between his knees whilst changing the drum and then forcing the gun back into place against the slip-stream was a nightmare which meant he did everything possible to keep his Vickers working.

Robert couldn't think of a flyer he'd rather emulate than McCudden. Richthofen perhaps, even though he was a Hun. Once, when he'd been instructing back in England, he'd seen McCudden performing unbelievable stunts in a Sopwith Pup. Robert had been awestruck as McCudden had looped from take-off and then continued looping a dozen times, until at a thousand feet he'd flown upside down until his engine cut out. He'd then continued gliding, before performing a perfect roll and restarting the engine with his plane flying on an even keel once again. Though flying skills might get you out of a scrape, they didn't guarantee kills. McCudden was, however, also an exceptional marksman, combining natural talent with hard work, meaning he could riddle a target using a tenth of the shots his fellow pilots needed. Though unable to match him, Robert was determined to come as close as possible. Hand-eye co-ordination and practice, practice, practice were vital.

He'd also been influenced by McCudden's tactics and attitude. Many considered aerial combat a form of medieval jousting conducted by valiant knights of the air. A pragmatist rather than a romantic, McCudden had little time for this. Not for him the need to prove his courageousness, to be another Captain Albert Ball, attacking irrespective of the situation, seeing overwhelming adversity as some irresistible magnet. Robert had wondered what this focal point of national fame and adulation was like in person, but shortly before he'd arrived Ball had been killed near Annoeullin. His death had come as little surprise to many, as his own safety had always been a low priority for him. McCudden thought Ball's fearlessness had been inspirational in difficult times, but also told Robert that the way to beat the Hun was at his own game. Use cunning. Don't attack when at a disadvantage. Far better to retire and seek an improved position. Except, of course, as every RFC officer knew: if an Allied aircraft were being overwhelmed, irrespective of the odds, join battle immediately.

The sky was lightening. Robert flew into an unaccustomed east wind. If, heaven forbid, he were forced to seek safe haven, then the wind would be a help. He could just make out the coast, but if on his return he was flying at seventeen thousand feet under one of those azure-blue skies never seen in England, the Belgian coast would be to the north-east, the French to the west and in the shadowy extremities of his vision would be the white cliffs of Dover.

As he gained height, a patchwork of myriad greens emerged below him, though a light ground mist had seeped into every hollow and depression and obscured some landmarks. Die-straight poplar-lined roads linked nameless small villages. The transition to another world was abrupt. It was a painting from which the artist had cast away all colours from his palette other than browns and greys. A few ruined and battered villages soon gave way to a lifeless landscape, a wilderness of shell craters across which snake-like trenches crawled, where not a single building or tree remained.

After he crossed the German lines he fired a brief test burst from his machine guns. As if in response, a few ugly round puffs of black smoke from German anti-aircraft fire appeared ahead of him, though his engine drowned out the sound of the bursting shells. Keeping an eye on the DH4s and the rest of his patrol, he checked for enemy scouts lurking above the barrage, but could only see cloud drifting in with the wind. There seemed little likelihood of the dull leaden sky their ack-ack gunners favoured most, though he would be silhouetted against the cloud, making his range easier to judge.

A dull, coughing, spasmodic chorus followed by the hiss of passing shrapnel told him that they had spotted him. Instinctively he took evasive action. He heard two wouffs of nearby shells, before there was a loud roaring explosion below him. The compression wave propelled his aircraft fifty feet up into the air. The smell of TNT in the smoke and the fine spray of burnt castor oil from his engine were overwhelming. He was shaken, and he leaned out and peered round the engine cowling – yes, the undercarriage was still there and his ailerons and elevators were working, so neither he nor the plane seemed seriously damaged. One of his landing wires, not a flying one, was dangling from its socket and there were a few rents in the fabric, though not enough to force him to turn back. As a second shell exploded, again too close for comfort, he kicked the rudder bar from side to side, so that the plane veered erratically before side-slipping to lose height. He looked to his left. One of the DH-4s had been less lucky. A curl of thickening smoke trailed behind it. With the petrol tank between pilot and gunner, an initial trickle of flame became a roaring inferno and engulfed the fuselage. It fell away below and behind him. Its fateful nickname of flaming coffin came to Robert. He felt momentarily nauseous. Guilty relief that it hadn't been him flooded through him. At least their quick deaths had spared them the agonising dilemma of stay or jump. A bullet, either German or self-inflicted, was preferable.

There was no more time to dwell on that. Regrouping with the remaining bombers and his patrol was the priority. The shells were now falling astern and Robert saw no sign of Richthofen's Circus or any other Hun Jastas. He breathed a sigh of relief. At sixteen and a half thousand feet, with the DH-4s still climbing, the SE5s left them and turned north.

Robert peered towards the horizon. It was the twinkle of light that first caught his attention. In the distance there was a black speck. A second brief sparkle convinced him. It was sunlight on metal. He waggled his wings to his patrol to indicate possible enemy aircraft. It was most likely a Rumpler heading west on reconnaissance. He turned to intercept it. He knew the

Rumpler had an exceptional operational ceiling, so gaining a height advantage would be difficult. Even with his greater speed, to overhaul it would take time. He had enough petrol but he could never match its four-hour capability.

He was over the lines before he finally caught up. He was right. A Rumpler, but he was stalking a pair, not one. Patience. Their black Maltese Crosses stood out on their camouflaged top wings a thousand feet or so below. He did not need his altimeter to tell him he was above twenty thousand feet – his aching head told him that. He had the sun behind him. He smiled. Arriving from the east should guarantee him an element of surprise. He craned his neck to check behind him. He pushed the joystick forward.

The air pressure increased as he dived, his ears sang and clicked as he hurtled down. His nervous tension melted away as he concentrated. His body was a part of his machine. One of the Rumplers saw him and sent off a signal rocket to warn the other, before banking and diving away. For whatever reason the second did not respond. Robert sought his firing position. He could see the gunner crouching in the rear cockpit. He was a novice, or pretending to be one, because he opened fire when Robert was still more than four hundred yards away. He continued wasting ammunition in long bursts. A novice. Robert waited. He glued his eyes to his Aldis sights. Not yet. A little longer. He could see the gunner's white face, his goggles, his helmet. At fifty yards he fired a burst with his Vickers. He was aware of bullets hitting his machine. When a collision seemed inevitable he pressed the trigger again, aiming ahead of the Rumpler to allow for deflection. His tracers raked its fuselage. He hit the pilot, who fell back, instinctively pulling on the joystick as he did so. The Rumpler zoomed upwards. Robert passed underneath. The Rumpler turned onto its back and fell into a steep out of control side-slipping spiral. Robert followed him down. The gunner's body, mirroring his aircraft, fell in a macabre twisting mix of flailing arms and legs. As they got lower the pressure on the wings became too much. Pieces came off, disintegrating and fluttering down like so much unholy green and lilac confetti. The wind pushed them westwards, well behind the lines. The wingless fuselage wobbled like a misdirected arrow as it plummeted earthwards and finally hit the ground in a flattish grassy field. Robert flew over.

One group of soldiers waved at him from an adjacent road. Others were already running across the field.

With the Germans fighting a defensive air war, most aircraft, on both sides, fell behind their lines. He'd once got permission to use a motor bike for a futile search for an LVG he'd downed near Ypres, but he'd got bogged down in mud near the front line. He'd returned covered from head to toe, but with an appreciation of the conditions the Poor Bloody Infantry put up with. This time he would not miss out. He turned into the wind and came in to land. He saw the observer's body a hundred yards from the remains of his stricken aircraft. Once on the ground he left the engine idling. He climbed down and examined his plane. The wings and fuselage had a variety of holes. Some from bullets, others from the shell. It was airworthy, and the sail-maker would work wonders and soon have it as good as new. He looked at the Rumpler. Frayed squares of Irish linen brushed on with dope wouldn't do *it* any good. It was completely beyond repair. Many of the Tommies had closed in on it. Others were clustered around the observer, doubtless bent on souvenirs. He'd heard they sometimes behaved badly towards the bodies, so he marched across to the plane. The soldiers parted for him as he arrived. He felt some hearty slaps on his back and heard a number of calls of "Well done sir." To his surprise, the pilot in the remains of his cockpit was still breathing. Barely alive, but alive.

"Get him out," he ordered. While they did so he looked round for an officer. "And get something to put him on."

Robert watched as they pulled the pilot out.

"Sir, he's dead."

"No. I'm sure..." He looked at the young man they'd laid out. In leaving his plane, he had breathed his last. Lying there on the ground, he looked remarkably peaceful, with little to suggest the violent nature of his death. Robert crouched down and pulled the German's flying goggles off. In doing so he noticed an envelope protruding from an inside pocket of his black leather flying jacket. Robert reached in, extracted it and examined the address.

Ltn Werner Schweren, Flieger Abteilung 5, Metz-Frescaly, Frankreich. Should he look inside? It seemed intrusive, but there was a photograph and he needed to see it. The dead pilot stared back at him. Assured. Confident.

Smiling. He had his arm round an attractive dark haired girl, who was smiling for the camera. Behind them some fountains and a number of statues were visible. He turned the photo over. In the same spidery handwriting as on the envelope was written

Werner und Erica, Märchenbrunnen im Friedrichshain 27. Juli 1917.

He glanced at the opening lines of the letter.

Mein Liebling Werner,

Sie haben mich der glücklichste Mensch in Berlin. Ich kann nicht warten, bis ich dich wieder zu sehen, und ich meinen Namen ändern von Fräulein Erica Gottleib an Frau Erica Schweren...

Robert shrugged. It was a pity Emily's Aunt Eleanor was not here to translate. Had this Werner written to Erica as he did to Emily? He looked at the girl and her address at the top of the page. She'd wait in vain for another at *Stargardtstraße 54*, wherever that was. He made an effort to pull himself together. It was unpleasant seeing the results of his work. If the Rumpler had come down in Hunland he wouldn't have given it another thought. It was no use getting sentimental; that only made it likelier that he'd end up stretched out like this himself. It might be callous, but his job was to kill and go on killing. He stood up, holding the letter. He was about to bend down and replace it, but something stopped him. He wasn't sure what. Someone would appropriate the jacket, patch the few holes and throw the letter away, but it wasn't just that. He shoved it into his Sidcot. He took a last look at the body. Would his comrades in *Flieger Abteilung 5* drink to him, sing defiant songs and toast his memory? He'd been to a few too many of these defiance parties himself.

He glanced back at the plane. The broken parts of propeller gave him an idea and it didn't take long to find the ideal piece.

An infantry officer arrived and agreed to post a guard until Major Blomfeld had examined the Rumpler. He also assured Robert that the Germans would get a decent burial.

Robert looked towards the body of the observer. He shouldn't delay too long. He didn't want to worry his crew, but he could afford a few more minutes. He walked across.

"Dieter Bodenschatz, according to his documents," an infantryman by the body said.

The observer, a large, rather overweight man, had lost his long fug boots and various bits of insignia from his uniform. And more too besides, if he'd had any watches, rings or valuables on him. Robert's face must have betrayed him.

"Not that they're much use to him now, are they, sir?" the soldier added, lighting a cigarette and looking at the piece of propeller Robert was carrying.

"No, I suppose not, Corporal."

"And congratulations, sir. Their gunners have been getting a mite too accurate of late, giving us a bit of a pounding. Now there's one less Boche to spy on us."

"Yes, you're right. Thank you, Corporal." Robert turned and, without giving the body a backward glance, strode back to his plane. He climbed in. He realised he was ravenous. He taxied away from the Rumpler and took off in search of the large breakfast that lay only a few short miles away.

September 17th, 1917
Westbourne Avenue

"It was very thoughtful of Eleanor to remember," Clara said, "especially..."

"Yes, yes. I know, I know. You're quite right," Alfred replied. "It was uncharitable to say otherwise. I will make an effort to thank her next time I see her. Don't look at me like that."

"I shall ask her round next Sunday afternoon, so that gives you a week to get used to the idea. This ridiculous business has gone on long enough." She gave him a steely look. "That's settled."

He gave her a weak smile, which she took as confirmation, before adding, by way of a last ditch defence, "You might warn her that I do not wish to hear her views on Kerensky's Provisional Government, or, heaven forbid, hear her sing the praises of those appalling Bolsheviks she doubtless admires so much. Their ferment! Their anarchy! If only the Czar had..."

"Alfred! She is only too willing to be tactful... to be conciliatory."

"Eleanor... conciliatory?"

The words pot kettle black came to mind but she finished her interrupted sentence. "And you know how she adores Emily."

Alfred saw a welcome opportunity to change the subject "Speaking of our daughter, will she be much longer?"

"She was a little late in and she's changing. And there's a letter from Robert."

He raised his eyebrows. "Is Alice aware tea will be taken at any time in the next hour then?"

"Alfred. Emily knows we are having a small birthday tea and she'll be here shortly."

"I hope the girl doesn't go on about this Lieutenant," he curled his lip up, "Poet?"

"It's nice that she's found a patient she finds so interesting to talk to. And I'm not sure why you object to him being a poet."

"Poet? Purveyor of gibberish doggerel, more like. What was the title of his latest effort, which she regaled us with?" he paused. "*The Tale of Tinúviel*. What sort of name for a poem is that? And what was that other one? *The Bridge of Tavrobel*. Sounds the sort of thing your sister..."

"Alfred." She gave him a warning look.

"But what sort of person spends his time recovering from trench fever by writing a gnomish lexicon, whatever that might be? And Emily may be fascinated by the history of this imaginary medieval earth but..."

"I think she said middle earth, dear."

"Muddle earth, more like. Where people speak Elvish of all things! Perhaps it's better he's not at the front."

"But he is a Lancashire Fusilier, like..."

"Edward. I know."

There was a short, tense silence before Emily's mother continued, "But she said he didn't remember ever meeting him." Her voice died away.

There was a second silence between them, before he reached out and held her hand. "Clara, I shouldn't have been so harsh the other evening. If you find it a comfort to visit this Spiritualist woman then you must continue."

She gave him a grateful smile. "I know you think she's a charlatan. That's one thing you and Eleanor do agree about. But it was hurtful to suggest, if she got in touch with him, that she should ask what Edward thought about David."

"I'm sorry I said that, but there's no getting away from the fact David's not acting normally. Whatever these doctors say, he just needs to pull himself together." He raised his hands in supplication. "I'm sorry. I won't say any more."

"You certainly won't. But you could always come along with me a week on Thursday?"

"Unfortunately not. I have a prior engagement." He held up Saturday's *Mail*. "I didn't notice this yesterday. Pemberton-Billing is speaking at the Metropole Assembly Rooms on bringing purity back into public life... police, the politicians and suchlike. And not before time. He'll be talking about his new society – *The Vigilantes* – as well. There's a piece in *The Imperialist*. Excellent idea! And he'll have something to say about this ridiculous peace offer the Kaiser's made to the Pope." He stopped abruptly. "You don't want to hear all this, do you?"

"Sometimes a little goes a long way, Alfred. But this is meant to be your birthday tea. Perhaps I could have asked this Pemberton-Billing to be here for you."

"That would be a treat," he said smiling at her.

"In his absence you'll just have to make do with your wife and your daughter, whom I think I can hear coming."

The door opened.

"Many Happy Returns, Father," said Emily.

October 11th, 1917
Flanders, East of the Menin Road

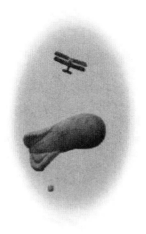

It was if he'd been hit by a sledgehammer. An excruciating pain shot up his left leg as the terrific kick from the bullet dislodged his foot from the rudder. When his leg would not move back of its own accord, he reached down, lifted it and forced it back into place. Seconds later a vicious whiplash reverberated through his machine as another salvo of bullets hit it. The sounds of wood splintering and glass shattering fused discordantly. His goggles immediately fogged up as the liquid from the compass in his wrecked instrument panel sprayed over them. He tried to wipe them clear but a bullet must have severed the elastic, as they came away in his hand. He threw the useless things over the side. For a second his sight improved before the rushing wind filled his eyes with water. He tried to keep his thought processes working calmly and methodically. Panic meant certain death. With his good leg he kicked full on his right rudder and pushed his joystick hard forward to the right.

#

As Robert had climbed to nine thousand feet, a few flaming onions thrown up by the Huns had exploded near him, before a bank of thick cloud had immersed him in an insubstantial world where wisps of grey vapour restricted vision to a few feet. In the thin, floating formlessness, part of Robert's mind had drifted. Why hadn't they come up to him this morning, tapped him on the shoulder and said "Pack your bags, you're off to Blighty. Now!" But no, four more days before his leave. He'd known it was due, but the confirmation warrant had been unexpected. He'd only had the chance to dash off a few lines before this morning's patrol. And then there was last week's news of the DSO. He'd be up there on the Squadron Honours Board with Capt. Albert Ball – *Ordre National de la Légion d'Honneur, VC (posthumous)*. They would hold a dinner for him on his return. At last month's, honouring Rhys-David, the Welshman had given a bravura speech in which he'd lauded the enemy's bravery. He'd finished with "Von Richthofen – our most worthy enemy". Everyone had risen and raised their glasses, apart from one non-flying officer who'd remained seated, announcing sotto voce, "I won't toast that devil".

And then Robert found himself in a different world. He looked around, but there was no sign of Richthofen's distinctive red Fokker triplane, only the other members of his patrol. Beneath him his plane's shadow was haloed against clouds. At thirteen thousand feet it was bitterly cold. The sun's rays were scarcely warming, and Robert knew that keeping the water in his radiator warm would be a real struggle. The clouds below him broke and thinned as the patrol moved in formation, working up and down the Menin Road.

McCudden saw them first – a group of Pfalz scouts, at a lower altitude, away north of Westroosebecke. By the time they launched their attack the Pfalzs, had been reinforced by a number of Albatrosses. Both sides' neat formations soon dissolved in a melee of diving, wheeling and zooming, with each pilot focussed on his own personal combat.

A red-nosed Albatross approached Robert head on. He saw the red-yellow flashes of its Spandau guns and heard their ominous clack, clack, clack. He fired a short burst in return, before both his guns seized up. The damned intense cold. Holding the control stick between his knees, he struggled to pull back the cocking handle on his Lewis gun. He could see the other pilot deciding which way to pass him, before he zoomed up and over Robert. His yellow fuselage and green tail were almost within touching distance. Once past him, the Albatross turned left to get on Robert's tail. It was the first time he'd wished for a Sopwith Camel with its acrobatic turning ability. He turned himself.

They swung around each other in ever-tightening circles, losing height as they did. A deadly tango for two, punctuated by staccato bursts of gunfire. Whoever the pilot was, he was good, and he was gaining a potentially deadly advantage. Robert could see that they were moving towards another bank of clouds. If he fell away in a full power spin and fled, would the Hun get on his tail before he reached them? He was still weighing up the probabilities when the bullet pierced his left leg.

He tried to ignore the pain.
Singing. Yes, I should sing.

He knew the Hun would press home his attack, and the clouds seemed his best hope.
Singing will help, but what to sing?

Before he could reach them, things worsened dramatically.
Something with a good tune.

His engine suffered a sudden loss of pressure, missing firstly on one, then two cylinders.

The Song of the Dying Airman.

His petrol tank had been pipped.
What better?

His worst fears were confirmed when freezing clouds of petrol vapour
swept back over him.
And ours is the best version!

Almost blinded he glanced involuntarily at the hot exhaust pipe on the
plane's side,
I don't think...

before putting the SE5 into such a violent side-slip that he could barely
breathe.
I'm going to get...

The sound of crackling flames behind him pitched him into a living nightmare.
Through all twenty-four verses...

He felt for the buckle on his safety harness.
But I'll try and hang around long enough for the first chorus, at least.

He pushed the control stick as far forward as it would go.
A handsome young aviator was dying...

Turned off the engine and raced earthwards.
And as 'neath the wreckage he lay, he lay...

Driving, he hoped, the flames up and away from him.
To the mechanics assembled around him...

For a few seconds the fire overtook the speed of the plane and was blown into his face.
These last parting words did say...

He could hear small detonations close to hand.
Did say...

He was about to be killed by his own exploding ammunition.
Take the cylinders out of my kidneys...

The flames were subsiding.
Take the connecting rod out of my brain...

He instinctively pulled back on the control stick as hard as he could.
My brain.

It was not responding.
From the small of my back...

Elevators were shot up.
Take the crankshaft...

No. It was slowly coming level.
And...

Heading downwind. Too fast for a landing glide.
Assemble...

Ground. Too fast. Undo harness.
The engine...

Padded. Braced. Hurled.
Again.

Free.
Emily!

#

My dearest Robert,

It's after midday and I should be setting off for Brooklands, but I had to reply straight away to your two pieces of news. How wonderful. Leave!!! Write as soon as you know the exact date. How much notice will you get? You might know by the time you read this? You could even be here on my first free weekend. I finish a week tomorrow on the Friday. I have read and reread it. It is real.

A plane has been over the hospital at least once a week since July and when I see it I imagine it's you, rather than a RNAS pilot who is besotted with the milkmaid at the farm on the corner of Newland Park. Are all flyers a little bit mad? I read about one who was summoned by Bourne Police for driving a car with only one light and was fined six shillings. He and three comrades then gave a fine aviation display sweeping above the Old Town Hall in which the court sat, looping the loop and 'attacking' each other before flying home with the cheers of a large crowd ringing in their ears. Quite mad!

There was talk of using a field by the hospital for an aerodrome, but it wasn't large enough, so you will have to arrive by more conventional means! I don't mind how you arrive just as long as you do.

I have had some news, too. A letter arrived saying I can take up a post at Byculla VAD Hospital in London. Don't worry, I won't disappear just as you return, as I wouldn't start until the middle of November. Mother has been better than I thought about it, though she doesn't like the idea of my being away at Christmas. And she's complained about London having more air raids, but no-one can guarantee anything, can they? Aunt Eleanor approves, as Byculla is an auxiliary of Endell Street Military Hospital, which is run by militant suffragists! She thinks it will be 'an excellent opportunity' for me, so I have made up my mind to accept the post and go.

Mother has just been in and reminded me of the time, so I must fly!

Your loving sweetheart,
who can't wait to see you again.
Emily
xxxx

P.S. as for your other news, I am so proud of you!

October 15th, 1917
Westbourne Avenue

Emily leant her bike against the railings and took her key out. She had thought about cycling straight to her aunt's, but couldn't resist stopping to check the post. There must be some by now.

"Emily." She turned. Robert's mother was coming out of her house.

"Hello, Mrs Buckley. Have you heard from Robert?"

"I'm so glad I've caught you. I thought you got back about now."

Was there a hesitancy in her voice? Her demeanour seemed different too.

"I've been looking. I wanted you to know. We've had some news."

Emily's heart sank.

"Robert. He's missing."

"But... I only had a letter a few..."

"It could mean anything. He told us if he were ever listed not to give up hope as it didn't have to mean the worst. One of his squadron crash-landed and wandered around behind the French lines for three days before news got back, so..." she shrugged her shoulders. "So I don't want you expecting the worst. No-one saw him shot down or crash, so try not to worry." She took Emily's hands in her own. "I know that's difficult – I haven't been able to think straight since this morning. All we can do is wait."

"I had a letter a few days ago. I was so proud of him," Emily's voice tailed off.

"Is anyone in? Your mother? Alice?"

"I'm not sure. I don't think so. I was going to call..."

"Do you want to come in to have a cup of tea with us?"

She shook her head. "I need to get changed and..." And what? "You'll let me know? If you hear anything... good... or bad? Can I see the letter or telegram?" She felt confused.

"Yes, of course. There's one of each." She reached into a pocket, pulled them out and gave them to Emily.

She read the blunt telegram first.

REGRET LT R.C.BUCKLEY 56 SQN WAS REPORTED MISSING 11.10.17. THIS DOES NOT NECESSARILY MEAN THAT HE IS KILLED OR WOUNDED.

"And the letter came an hour ago."

Dear Mr and Mrs Buckley,

You will be hearing through official channels but I wanted to let you know personally that your son Robert is missing. He was last seen engaging a German aircraft during a large-scale dog-fight over enemy lines on the 11th October. As you must be aware, these situations can become highly confusing. I have questioned the other pilots returning from the sortie and no-one reports seeing Robert crash. I would therefore urge you not to give up hope, as there is every possibility that he may have made a forced landing. Rest assured that I will inform you if I receive any definite news. Robert is a resourceful young man and you should draw great strength from this. His recent decoration was richly merited.

Major R.G. Blomfield

Emily held the letter in her hands, finding it difficult to share the Major's optimism.

"I'll let you know straight away. Don't worry. The Major says missing means just that... missing. Robert will turn up. I'm sure he will."

Could that be true?

"Remember, you can come and talk to me whenever you want." Mrs Buckley hugged her before going back inside.

Emily felt as if she were rooted to the spot. She forced herself to move and to take out her key. Her hands shook as she fumbled with the lock. With difficulty, she opened the door, stepped inside and closed it behind her. The hall was still, an oasis of peace and calm, the opposite of the thoughts racing through her mind.

"Mother?... Alice?" she called. Her words echoed back to her. Silence. Standing there, alone, she became conscious of her pounding heart. She felt as if it would race away with her, faster and faster, until... until what? She tried to control her breathing, but couldn't. There were letters on the hall table. The one on top was addressed to Miss Emily Walker. She snatched it up, ran upstairs and threw herself onto her bed. What would it say? She tore open the envelope.

Dear, Dear Em,

No time for a proper letter. Just letting you know leave fixed. Home late on the 15th or definitely 16th. Will try to write later,

Love you
R xxxxxx

"Please be just missing, Robert," she whispered. "Just missing."

October 11th, 1917
Rumbeke, West Flanders

In the distance a pack of grey wolves loped menacingly towards him. He tried to push himself up. The fingers on his left hand dug into the grass and he collapsed onto his front. He lay for a few moments. The ground was almost deliciously cold. From somewhere he summoned enough energy to roll over onto his back and pulled his hand back to his face. He could smell fresh earth, but mixed with it was the pungent smell of smoke. He turned his head. Was that his plane? If it was, it had been reduced to a smouldering skeleton. Irritatingly it refused to stay in one place. He struggled to judge how far away it was and failed.

Memory seeped back. The dog-fight. The green-tailed Albatross. The crash. He started shaking, then laughing. Tears ran down his cheeks. He felt the grass again, stretching his arms out as far as he could. His vision was clearing and with an effort he half-turned and pushed himself up on his elbow. He remembered the bullet wound. At least his leg wasn't hurting.

A broken line of grey uniformed soldiers was running towards him. As they came closer he could hear them shouting. He was surprised at how calm he was. They circled around him. An officer stepped forward and stood over him.

"*Glück gehabt, junger Leutnant. Normalerweise würden wir Ihre Überreste aus dem Flugzeug ziehen. Sind Sie verletzt?*"

Robert gave him a blank look.

"*Können Sie aufstehen? Ich hole ein paar von meinen Leuten, um Ihnen zu helfen.*" The officer gestured and said something to a couple of the soldiers who came forward and pulled Robert to his feet. He winced – his left leg felt stiff. He could only just manage to put his weight on it. One of the soldiers pointed at Robert's back. "*Das muss doch am Hintern ziehen.*" Some of the soldiers laughed. "*Der Kapitän hatte Recht gehabt. Sie können froh sein, am Leben zu sein.*"

Robert felt behind him and pulled charred pieces of his Sidcot away.

"*Ein paar Zentimeter weiter vorn, und Sie hätten sich mehr als den Arsch verbrannt!*"

This provoked great merriment, with which Robert found himself joining in. He reached inside his jacket, unpinned the red ribbon and kissed it.

"My lucky charm." He brought it to his lips again before returning it to his jacket.

The officer understood. "*Ihre Glücksbringer!*" he said and laughed. He pointed at Robert's right leg pocket and held out his hand. "*Ich denke vielleicht Ihre Leuchtpistole.*"

Robert took out his Very Pistol and handed it over. He pointed at the wreckage and shrugged. "No need to set the dear old bus aflame. Your chappie did a decent enough job himself." He gave his plane a last look and turned away.

The soldier helping him indicated himself. "*Ladekanonier,*" he said, and mimed firing a gun upwards. "*Maschinenkanone,*" pointing at Robert. He laughed and slapped him on the back and gestured in the direction they were going. "*Kraftwagen-Flak...* Archie, Archie!"

"Yes, Archie," he agreed. They moved away. Robert leant on his jovial captor, settling into an ungainly rhythm – more of a hop, with the drag of his weaker leg.

"*Wir sind ganz in der Nähe eines Flugplatzes. Fünf Minuten.*" He tapped Robert's left leg. "*Dort kann Sie ein Arzt sehen... Doctor... Sie werden Ihnen etwas Gutes zu essen geben. Sie sollten froh sein, für Sie ist der Krieg zu Ende.*" He took more of Robert's weight. "*Lächeln Sie, für Sie ist der Krieg zu Ende.*"

#

"Take a seat, Lieutenant. You have seen the doctor? Your leg?"

Robert examined the rather portly middle-aged German officer sitting behind the desk with interest. He spoke with a slight accent that Robert could not quite place.

"Thank you. I was lucky. The bullet went straight through and missed the bone. He's patched me up." He took a guess at his rank, "Major?"

"Correct. Major Ernst Sattler... and you are Lieutenant..."

"Robert Buckley."

"So now we have been properly introduced to one another," he smiled and laughed. "And we will not be shooting you as a spy because you are no longer in uniform."

Robert examined the ill-fitting overalls he'd been given to replace his burnt Sidcot. He felt in a pocket to check the contents: ribbon, Emily's last letter and some money.

"You were extremely fortunate that you landed here. The *Fliegerab-wehr-Abteilung* are part of the German Air Service, as am I. They respect you flyers. If you had crashed nearer the front line your reception might have been more... what shall we say? Problematic. Some there are in no mood to treat a downed pilot in a civilised fashion. And my Army colleagues sometimes handle these..."

"Interrogations?"

"No, nothing so formal, Lieutenant. Army Intelligence perhaps, they always behave more like a bull in a china shop. So you see," he smiled, "for you it could be worse."

"This seems to be turning out to be my lucky day, Major."

The Major chuckled. "One of the things I love – your English sense of irony. I would not, however, tell my colleagues that I am an anglophil."

"Anglophile," Robert corrected him.

"Thank you, Lieutenant. The German does not have the e. Please feel free to correct any other little errors."

Robert had been well briefed about how to behave if captured but he couldn't help being intrigued, despite himself.

"Your English is excellent, Major. Almost flawless. How did you learn to speak it so well?"

The Major beamed. "You have heard of my place of birth, Windhoek? In Deutsch-Südwestafrika? No? From an early age I spent many years in neighbouring Cape Colony. In Cape Town. I had many English speaking acquaintances and friends there." Robert could now hear the slight South African lilt to his words.

"But didn't Germans volunteer and fight with...?"

"The Freikorps in the Vryheidsoorloë? The Boer Wars? Certainly. But the Boers who fled to Windhoek afterwards were ghastly, whereas the British in the Cape were much more refined. As I ended up doing much business with them, I made the effort to improve my English, and I enjoyed learning." He shrugged and smiled again, "I am fairly pleased with the results."

"And do you speak anything else?"

"Being close to Afrikaans, my Dutch is more than adequate and my French is improving." He smiled, "So I cannot complain. But I am forgetting my manners. I have not offered you a drink. We are a little early for afternoon tea, but perhaps we can make an exception?"

"As I did not give you advance warning of my visit, it would be churlish of me to object."

The Major laughed. "Excellent, Lieutenant." He stood up and walked over and spoke to the orderly by the door before returning.

"Cricket, Lieutenant. Do you like cricket? Do you play perhaps?"

Robert couldn't help nodding.

"Batsman or bowler?"

"I have turned my arm over a little. Leg breaks mainly."

"What a pity you cannot teach me the googly then, though too much time sitting behind a desk might make me a bit too slow in the field." He patted his large stomach. "I wonder does Mr McCudden bowl too?"

Robert attempted but failed to keep his face impassive.

"Do not worry, Lieutenant, an inspired guess. I pitched the ball, and like the googly it went the opposite way to what you were expecting. The 56th seemed likely. And no need to confirm or deny it. You'd be surprised how much we do know so it doesn't matter a great deal. It's just a snippet of information to keep my superiors happy. I can hardly discuss the LBW law with my Obersleutnant."

Robert didn't let the Major's minor success worry him. He found he actually liked this rather eccentric and enigmatic German. He only had to provide name and number but after today's earlier traumatic events this was proving quite soothing. The alternative of being left alone with his thoughts was less appealing.

The Major continued in the same vein. "Newlands Cricket Ground – such a magnificent setting. Jack Hobbs scored his first Test century, a hundred and eighty seven before he was out, hit wicket. An unusual dismissal, though not as rare as handling the ball, I believe. Charlie Blythe took ten wickets in the match with his slow left arm spin. So there you are, a Hun who's seen England beat South Africa, in South Africa, by nine wickets. But South Africa emerged victorious in that series, so perhaps England will not win this war. A pity we are not both fighting the French. You spent hundreds of years doing that and now you are allies." He sighed. "But we are where we are. Have you read much Shakespeare, Lieutenant?"

Robert decided he would not be surprised by any turn in this conversation. "At school I've seen the odd play. My girl is..." Robert stopped. "So yes. I've seen some."

"He is very popular in Germany. Some talk of Shakespeare as *ganz unser...* entirely ours. There is a poem by Freiligrath which starts '*Deutschland ist Hamlet*'. Goethe? You know of him? No? Our greatest writer? Do stop me if I get too carried away."

Robert smiled. "It's not as if I have any other pressing engagements."

"Indeed!" The Major laughed. "Goethe said Shakespeare freed us from the shackles of French theatre. I have an early copy of Schlegel's translation so, unlike the French, I read his lines as verse rather than their ridiculous prose – but as Goethe put it in his Faust, "*Ein echter deutscher Mann mag keinen Franzen leiden, doch ihre Weine trinkt er gern.*" He smiled. "'A real German man likes no Frenchy, but likes to drink their wines'."

The orderly returned and placed a tray on the desk.

"Good, here is our tea. I'm sorry I can't provide anything stronger. Not even the particularly bad vin rouge served at the local estaminet, let alone a good vintage Goethe might enjoy. Perhaps the estaminets in Liettres are superior? If you ever visit South Africa, you must try one of the Vergelegen reds."

"Thanks for the recommendation." Robert said, "I shall drink some whilst watching the cricket – though South Africa hardly fits into my current travel plans, unfortunately! Have you ever visited England, Major?"

"A few times. Generally in the winter months, so my ambition to see the captain of England lead his side out on the first morning against Australia at Lords remains unfulfilled."

Robert studied him. He seemed serious. "My father took me to see Australia at Headingley in 1909." An occasion that seemed an impossibly long time ago now.

"Yorkshire? You are from England's most successful county?"

There seemed little point in denying it. "We get a County game every season only ten minutes' walk from my home, but how..."

"Do I know that? I was given a copy of Wisden by the friend who introduced me to cricket in Cape Town. I have several and at one shilling each they are excellent value. They are quite soothing to read. A reminder of better days. Though one thing I have never understood is the way you divide people. The England captain always an amateur. Mr C B Fry on the scorecard not Fry C B as he would be if he was a professional. And you have carried this divide into this war. Your Royal Flying Corps. I have had Sergeant Pilots sitting where you are now."

It was true there were pilots who had come up through the ranks – who inhabited their own no man's land, excluded from the officers' mess and forced to spend their time with non-commissioned fitters and mechanics instead. Robert found this difficult to defend.

"I see you are not happy about it." The Major smiled then indicated the tea. "Shall I be mother?" He leant forward. "Such an interesting expression. But perhaps you can advise me. Milk? First or last?"

"Last is better."

"Exactly as I thought. When I take tea at Claridges I want to behave like a Gentleman not a Player. Sugar?"

"No thanks." He watched the Major pouring the tea. "With your grasp of the language you should read Shakespeare in the original. No offence to you or Schlegel but I don't see how any translation, however good, can be the same. Last year we commemorated the three hundredth anniversary of Shakespeare's death. We remembered, above all else, his Englishness. Some things are untranslatable and his inspiring Englishness is surely one. You only need to read Henry V's St. Crispin's Day speech to know why we'll win this war. But I'm not sure a German could understand that, and for all their many faults the French didn't invade Belgium."

The Major seemed unperturbed. "I am not offended, Lieutenant, and, with Schlegel being dead these last seventy years, he will not be too worried either. But it's good you can show some spirit, despite your difficult day." He passed Robert a cup. "I shall take comfort in the fact that Henry defeated French rather than Teutonic knights. Doubtless the victors will decide who was to blame for all this. Now, how is the tea? Not too strong?"

"Very refreshing, Major, thank you."

"I realise you won't confirm where you patrol or give away military secrets, but as an impartial observer, humour me. Sopwith Camel or SE5a? A silly question. You are hardly likely to betray your aircraft? And flying with the first squadron equipped with them, too, though more are arriving in France every day? Don't worry. I'm not trying to catch you out. I've had little talks with people who aren't quite what they seem, who try to conceal important things, but with you flyers... it's different. Exchanging these pleasantries is excellent practice for when I have... what is the expression?... bigger fish to fry." He changed tack again. "I wish you SE5 pilots could be put in a room with your Sopwith comrades to battle it out. But I am with you. The Camel is nose-heavy and harder to fly and develops engine trouble when it matters most? Isn't that correct? I heard many of your inexperienced pilots have crashed on take-off. Such things must be demoralising."

He studied Robert's face. "It's only natural to worry, don't you think? It must be an anxious time this afternoon at your airfield. I hope none of your comrades saw your plane on fire and jumped to the wrong conclusion."

That thought had been nagging at the back of Robert's mind.

"Sorry, I didn't mean to upset you... I hate to think of a sweetheart hearing that you are *gefallen* instead of missing.

"*Gefallen?*"

"K.I.A. Isn't that how it is recorded? But again I apologise, Lieutenant. You look unsettled. Rest assured, the Red Cross will send news at some point, but there's bound to be delay." He smiled. "Cheer up, you are sitting there alive and well and have not been killed in action. I have seen the remains of your plane and you are a very lucky young man." The Major drank the last of his tea. "Think how overjoyed your sweetheart will be when she eventually hears you are safe and well."

Robert was silent.

"A pity we can't get back news that you are alive, but my hands are tied. I might persuade my Obersleutnant, but before you tell me, all communications are to go through Cox and Co. in London and not to your squadron – all I can say is that unofficial channels do exist but the Obersleutnant..." he shrugged, "needs more than little snippets." He sat back in his chair and clasped his hands in front of him.

Robert looked at him. "I'm afraid, Major, your back foot landed a good six inches over the bowling crease, and knowing the Laws you'll realise you've just bowled a ..."

"No-ball! Very good, Lieutenant. And I never expected you to play my indiscreet request with anything other than a straight bat – but like you, I have a job to do. An Australian pilot recently told me the number of aircraft written off in the previous nine months, and much more besides. He liked cricket too. Victor Trumper was his hero. But he was demoralised, as some people in your position are. But you?" He smiled. "So!" He leant across the desk and offered his hand. "No hard feelings, and I do wish you all the best." In yet another strange turn of events for the day, Robert had little difficulty in shaking the Major firmly by the hand.

"Time for you to move on," continued the Major. He spoke in German to the orderly.

"Might I ask to where?"

"The next few hours should be quite pleasant. The pilot who shot you down is taking you to his Jasta. He plans to show you round his aerodrome and give you a good meal in their mess, before you join a group of your fellows whom we have been collecting in a small house nearby. And when we have a full eleven," he gave Robert a pointed look, "you few, you happy few, you band of brothers... you will be sent east. So, please, go with the orderly."

"The quotation?"

"Did I not say? I had an English governess for many years. She often read to us. She loved Tennyson too. Did you know that the Charge of the Light Brigade was also on St. Crispin's day?" He smiled. "Unfortunately she hated cricket."

Robert stood up. "Goodbye, Major." He walked over to the door before turning and holding up his right hand and twisting his hand back and forth. "It's all in the wrist action, Major. Bend it sharply from the normal as you deliver and let the ball roll out of your hand. But practice with a tennis ball first. Don't want you being hit for six."

"Thank you, Lieutenant. I'm sure there'll be a few more googlies bowled by either side until a time when we can play up, play up and play the game." With that he picked up a pen and started writing while Robert followed the orderly out of the room.

November 24th, 1917
Byculla Hospital

"You must be Emily. I'm Dora, but my friends call me Fish." Emily hesitated, then shook the assured looking young woman's outstretched hand. "A house we lived near had a memorial to a fish in the garden. Strange, I know, but when I went to Cheltenham I made the mistake of mentioning it in the dorm and the name stuck.

Under the soil
The old fish do lie,
Twenty years he lived
And then he did die.

There are more verses," she laughed, "It could have been worse... they might have called me Trout."

Emily, immediately reassured, joined in with her laughter.

"Hello... Fish – but I'm afraid that I am plain boring Emily."

The young woman looked at her in surprise. "I'm sure you're neither plain nor boring. I hope not, anyway. But come in." She stretched her arms out expansively. "What do you think of our abode?"

Emily looked round her. "It's... cosy."

"It could be bigger," Fish smiled, "so let's hope neither of us have too many annoying habits. But at least there's a decent fire, even if it means bringing the coal all the way up here."

Emily had already decided that the three long flights of stairs up to the attic would keep her fit. She took her coat off, put her things down and looked around the room.

"We could partition it, if you want. I've been here five weeks and I've tried not to let my things spread too much. There's space in the wardrobe and you're welcome to one of those large wooden boxes. Turned on their sides, they're fine as a bookcase cum cupboard."

Emily couldn't resist a glance at the contents.

"And the staff here are hunky-dory," Fish continued. "Did you meet many before coming up? They don't act as if we are semi-intelligent tweenies. The higher-ups at Endell Street seem determined everyone here is treated as a responsible adult."

"I had hoped I might be at Endell Street rather than in one of its auxiliaries, but no, I only had a quick word. I was told to come up first, but... oh, you're keen on E. Nesbit!"

"You've seen my extensive library! My guilty secret. After a twelve or thirteen hour day I haven't the energy for anything demanding or worthy, so I've retreated into my childhood. But I never tire of re-reading them."

"*House of Arden* is my favourite, then *Harding's Luck*..."

"Then rather than plain boring Emily, I shall call you Mouldiwarp."

Quick as a flash Emily responded. "And I shall whisk us both back in time and we'll have exciting adventures seeking family treasure."

They laughed again, already at ease in each other's company. Emily felt closer to this rather odd young woman she'd just met than to many people she'd known for years.

"Come on, Mouldiwarp, sit down by the fire. Would you like one of these?" She handed Emily a crumpet. "The fire's died down enough. And you can use Beelzebub."

Emily examined the handle of the toasting fork she'd been given, as she skewered the crumpet.

"He's rather splendid," Fish continued. "The Devil not only has all the best tunes, but toasts the best crumpets too. Are you musical?"

"No, I'm hopeless."

"Shame. That's two of us. There's a piano downstairs. I was hoping you'd bash out more than the few poor melodies I can manage."

They both examined the progress of their crumpets. Emily indicated Fish's fork.

"Yours is different."

"Omfra. My Cornish Pixie."

"Omfra?" said Emily, once again bewildered.

"Omfra. Lost his laugh. Searched high and low for it amongst the barrows of the ancient Cornish kings, waded through the bottomless Dozmary pool before meeting a bird who, happily for him, turned out to be King Arthur in disguise and restored his laugh." She laughed herself. "Hope it never happens to me. But I always pack Beelzebub and Omfra. Vital travelling companions. Look, they're done. The plates are by your foot."

Emily had never considered packing toasting forks before.

"Do you want jam? It's home-made. Blackcurrant."

"From the house with the fish?"

"Afraid not. My family have seen the world. We moved forty odd miles to the southern edge of the Cotswolds. Wotton-Under-Edge? No? I wouldn't have expected you to know of it. Handel played the church organ when it was still in some London church, but apart from that..." she smiled, "however, it's home."

They spent the next few minutes eating the crumpets.

"The jam is excellent." Emily said when she'd finished. "But you meant it? About the staff being fine? I did a stint in a local hospital but I was living at home – thinking of which, I must write a reassuring letter to my mother."

"She worries? They do, don't they? But Matron's quite a sport. The food is pretty good. And I've found someone who does shampoos. And three to five thirty off on alternate days and a half-day holiday every so often." Fish smiled. "When we do get one we shall go out on the razzle. No point in not taking advantage of being ten minutes' walk from Highgate Underground, is there?"

"A razzle sounds great fun, but perhaps I'll leave that out when I write." Emily stood up and examined the photograph next to the books.

"George. George Graydon. My private fiancé." Fish's voice lost its vivaciousness. "Was, I should say. Could do with your time travelling, Mouldiwarp."

Emily stretched out her hand, surprised at her own confidence. "Where?"

"Gallipoli. Chunuk Bair. He was there with the Gloucesters alongside two of my brothers, but they came back."

"Your private fiancé?"

"He signed his last letters with that. I met him in Bristol. An artist. My parents didn't approve, so we hadn't made it public. He joked that of all the fish in the sea he had to fall for me."

Emily smiled.

"We used to walk up a path near my home called Adey's Lane. He claimed all the most wonderful maidens in England were to be found within a stone's throw of it... he was a great flatterer... and he said that when we were old and grey we'd move into one of the almshouses at the bottom of the lane." She faltered, shook her head and sighed. "I'm sorry, I shouldn't get maudlin. I wanted to make your arrival a cheerful one."

"You're not. Honestly. One of my brothers went west last year and I still miss him dreadfully. It's strange. This war. Some can't or won't talk, but... I hope you don't mind me saying... with others it's so natural. I'm glad you can. I'm so sorry about your George. He sounded so romantic."

"Thank you, Mouldiwarp. I think we shall get on most famously. But what about you? Is there anyone?"

"Yes. Robert. He's in the RFC. He was shot down early last month. But... I feel... almost guilty... he survived. He's a POW."

"Guilty? Don't be ridiculous. Why should you? He'll come back to you, so one day you may introduce us. How is he at flying magic carpets?"

Emily laughed. "*The Phoenix and the Carpet*?"

"Yes. My favourite of the children, and the Phoenix's too, was Robert, so that must be a good omen."

"I hope so. Yes." Emily paused. "It was pretty grim for ten days. And then the second telegram came." Her voice wavered, her sense of relief still overwhelming. "ROBERT BUCKLEY 56 Sq. WELL. WIRING CAMP WHEN KNOWN – PRISONERS SOUTH KENSINGTON. Not many words but..."

"Have you heard any more?"

"Very little. The Red Cross confirmed they'd had an official postcard from him. We've had letters from people in his squadron. They're sending his things. I'm hoping there might be something for me. His father had his mess bill for eighty-eight pounds and tuppence. He was glad enough to pay it, but it was the tuppence that surprised me. But there's been nothing yet from Robert. It can take six weeks, even two months for letters to reach home, but his mother is forwarding any news, and my mother too, so I'll just have to be patient."

"Have you written?"

"Not yet. I'm not sure what to do. The War Office advice is confusing about writing before there's a definite address. I might give it a go later." She smiled. "New place and everything. After the first telegram I wasn't sure about taking up this post, but for better or worse Fish... here I am!"

"Undoubtedly the better!" Fish replied with gusto. "But I must be going. I'm on duty at five, whereas you need to unpack. And make the most of your evening. Nose to the grindstone tomorrow. So I'll say adieu, Mouldiwarp." She turned back as she reached the door. "Hot meal at seven fifteen - I'll see you then."

#

Dearest,

I am writing this short note following War Office advice NOT to write before now. We heard you were missing on 15th October. Telegram arrived on 25th saying you were POW but unknown camp. Thankfully well! Have taken post Byculla VAD Hospital, Broadlands Rd, London, N6.

I am so relieved that I shall see you again,

Love always
your Emily
xxxx

Emily sat back and looked at the letter card. It seemed so inadequate. Even writing that had involved much indecision. She looked at the time. Fish would be back soon. She had better get it done.

Dear Mother and Father,

The journey down was fine. I have a nice room-mate. I am looking forward to

She screwed up the paper, threw it into the fire and picked up her pen again.

My dearest darling Robert,

I have written an 'official' letter-card, but this is letter ONE. I shall number my letters so you know if any are missing, but I have no way of knowing if you get this or if you do, when or where? Someone in the War Office may be reading this and crossing out the military secrets I am revealing. Mysterious Person in the War Office, please accept that all I want is to write to the person I love and I promise that nothing in this letter will be of help to the Germans.

I was desperate to write earlier, but at every turn was told there was no point. One of Alice's cousins works at Reckitts, and they have helped families of former employees get in touch with prisoners. Letters have got through in the most unpromising of circumstances.

All sorts of people have written to us about you. It is agonising not knowing what you have been through and what you are doing now. I long to see something in your own handwriting. Time never moved as slowly as in those ten days. I thought I had lost you. Even now I shudder at the thought. I might have lost you. I knew it was illogical but I was so angry with you. I might have lost you! How could you do that? It made me realise how unbearable life would be without you. It made me so angry that you and your stupid plane had torn us apart. That you are one of millions fighting a war could not stop me feeling that. No matter what other people have been through, for those ten days all I could think was Robert please, please be safe. I could not care less about anyone else's fate, all I wanted was you. And then the best telegram ever arrived. I had not lost you! I was in the most delirious daze when your mother told me and showed me the words in black and white. I might have lost you but I hadn't. I had been given a wonderful second chance so don't you dare do anything to put that at risk. Never ever do

"Are you all right, Mouldiwarp?"

Emily looked up.

"I don't think you heard me come in."

"Fish. I was just..."

"Are you all right? You look a little..."

"Emotional? I should have stuck to writing home. But I'll finish this tomorrow. I can add a bit about my first proper day." She folded it carefully and took out a fresh piece of paper. "I'm quite tired. I don't know why. You're the one who's been working. I'll write to my parents. It won't take long, and then we can sit and have a chat before bed. I haven't told you anything about home and I want to hear more about the old fish, and about your family." She smiled and waved her arms vaguely. "Everything."

"I'll get changed while you do that. Don't you find these starched collars irritating? I do."

Emily picked up her pen again.

Dear Mother and Father,

    Just a short letter to say I've arrived. My room-mate seems...

December 9th, 1917
Epsom

He opened his mouth to scream as the side of the trench collapsed. His legs gave way and he slithered downwards. It was raining thick heavy globules of mud. Desperately he swam against the onrushing enveloping sea of mire. The more he pushed the cloying morass away, the faster it came, forcing its way into his eyes, his ears, deep into his nostrils. He reached out and touched a dead, lifeless hand, which turned hard, bony, brittle, before disintegrating in his grasp. His ears were ringing. He was in a strangely muffled world where his ears would not stop ringing. On the far side of the ringing he could hear someone screaming. He opened his mouth to scream too, and the mud rushed in. Choking. Asphyxiating. Solidifying. He screamed deep from his smothered lungs. In his head the scream went on forever.

"Captain... Captain Walker... It's all right. You were having a nightmare."

He could feel the touch of warm, gentle hands that did not decay or de-compose. The shaking took over his whole body and a fresh wave of panic threatened to overwhelm him.

"Try to breathe more slowly. Come on, take a deep breath."

It seemed easier to David to give in to the driving surges of adrenaline. A feeling of sickness rose up and down in his chest. The pounding of his heart rang in his ears.

"Don't worry, Captain. You're safe. You're here in hospital. Don't you re-member? Try opening your eyes. You'll see."

He tried but they were glued together. His eyelids felt so heavy. He struggled again to open his eyes, without success.

"Come on. Squeeze my hands as hard as you like. I don't mind."

David took a deep breath. He contorted his face, moved his head from side to side, and slowly forced his eyelids apart.

"There! I knew you could do it."

A woman's face gazed down at him. She was smiling. He felt he should know her. He let go of her hands.

"You've had a bad turn. We'll have to tell the doctor. Look, you're soaked in sweat. Let's get you out of that pyjama top and I'll get you some-thing dry to put on."

He looked at her silently as she helped him change.

"Do you know it's my birthday today? Twenty-four, now you ask! I wasn't expecting a card or anything, though it would be a special treat if you wished me Happy Birthday. You needn't bother with the Nurse Fel-lows part. And there's no need to sing Happy Birthday to me. I'll settle for a smile instead. No? Not yet?" She stood back from the bed and tried to mask a sigh. "It's not long until Christmas, so we'll exchange greetings then. That will be something to look forward to, won't it? Lean forward and I'll plump your pillow for you."

She put her arm round him to pull him forward. "That's better, isn't it? You're more settled now. Your parents are coming this afternoon, aren't they? They must be looking forward to that."

David turned onto his side and pulled his knees up towards him. For the time being, the noises in his head were stilled.

#

"It's such a shame it isn't a better day. You could have taken us round the grounds. The doctor says it's good for you to get up and about." Mrs Walker struggled to keep her voice optimistic. "Never mind, there's always next time." She gave her husband an imploring look, inviting him to speak; the last half hour had not been easy.

"Yes. A brisk walk in winter sunshine. Nothing more invigorating," he agreed, before gazing at the rain battering the windows. His hand moved towards his pocket watch. "Yes, a brisk walk."

"And they've said they might move you in the New Year to a hospital near Edinburgh. Craiglockhart. There are all sorts of sporting facilities there – golf, tennis, swimming. It sounds marvellous, though I can't see why they don't find you somewhere nearer home." She looked at her husband. "Emily came across officers suffering from... but the doctors know what's best. And getting you better is the most important thing," she added, with a confidence she didn't feel. "I'm sure it's just a matter of time. Of course, we'll still come to see you even if you do get moved to Scotland. And Emily has said she will visit when she can; it's only an hour on the train. She said she'd written, but perhaps you haven't had a chance to read it yet. She's settled in really well, which is a relief. I must admit I wasn't sure about the whole thing, but she was so determined, and then with Robert reported missing and then a prisoner... it was all so topsy-turvy for a while. She'll tell you all her news. She's made an excellent new friend, whom she insists on calling Fish in her letters – which does strike me as somewhat odd. I had hoped she'd be back for Christmas but that seems unlikely, so there'll be just the two of us. And Alice." She looked at her husband for support again. "Alfred, there must be something you could tell David about?"

"Yes... um... Weather's been pretty awful back home too. Yes." His gaze returned to the window, before he continued with an effort. "The Unseen Hand. Have you been following things? No? Fascinating article in the *Imperialist*. Germany is under control of these..."

"Alfred, I don't think David wants to hear about your obsession about that. I know I don't. All very unsavoury. Surely there's something else? Is there nothing in yesterday's *Mail*? I thought you'd brought a couple for David." Emily's mother lowered her voice. "Something local perhaps."

He unfolded a paper and scanned it. "Chap's been fined for taking a wedding party to St. Barnabas's in his car. Says he had a carriage and two greys booked but the cabman hadn't turned up, being delayed at a funeral. He knew he was breaking Petrol Regulation Orders, but the bride was half an hour late and the groom was a Chief Engineer who had to join his ship straight after the service, so if he hadn't there wouldn't have been a wedding. The bench told him it was only seven or eight hundred yards to the church and they should have walked. Two guineas' fine. What do you think, David? Bride running down Hessle Road to get to the church on time. Would have made a rum sight." He waited. "No? Let's see... what else?... There's been a dreadful disaster in Novia Scotia. A munitions ship blew up and they think thousands have been killed. Three thousand tons of TNT. People sixty miles away felt it and..." He noticed the warning look from his wife. "No, perhaps not... um... Heavy snow in North Wales and fifteen degrees of frost recorded near Huntingdon on Thursday. Your mother was saying people have been skating on Clough Road fields. Perhaps when you're better... Lloyd George has come back from Paris with a dreadful cold." He turned a page. "There's a rather good piece about War Bonds – 'If Sanatogen is good for personal health then War Bonds are good for the nation's health'. Yes, I rather like that. So there you are, David. I'll leave the papers with you, and then if you... Clara. I'm sure you must have more to tell David before we have to go." He sat back in his chair and reached for his pocket watch.

#

Mrs Walker examined the window blind. She longed to reach forward, release it and gaze illicitly into the darkness. She looked at her husband dozing in his seat opposite and sighed. He had his mouth open – would he snore? She couldn't let him inflict that on their fellow passengers. She would have to poke him if he did. She let her own eyes close. She'd felt like giving him a sharp poke in the ribs earlier when waiting for their train, even though he'd only voiced the dreadful thoughts she herself had been trying to suppress.

"Perhaps it would have been better if the men who pulled him free had left him."

"Alfred, that's unforgivable. You can't mean it."

"I don't know what to think, Clara. You saw him. If you can honestly tell me that he's improving... No. You don't have to say anything. It's written as clear as anything in your face."

"But the doctors..."

"Clara, they don't have any idea. His vocal chords are undamaged. He screams sometimes at night."

"Alfred, don't."

"You heard what that nurse said."

"This new hospital they are sending him too? Surely..." Her voice petered away.

"We might as well be perfect strangers. You sat there holding his hand all that time and what response did you get?"

"They said this Craiglockhart place has done wonders for some people, Alfred. We can't give up hope."

"I'd have more confidence in that London hospital. This Dr. Yelland has the right idea. Sufferers from the hysterical disorders of warfare need shocking out of it. It's what the lad needs."

"I can't bear the thought of David receiving electric shocks."

"Then perhaps neither of us should place too much faith in miracles, Clara. It's hard to say it, but shouldn't we accept that he's gone?"

"No, no, no! It's far too soon to give up hope. I don't know how you can. Wherever he is, he will return – and I promised I would visit him and visit him I shall... with or without you, Alfred."

"Of course I shall accompany you, dear. I just worry that it will grind you down. You already look so worn." He looked along the platform. "Ah, this must be ours." He gave her a sympathetic smile. "It's been a long tiring day. And I know, he is our son. It's just..." The rest of his words were lost as the train came to a halt in front of them.

She opened her eyes, unsure whether she had drifted off. The train had come to a halt. She risked a peek behind the blind. Goole. Nearly home.

#

He lay awake. The sensation of sinking ever deeper into the bed grew stronger. For the last hour the ringing in his ears had been incessant. He lay awake and stared at the ceiling.

#

"It won't be long, sir," the RAMC sergeant said. "Soon get you somewhere a little more comfortable. Get you cleaned up. You've brought half of Flanders' mud with you." He looked down at the young captain lying on the stretcher. He was almost encased from head to toe. He seemed to have lost his boots.

"Look after him, will you." A second voice said. "He's a pretty decent sort. Hell of a job getting him out. Just see his feet at first. Thought he might have suffocated before we got to him, like one or two other poor buggers. It was a big one. Done a lot of damage. Anyway, must get back up the line, I'll leave him in your capable hands."

#

Renewed shelling threw him into a raving paroxysm of screaming and slobbering.

"We're going to have to strap him down, Sarge," the corporal said. "He'll do himself an injury." As he endeavoured to get away, six of them struggled to hold him down, until after several minutes he was securely tied.

"Don't know where they get the strength from, sometimes," the sergeant said. "Still, he's a bit calmer for the moment so we'll lift him on three and try and get him to the CCS before the bleeding Boche starts his barrage again." He looked down at his charge. "Ready, Captain?... One, two, three."

#

The doctor walked down the long line of stretchers that filled the Casualty Clearing Station's large reception tent almost to overflowing. Some casualties were pale and cold and made little response. He peered at their labels – 'Re-suss' 'Pre-op' 'Evac'. His orderly made a careful note. Some had the small, innocuous, tell-tale holes of a bullet entry. These men lay there and gave him anxious looks, afraid to be touched. Their drawn mouths, rigid muscles and thready pulses suggested untold disaster awaited within. He stopped by an infantry captain who was strapped to his stretcher. There was no obvious sign of physical injury, though he appeared to be having an epileptic fit. With difficulty the doctor looked into his eyes and sighed. "Evac" he said and moved on.

\#

Every few seconds the captain clawed uncontrollably at his mouth. The VAD nurse watched him. When he had managed to speak he had stammered so much his words were unintelligible. The flesh on his face had gained a life of its own, shaking spasmodically.

"Nurse! Nurse!" a soldier behind her called out for attention, "are we going to be here much longer? I'm gasping for a fag." He waved the bandaged stump of his right arm and grinned at her. "Good job I'm left-handed."

"Another two or three hours, I should think, Corporal, and then you'll all be off." And you'll be easier to treat than that captain, she thought.

\#

The doctor swayed as the train clattered over the points, but being used to it he avoided bumping into the double tier of cots running along both sides of the long carriage. He moved along, glancing from side to side at his ninety-three charges. He hadn't lost anyone on his train yet, even if some didn't last too long once they reached their destination.

Most men in the cots had turned on their sides away from the light. Apart from the regular rhythm of the train, everything was still and quiet – except for the low, barely audible moaning coming from a cot at the end of the coach. Its occupant lay on his back. The white of his arms contrasted with the grey blanket on which they were stretched. His eyes wide open, he appeared to be studying the white domed roof. The doctor reached out and gave his hand a reassuring squeeze. As the train moved closer to the coast, the captain shut his eyes and gave in to the need to sleep.

#

Since leaving Le Havre a heavy sea had been running and he lay in his bunk, intermittently seasick. At eight p.m. the torpedo struck the *Donegal*. The explosion ripped through the hospital ship's engine room, reducing gargantuan timbers to matchwood, smashing glass and buckling steel girders. Rushes of steam hissed out of its boilers. An ominous tremor resounded throughout the vessel as its stern settled more deeply into the water.

Despite some urging, the captain did not stir until forced onto the deck. As one of the last to arrive, he was unceremoniously thrown over the side. A lifebelt held his head, from the chin upwards, just above the violent swell. The bulk of the ship loomed over him, its twin funnels now projecting out at an alarming angle, before it slowly slid, almost effortlessly, below the waves.

He was sucked down. Deeper and deeper. Spun around. Twisted. Lungs bursting. The shock wave of the ship's exploding boilers propelled him rapidly upwards. He broke the surface, opened his mouth and swallowed a large quantity of water. Hands grabbed him and pulled him out. Unaware of his rescuers, he lay in the bottom of the lifeboat gasping and shivering uncontrollably.

#

Over the months, the ceilings had undergone numerous transformations, as had the doctors and nurses. He was aware of them talking about him and to him but he did not feel any desire to communicate. He was locked away. The part of his brain that told him that he should speak to doctors, nurses, to visitors when he had them, was completely overwhelmed. Even the obvious distress of his mother was insufficient to break through. The ringing in his ears subsided. He stared at the ceiling. For the moment neither it nor the walls seemed in imminent danger of collapsing in on him. He shut his eyes and tried to think of nothing.

January 13th, 1918
Highgate Cemetery

Emily looked across at her aunt as they walked along between the memorials and gravestones. She was still taking in what she'd just been told.

"What I can't understand is why you didn't tell anyone last July, as soon as you came home from London," she said.

"I thought of it," Eleanor replied. "I could have regaled people with tales of my great London escape and been the centre of attention!"

"I'm sure you would have hated that!" Emily laughed.

Eleanor smiled. "In the end I decided not to. I knew you were thinking about coming down here. Your mother is a great worrier, and I didn't want her using my narrow escape as the excuse for stopping you."

"You're right about Mother worrying! There's no point telling her that you can't guarantee safety anywhere. I sometimes think I should be writing home every day just to reassure her."

"One thing you can do, Emily, is promise not to do anything silly. I heard about a young soldier who pulled his girlfriend out into the street to get a better view that day. It was the last thing they ever saw."

"I promise I will be sensible, Aunt. I don't want you to worry, either. We haven't been affected at all out here, not even in the December attack. Robert once told me that German raiders preferred clear nights and full moons, so I'll take particular care on those evenings. I know people can become fatalistic, but I shall try not to!" She looked around her. "Are we nearly there?"

"Yes, I think so. That one over there looks as if it's the one we want."

Emily stopped in front of the impressive monument and read out the inscription.

'Of those immortal dead who live again
In minds made better by their presence.'

"It's a quotation from one of her poems. And whatever you believe about an afterlife, Emily, living on in the thoughts of others is the only true immortality."

"I understand, now, why you quoted her as we came through the gates, Aunt." Emily paused, deep in thought, before continuing. "Our dead are never dead to us – until we have forgotten them. Yes, there's a real element of truth in that."

"I'm glad you think so, dear."

"I remember your giving me Middlemarch. It took me quite a time to realise that the author wasn't actually a man. You should have told me!"

"I wanted to see how soon you would guess." Eleanor smiled. "You were much younger, and I wouldn't have wanted to discuss her rather unconventional life with you back then." She pointed at the memorial. "My only argument with her was that she was an ardent anti-suffragist, but her books are so sublime that I'll have to forgive her for that. I hope you didn't mind coming here. It seemed an ideal destination for a walk on such a lovely afternoon, even if it is a bit chilly."

"It is, isn't it? I'll be glad when this cold snap ends, but I love coming here. It's so peaceful. I do need to get back soon, though, as I'm on duty again at five. Wasn't there another grave you wanted to find?"

"Yes, Marx's, but I'm afraid he only warrants an obscure spot down one of these side paths. Nowhere near as important as Britain's finest female Victorian novelist! The light's going a little, so he can wait for another visit. I don't think you would find him interesting, anyway." She looked at her niece. "No, I thought not, so instead of boring you with his ideas, I've something else for you instead." Eleanor reached into her bag. "You are an intelligent, independent young woman and I've had this long enough. I'd have given it to you at Christmas if you'd been home." She indicated the memorial, "For all her achievements as a free-thinking woman, she never, to my knowledge, did what you did." She handed Emily the package. "I've had it framed."

Emily unwrapped it. "The photograph of me climbing! How wonderful!" She hugged her aunt in delight. "It will have pride of place on my mantelpiece when I'm home, and here too till then. Fish will be fascinated. I've never told her about my climbing exploits."

"I'm glad you're pleased. Shall we say farewell to Mary Anne Evans?"

"Yes, Aunt." She looked at the grave. "Goodbye, George." She took her aunt's arm and they walked away together. "David's been in Scotland a week now. Has Mother had any news? You know I went to see him just before he was moved?"

"Yes, so I heard. You must tell me all about it on our way back."

The shadows lengthened across the cemetery. Emily was briefly silent as she thought of her visit to her brother.

January 3rd, 1918

Epsom

This is so much harder than I ever imagined it would be, thought Emily. He hasn't improved at all since my last visit. She sighed. I'm not sure that I'm ever going to get a response. No, don't give up. Try to be cheerful. Try to be cheerful.

"I've found some more words for your glossary of slang, David. Remember? When you were last home? We only got as far as D, so here's an E for you. It's Erk. Any ideas? Take your time. Robert told me, if that helps." She waited. "No? I'll tell you then. An Erk is an air mechanic." She leant forward and took his hand. "My friend Fish suggested the next one. F for Forby? You'll have had one... the cloth to clean your rifle. And the G was the suggestion of one of my patients at Byculla. Ready? Gas-pipe brigade! He was stationed in Withernsea with the East Yorkshire Mounted Brigade back in 1914 on... you'll have guessed it... on his bicycle. You might have seen him when you were stationed at Atwick before..." Her voice wavered.

"Oh, I'm sorry, David. I should have realised that in February that you weren't well. I'd seen patients with neurasthenia. I know I'm not a doctor nor even vaguely qualified, and I'd only been at Brooklands for a month or so, but I can't help feeling guilty... Mother is so upset. I shouldn't say so but...

I've said it now, so..." She dabbed at her eyes with a handkerchief. "I'm just so useless and I don't know why I even thought of asking people for this stupid slang!" She started in surprise and stopped speaking. Was she imagining it? Had he squeezed her hand? She looked at him. Was he looking at her or just staring in her direction? She took a deep breath. "Let's get on with the alphabet... H is for Hard Tack... you'll have eaten plenty of that. They might have been pulling my leg, but I was told that dry army biscuits can be used as fire-lighters. And I like my I... an Iddy-Umpty. It's lovely to say. An Iddy-Umpty. A signaller. And J is... J is for Jippo, which is bread and..."

"Gravy."

She froze. Shocked. It had been no more than a faint whisper. And a cracked one too.

"Jippo is gravy... Japan is bread... le pain... Japan." David stopped and subsided back into the bed, as if the effort had been overwhelming.

Emily stared at him. A tear formed in the corner of her left eye and rolled down her cheek.

"K?"

She thought for a moment. She couldn't think straight. She ought to tell someone. But he'd asked her for a K. She must continue. What if he retreated into his silence? Her mind went blank. Where had she heard it? From the Scotsman on the ward. That was it. "A Kokky-Olly-Bird?"

He gave a slow, uncertain awkward shake of his head.

"Don't... know."

"I was talking to one last Tuesday. A King's Own Borderer." She smiled at him, and was encouraged by the tiniest movement at the corner of his mouth in return. He shut his eyes.

"Tired."

"I'll go if you want – or I can stay a little longer?"

"Few minutes. Carry... on."

"A few minutes, then. And I won't go all the way to Z. Just two I particularly like. P is Pip-emma. That's now, as it's afternoon. My last one's a T. I had a choice but Trez Beans it has to be – Three Blue Lights. My Kocky-Olly-Bird told me to look out for three dark blue signal flares at night, because if you do see them it means the war is over. Of course, everyone uses that to mean something highly improbable has happened." She gave his hand another squeeze. "It's not night yet." She leant forward. "But it's getting dark." She kissed him on the cheek. "So I'd better get outside and set off Three Blue Lights!"

#

Emily flopped down into her seat in the empty compartment, thinking of the telegram she had just sent. GOOD NEWS. VISITED DAVID. HE SPOKE. WRITE FULL DETAILS ASAP. The afternoon had been emotional. She let out a long sigh, feeling both drained and overwhelmed – but also happier than she could have imagined when she'd set off for Epsom. She reached into her bag and took out the letter that she already had read innumerable times since receiving it that morning. She examined the franking mark on the envelope. *Offizier-Gefangenenlager Trier Geprüft FA.*

My dear Emily,

   We have settled into a permanent(?) camp here in Trier and at last been allowed to write proper letters. The journey was tedious in the extreme and I saw some grim sights especially at ******* ********* where a large number of ******* ********* were on the platform. I will never complain again about

For the umpteenth time in the last two days, the train lurched to a halt. Robert's stomach gave an involuntary rumble. Since the night when he'd been entertained by the German flyers, his diet had been a meagre affair. A slice of wurst, some hard sour bread and weak cabbage soup had been monotonous fare. The cigars he had managed to buy had at least proved excellent appetite suppressants. Robert and the other prisoners had taken escorted walks from the house into the countryside, but the fields had been devoid of their last heads of corn and the birds had beaten them to anything worth scavenging in the hedgerows. A number of old Belgian women dressed in black had pushed crusts through the barbed wire of their thirty-yard-square exercise cage and, though Robert felt guilty, it hadn't stopped him eating them. Yesterday they had been allowed out onto the platform at Ghent and had been given a lunch of watery soup, bread and ersatz fish-cakes, which had been a welcome addition to their journey's ration of two small loaves.

The train shuddered, moved and stopped again. It was impossible to know whether they were in a town or the middle of nowhere, whether they would move again in two minutes or two hours.

The doors to the cattle wagon were flung open. Robert stood up. In the long hours since exercising in a barren field next to a railway siding, he had stiffened up. He stumbled out onto the platform alongside his nineteen compatriots. God, it was cold. He looked up at the sign – *Köln*. He tried to ignore his hunger pangs.

A train pulled in on the other side of their platform and Robert watched, horrified, as the guards unlocked the wagons, disgorging the most pitiful members of the human race he'd ever seen. He saw several bodies lying on the floor of a wagon before a guard pulled the door shut, after the last prisoners had dragged themselves out. The smell was overpowering. Many looked barely alive. Their tattered uniforms scarcely covered them. They stood in silence. Emaciated ghosts. One, cheekbones protruding from his face, stared at Robert. Robert smiled at him. There was no flicker of response; the man just looked back with hopeless hollow eyes. A guard shouted, and the man turned and shuffled off with his comrades along the platform, down some steps and out of sight.

"Russkies, poor sods," Stan Bennett, a fellow prisoner who spoke good German, said. "The guards say they're heading west to build trenches. Not many will see their homeland again. Awful. Hope they don't stick us all in with them tonight. Don't suppose any of them has two marks fifty, either."

"Two marks fifty?" said Robert.

"For bread and sausages to supplement the soup. Costs two marks fifty. And we'll be here overnight."

As they queued for food, a woman stopped, said something in German and spat at them.

Robert looked at his friend for explanation.

"She wasn't complimentary." Stanley glanced upwards. "Perhaps she was on the receiving end when I flew my Handley Page over here." He smiled. "At least our guards seem reasonable. One says we're off to Karlsruhe in the morning. Fritz assembles all us RFC types there, before moving us on, but for now downstairs and not, thank God, sharing with our unfortunate allies."

It's been very cold here since we arrived. The commandant seem reasonable enough...

"Top or bottom, Stan?" Robert surveyed the rickety bedsteads. Of the six sets of four in the room, two berths were free.

"Top."

Robert threw his canvas sleeping bag onto the bunk, along with a collection of old children's exercise books he'd been given to use as padding. He sat down. "One moves, everyone moves," he said. "God, they're hard." He lifted the thin mattress and tapped on the boards underneath. "Hardly Home Sweet Home. No danger of us going soft."

The door opened and an officer came in.

"Hope you're settling in." He proffered his hand. "Andrew Butler, former 32nd."

"Robert Buckley. 56th."

"Stan Bennett. 100th."

The newcomer laughed. "100th? My last sortie was escorting some of your Bloody Paralysers... but no hard feelings!"

"Perhaps if you'd flown a decent bus rather than a DH5, you might not be here too!" Stan answered, laughing in return.

Butler sat down on the neighbouring bunk. "You'll both be glad to be out of quarantine. Pickle baths never get any better, do they? God knows what they put in them. Anyway, it's my job to fill you in on a few things. The Oflag Commandant was once a military attaché in London and speaks excellent English. He's a decent sort. Some Commandants aren't. It makes all the difference. Either of you vegetarians? No? Might as well be. Get used to barley, bean and vegetable soup with an occasional bit of meat of dubious provenance thrown in. And you'd best like beetroot. It just about keeps the wolf from the door. We all rely on Food Parcels. Don't worry, we set a little aside for newcomers until something gets through. Mess in groups of four as it makes parcels easier to share."

"What's the food like in them?" Robert asked.

"The parcels? Each contains two loaves per officer. As to the rest, it's all down to luck. They vary tremendously, but nothing goes to waste. We had some loaves of bread recently that needed hammers to break open. God knows how long they'd been in transit. Lots of holes inside were filled with mould. We soaked them, squeezed out the green slime and cooked what was left." He smiled again. "Most aren't as bad as that."

"What about the other prisoners?" asked Stan. "The French, for instance?"

"Some are sociable, some aren't." Butler shrugged. "They have their own courtyard. They don't treat their orderlies well. Food and so on. There was a knife fight over a single lump of sugar, if you can believe it! Do try and be near their water pump when they send the orderly down who used to be an opera singer. Sings some fantastic arias whilst he's filling up the containers... And there are a few Russians too. One or two have basic English and some speak good German."

"What about the guards?" asked Robert.

"Generally okay. Some are bribable, if you've anything to bribe them with. Deutschmarks, if you've got them. Your pay's about a hundred a month in camp money – lagergeld. They take fifty off you for your food and lodging! Your people can send you extra money and the Germans will add it to your account, but they'll only issue it as camp script. Four good bottles of beer for a mark in the canteen. But cigars are harder to get, so you'll have to devise your own mix of wood shavings and tobacco. A barber's here every day, a tailor and cobbler a couple of times a week, and several washerwomen come on Saturdays. And," he opened his mouth wide, "one platinum and two gold fillings – eighty marks." He smiled. "Any other questions?"

"What if you don't want to spend the rest of the war twiddling your thumbs here?" asked Robert.

"No successes on that front. There have been attempts. But if you have plans, be careful who you talk to." He gave them a meaningful look. "Most chaps are more likely to indulge in escapist reading. You haven't any reading material with you?" Robert shook his head. "Shame. Book parcels arrive occasionally, so there's a small camp library. Hope you like old Rider Haggard?" Butler stood up. "I'll leave you then. Roll call is at five." He pointed at their sleeping bags. "Best to crumple the pages for the filling. Much better than tearing them into pieces. And you can add these." He gave them a couple of rolled up newspapers. "*The Continental Times*. Propaganda rag. You'll get questioned about the latest state of things for a couple of days." He stopped near the door. "One last piece of advice. Some chaps come down with barbed-wire disease. Go a bit strange. Too long cooped up. So best try and keep busy. See you at roll-call."

Robert took no more than a few minutes to organise his few belongings, before picking up one of the exercise book and starting to tear and crumple the pages for his makeshift bedding.

...sent my parents a long list of requests. Our letters are rationed so will write asap, but there are no limitations on receiving them!

Always thinking of you, my darling Em,
your Robert
xxxxx

The rhythm of the train changed as it slowed. Emily looked up and, to her surprise, saw that they were nearing Waterloo. She folded the letter, returned it to its envelope, then stood up as the train came to a halt.

February 1st, 1918
Byculla Hospital

Fish collapsed into an armchair. "Well, Mouldiwarp, what did you decide?"

Emily was lying stretched out on her bed. "About what, Fish? Whether it's better to be worn out from an afternoon's shopping and gallivanting around town or to be exhausted from providing bed-pans for Major Caswell? What about cleaning him up? Five times! I won't go into the gory details. Sister was an absolute brute, in a foul temper. And I think I'm getting a chilblain. On my nose of all places... I'm sorry, I'm sorry." She held her arm up in supplication. "I'm just a bit tired – I've been on my feet all day and I haven't written any letters. The more I think of things I should be doing the more weary I feel... but I didn't mean to snap."

Fish stood up. "Why don't you sit over here? The coal scuttle needs filling. I'll do that, and then come in again."

"Okay. I shall try and be more..."

"Reasonable? Optimistic? Cheerful?"

"Yes," said Emily, swinging her legs off the bed. "More reasonable, though we'll have to see about the optimistic and the cheerful."

Fish smiled at her. "I have faith in you, Mouldiwarp. Five minutes."

Emily knelt down. The fire was dismal. She pulled out the fender and poked half-heartedly at the coals. After a minute or two it started to draw, the embers changing from dull red to a red that was a bit less dull. She picked up a newspaper and held it stretched taut across the grate until she heard the satisfying sound of the air rushing in, sucking the paper towards the chimney. She'd been more careful since setting a paper alight a few weeks ago, so she pulled it back in good time. She was pleased to see flames reviving around the edge of the coals. Watching the fire come back to life, her mood lightened and she determined not to take out her troubles on her friend.

"Coal," Fish announced, coming back in and depositing the scuttle on the hearth. "Good, you've got it going... and we also have cocoa. Mind, it's hot." She passed a mug to Emily. "That's better."

"What is?"

"You're smiling." She sat down next to Emily. "So, Mouldiwarp, have you made up your mind?"

"This cocoa is excellent, Fish, thank you. I meant to make some earlier but I couldn't be bothered." Emily took another sip. "Made my mind up? About what, Fish? About whether a glittering stage career awaits you after your performance yesterday evening? With regard to that, I've decided that sadly it does not."

"That is a trifle unfair. I was quite outstanding. And theatre critics from the papers will feel exactly the same."

"So Matron will need replacements when we transfer to the West End?" Emily smiled.

"She'll be more worried about losing Cook than four of her nurses. And we'll need more bicycle lamps than you scrounged last night, for the foot-lights, when we walk out on stage in Shaftesbury Avenue."

They laughed together.

"I'm glad you persuaded me to take part. It was fun, wasn't it?" Fish continued.

"It certainly went down well with the men. Two Lieutenants said this afternoon that after seeing your Cinders they couldn't wait for your Jack, as they longed to see you shinning up the Beanstalk. You've won yourself two admirers! My Ugly Sister hasn't had them flocking to my door in quite the same way, though Matron was quite complimentary. Did you see her actually laughing out loud? But talking of Matron, I saw her this afternoon. And yes, I did make up my mind... I've agreed to stay until the end of June. I'll finish on Friday the twenty-eighth."

"Excellent!" exclaimed Fish. "Same day as me. And what about my Grand Plan?"

"Three weeks scrambling around on my hands and knees picking fruit in your glorious Gloucestershire? Why not? It will be fun."

"Even better. But what about your leave? Did she agree?"

"She could hardly object if I was signing on. Two weeks. I'll go home next month for a week, and save the rest. Don't worry – I'll take the twenty-third as leave. Can't miss your favourite magician. What's his name... Ching Lung Soo?"

"It's Chung Ling Soo, not that it matters."

"Ow!" Emily exclaimed and moved her head from side to side. "My neck!"

"Come on, move that cushion onto the floor and I'll rub it."

"Ahhhh, that's so much better," Emily said a few minutes later. "Did you see that advertisement about massage courses? Some start in August and they want VADs to train. We could both do it, though I'm... down a bit, please. Left. Yes, just there... nowhere as good as you. You've got a gift for this. You're not too tired?"

"No. And yes, I saw that advertisement too, but I think I'll wait. I'd consider coming back here, but who knows what will happen? Even if the war finished tomorrow, all the wounded aren't going to disappear, and August seems a long way away, especially on a day of such dismal weather."

"I'm sorry, Fish, I haven't asked how you got on. Was it as bad as yesterday?"

"Much worse than up here, a real pea-souper, but I was hardly going to miss a chance to get into mufti. Coming out of Piccadilly Circus underground I swear it was green. You could hardly see ten feet. I almost turned right round and came back again. But then I bumped into, literally bumped into, Louisa Eden, outside the Lyons Corner House in Coventry Street. Remember I was telling you about her? So we went in and, considering it was a Friday afternoon, it was so quiet. One of the Nippies said it had been like that all day what with the fog, so we were able to sit there for ages, which reminds me... would you mind passing my bag?"

Emily stretched forward to reach it.

"Now don't say I never think of you," Fish said, pulling out a paper bag. "One of their pastries. A little bit battered, but it's..."

"The thought that counts. Carry on. Mustn't talk with my mouth full," she said, taking a bite.

"Exactly. Manners maketh a rather tired, if no longer quite as grumpy, Mouldiwarp. Not bad, is it? Nothing like as good as pre-war, but not bad all the same. Where was I?"

"Louisa Eden?"

"Yes. She was with a friend in Covent Garden last Monday night when the maroons went off, so they headed for the public shelter at Odhams, in Long Acre. There were hundreds in their basement when they got there. They'd been in there four hours when a bomb hit the pavement right outside. Luckily they were at the opposite end from the full force of the explosion. She said the most terrifying thing was that they were almost drowned, when the Fire Brigade deluged the building to put the fires out. And to think we were complaining about the all-clear not going till one thirty."

"Was she injured?"

"No, she was one of the lucky ones. Her friend was, not badly, but was taken to hospital —and there were many worse off there. About forty people died, apparently. She heard some people claim that the Germans targeted Odhams because they print *John Bull* there. Louisa still had some printer's ink on her hands that she hadn't been able to get off." She took a sip of her cocoa. "You know those two separate stampedes to get into shelters? There were people in the hospital from those. The worse of the two was at Mile End tube. Hundreds were queuing for the second show at the Olympia when warning maroons went off. Unfortunately they were mistaken for bombs and everyone panicked and rushed for the tube. Fourteen dead as a result! I was in a lift at Covent Garden and heard two women discussing how inconvenient it was when the poor flocked into the tube, with no respect for regulations, and how they sat on the stairs blocking them.

They suggested the poor should be banned from using the Underground as shelters."

"What an appalling idea!... But I'm surprised Louisa was back in town so soon."

"She shrugged it off. Said she might not go up to town on clear evenings with a moon again, but apart from that... and she'd wanted to see *Hindle Wakes*, so we got tickets for it. Hayford Hobbs – so adorable – and Colette O'Neill. Some people might find it a trifle scandalous, but sophisticated ladies-about-town like myself take it in their stride."

Emily laughed. "Yes, sophisticated is the first word that comes to mind when I think of you... No, don't stop. It's so relaxing. You're a godsend, dear Fish. One more minute? Please!"

"One more minute and that means *one*, not, with your curious use of mathematics, extending it to five."

"As if I would," Emily said in mock disbelief. "And then I'll top up these cocoas."

"Very well, Mouldiwarp. One more minute. I'm on earlies tomorrow so I ought to get to bed."

Emily leant back and let Fish's fingers melt away the last of her earlier tension. Three minutes, perhaps four, of blissful relaxation left.

March 7th, 1918
Westbourne Avenue

"You won't be too bored, Emily?"

"Mother, I've told you. I'll be fine. I'd like the chance to not do much for a few days. The occasional lie-in will be bliss. Father may not approve, but I won't be up bright and early every day." She saw her mother's anxious look. "Don't worry, it wouldn't feel as if I'd been home if I returned without hearing him grumbling away behind his paper over the breakfast table."

"You won't argue with him, will you? It's bad enough treading on eggshells with one member of the family, and he has been looking forward to seeing you."

"I plan to tell him it's wonderful the Russians have signed a peace treaty and..."

"You weren't? He was upset yesterday with the Germans occupying Petrograd and he won't refer to the Bolsheviks by name. 'Those ignorant madmen who've launched their Godless reign of terror' he calls them. You mustn't say anything…"

"Mother! Stop worrying! I shouldn't tease. Of course I wouldn't say that. If I disagree with him, I shall be careful. I won't mention it. But how are things?"

"Between your Father and your aunt?"

Emily nodded.

"I wish I could put them in a sack and throw it overboard from the ferry. You mentioned Russia. Your aunt was at some Labour Party Conference in Nottingham where some dreadful Bolshevik spoke, and your Father said something to her about Clydeside anarchists…" she sighed. "But at least they are talking. And you mustn't worry about that now. Having you home is the main thing. I just wish it were for longer."

"Ten days, Mother. And longer in the summer."

"But you're planning to go fruit picking."

"Mother, please don't look like that. Yes, I am, but I'm here now, so what shall we do?"

"I'm sorry, I was just a little disappointed, that's all. As to now, there are a few things you might enjoy. The Tivoli's got an American musical burlesque, *The Mirth and the Melody,* which sounds fun. And *Dombey and Sons* is at the Central."

"Having attended all those Dickens Society meetings, I must go with Aunt Eleanor, though she always complains about the Central calling itself 'The Rendezvous of the Elite'." She smiled. "If this is the elite, heaven help the hoi-polloi."

"I believe I've heard her say something similar, Emily. She has no complaints about the Palace, as I've got tickets for a charity do there next Thursday afternoon in aid of Mother Humber and the Daily News' Tobacco Fund. Robert's mother is keen, as it's organised by the *Killinghome Koncert Krowd*, who are flyers from the RNAS base at Killinghome. There's a rather unusual auction, too."

"I'm intrigued, perhaps I'll…" Emily stopped as she heard the front door being opened.

"It's Alice." her mother said. "She's been to her sister's and done some errands as well."

"Do you mind if I go and say hello?"

"No, you go, dear. I've things to do here."

Emily rose and went into the hall.

"Let me help you with those, Alice."

"Miss Emily!" Alice put her bags down and opened her arms wide. "Come here, that's if you're not too old for a hug?"

Emily stepped forward and found herself engulfed.

"You weren't expected until later," Alice said, finally letting Emily go. "But now you're living all grown up and independent in London, I suppose we shouldn't know what to expect." She gave Emily a beaming smile. "Can you help me with these bags? My arms are dropping off. You can come and sit in the kitchen whilst I make a cup of tea. What about your mother?"

"She'll be fine." Emily picked up the bags and followed Alice into the kitchen "How is your sister's family, Alice?"

"They're not complaining, apart from my eldest nephew, the one who's a prisoner like your Robert. You can't be sure from his letters, what with the censors, and he's not a great one for letters anyway, but I think he's not having it easy. Do you want a cup of tea?" Emily nodded. "They work them hard. From hints he's dropped, he's in a coal mine, and there's only straw pallets to sleep on. My sister sends parcels when she can, and Reckitts have been so helpful. It's been two and a half years now, so he's used to it. He was shifted east... here you are, dear... and it's been much colder this winter."

Emily felt guilty. As an officer, Robert didn't work and had much better conditions.

"But what about you, Emily? I shouldn't prattle on. How are you? You haven't forgotten us all? And what about London? And the hospital? Have you made friends?"

She thought of Fish. She'd be leaving now for Kent to stay with her aunt and uncle.

"I've never been to London," Alice continued, "but you never know, I might get a call from the King. Though your mother's been worried sick whenever there's news of an air raid. It must be..."

"Alice! Alice! Stop! There's plenty of time. I'm not going back tomorrow morning!"

"I'm sorry, Emily. We've all missed you, that's all."

"I know." She reached across the kitchen table and squeezed Alice's hand. "How have my parents been?"

"Your mother's perked up with your brother improving. She wants him better, but she doesn't want him returning to France. From what she says, though, they aren't sure if he'll ever be normal again. Still, whatever he's like, it's better than all those months when he didn't speak. They ought to send him home. A bit of home cooking and proper attention is what he needs."

There was a tap at the back door. Alice stood up, and went across and opened it.

"Your spring greens, Alice, and some leeks too... Is that Miss Emily?"

"Yes it is, and don't you be bringing your muddy boots in my kitchen, Fred Barber."

"Don't fret. I've known you long enough to know where my boots aren't wanted. You all right, Miss? You're looking well."

"Thank you, Mr Barber. I'm afraid it's a bit late to help you in the garden."

"Never mind, Miss. I needed to see how much manure to order. Prices are ridiculous. Four and sixpence for a quarter hundredweight bag from Spencers. But I've decided to give this Govo special potash potato manure a try as..."

"Fred Barber, I thought I was bad enough. Miss Emily doesn't want to hear you rabbiting on about that. And letting all that cold air in."

"True. I'll be here Monday afternoon, Miss, if you want to give me a hand." He laughed. "Though I dug the last parsnips the other week and I won't be sowing any new till next month, ground's too cold."

Emily laughed too. "I am bereft, Mr Barber. I bet the soil can't wait to be warm enough. Yes, we'll have a proper chat next week."

"Right, Miss. Very good. I'll look forward to it. Enjoy your tea." He doffed his cap and shut the door.

"Where was I?" said Alice, sitting down.

"You were telling me how my parents are."

"Yes. Your mother keeps herself busy with her volunteering, and she's so pleased you're back. She just wishes..."

"That I were back for good. I know. And my father?"

"Your father? Mr Walker is as he always is. Goes on about things that are a bit above my head, but as long as he's got someone prepared to listen to him, he's happy." She smiled, then looked concerned. "He's taken some aspects of your brother's condition even harder than your mother. A regular injury would have been far easier. Even something serious, I suspect, but you'll have to judge for yourself. He's due back about six, as dinner is at seven. And thinking of food, there's all next week's changes to worry about."

"The ration cards? We've had them two weeks, but at the hospital we haven't noticed much change. I heard you could buy forgeries in Bermondsey at sixpence a time, and one woman got two months for having one for a fictitious member of her family. I hope you've not invented a whole household here, Alice."

"As if I would! I dropped our counterfoils off earlier, so we get served after the weekend. Your mother said there's a meeting tomorrow at the Queens Hall explaining everything, but if I'm honest," she shook her head. "I don't think I'll go. If rationing does shorten the queues, I won't complain. Twenty-five minutes I stood for the bit of beef I've got for Sunday."

Emily thought to herself that Alice enjoyed standing in a queue and then grumbling to her neighbours about standing in a queue!

"The butcher reckoned the beef would need fourteen coupons after Monday." She sighed. "One and threepence of meat each a week! And how we're to manage on five ounces of butter or marg, I don't know, but we'll just have to, I suppose. So you'd better make the most of the beef. And no complaining about my Yorkshires."

"Why would I do that?"

"I don't care what Hawleys claim. Their Yorkshire Pudding powder is not the same as the real thing. I've told your mother that, and as to it being as nourishing as meat... ridiculous! But I might get hold of some eggs. Since Christmas it's been almost..."

"Alice, you are so funny. Don't worry, your Yorkshire puddings will be wonderful. One of the things I've been looking forward to most is your home cooking. My stomach's been rumbling in anticipation since we left Kings Cross. Aunt Eleanor was complimenting your cooking in one of her letters recently."

Alice gave Emily a beaming smile. "I bumped into your aunt earlier, coming out of this new café that's opening on Princes Avenue on Monday. Pleased with herself, she was. She might take you to it. On the corner of Welbeck Street. A community café and canteen, whatever one of those is, but she says it's the first in the country. There's going to be more across the city. But it's not charity. The local Food Control Committee insisted on that. Your aunt said it meant people could get a hot meal without the necessity of lighting a fire, and prejudice was not to stand in the way of its success. She showed me Tuesday's menu. A three-course meal for sixpence. Half a pint of Brown Windsor soup, savoury rissoles, rice pudding, all tuppence each. Wednesday's Shepherds Pie is threepence though. She's expecting most to take their food home as there's only room in there for twelve to sit down. And you take your own plates."

"It sounds an excellent idea. You should suggest some recipes."

"Perhaps. All very charitable, I'm sure. Can you pass me that pudding bowl? And the flour."

Emily stood up and fetched them.

"The butcher had some suet and a few bacon bits," continued Alice. She stood up and moved to the sink. "But I'd better wash and chop these leeks first. You can always have a try at making the suet pastry, Emily."

"I want to enjoy my first meal home, not ruin it, Alice, so if you don't mind, I'll let you get on." She paused by the door. "I was meaning to go next door, so I'll tell you all about London later... The streets..."

"The streets?"

"They're all paved with gold," she laughed.

"Get away with you, Emily. You must think I'm as daft as a brush, but I'll look forward to hearing what it's like later. And it is lovely to have you home."

#

Fish drew in her breath. It was a quite breathtaking sight. Her uncle's house outside Sheerness was isolated, and on moonless nights everything was pitch black. But tonight what should be invisible was visible: silhouettes of trees, hedgerows, outbuildings, even some animals in the fields. If London's buildings, miles away along the Thames estuary, had only been high enough, she felt she'd have seen them too.

It was the view northwards, however, that was astonishing. Streaks of high hanging cloud were reflecting a great red fire that appeared to be raging over Essex. Fish realised slowly that this was an illusion – what she was witnessing was neither fire nor cloud, but a rare appearance of the Aurora Borealis. Over the sea, bands of red and white light, brighter than a full moon, shone and rippled elusively. Even the brightest stars were barely perceptible against the ghostly, pearly light.

She lost track of time, following the ever-changing movements in the sky, until she was shocked out of her reverie by bright shafts of white light. Fish was mystified. They couldn't be searchlights – everyone knew that aircraft only came attended by the moon, and there wasn't one tonight – yet the unmistakeable sounds of a distant deep rolling barrage of anti-aircraft guns soon convinced her otherwise. An air raid must be in progress. What must Londoners be feeling? They would have anticipated a safe and undisturbed night's sleep, but now they were threatened by German bombers navigating in the dark of the moon. Fish was shocked, but at the same time mesmerised, by the spectacular combination of natural and man-made celestial light shows.

"Dora," called her uncle, "it's well gone eleven. Shouldn't you be coming in now? You'll catch your death out there."

To her left, sporadic flashes mingled with the roaming lights seeking out the raiders. Over there, in reality, people would be catching their deaths. "A couple of minutes," she replied. "You should come and look. I've never seen anything like this before. The colours are incredible." She pulled her jacket around her, before saying to herself, "Can you see it too, Mouldiwarp?"

#

Emily stretched, yawned and looked at the time... gone twenty past and she'd meant to have an early night. How had the last hour passed? She knew very well where it had gone. She'd only got *Castle Blair* out as she'd promised to lend it to Fish on her return, but then hadn't been able to resist opening it. She ought to get to sleep. She put the book down on her bed-side table – but instead of turning her light out, she picked up two of the items that Robert's mother had given her earlier.

#

"Come in Emily. I'm so pleased you've popped in."

Emily followed Robert's mother into her drawing room.

"A letter arrived on Tuesday and Robert says there are two on their way to you." She smiled. "Why he writes more to you than us I can't imag-ine! And yours, presumably, are also long lists of things he wants us to send him, with an occasional snippet of news thrown in as an afterthought!" She laughed. "But I shouldn't tease you. Have you heard recently?"

"Not for a week or so. It's so erratic; letters arriving out of sequence or not at all. What did he have to say?"

"He's been playing hockey on ice using walking sticks. They piled up the snow in a courtyard in a rectangle and then flooded the ground inside it to make a rink."

"They've had a good deal of snow." Emily said. "And I'm not surprised about the hockey. He said some officers tried cross-country skiing. It's hard to believe that they can give them parole and allow them to wander round outside the camp. Their problem always seems to be occupying themselves and filling up their days."

Robert's mother walked across to the bureau. "This arrived after his other things. I wanted to check with Robert as I wasn't sure if I should give it to you now or hang on to it until this dreadful war is over – if it ever is."

Emily had heard this view expressed increasingly often from the grow-ing bands of the war-weary.

"And now I have Robert's reply." She handed Emily a small metal box. "He arranged for this to be made for you, but he was shot down before it was finished. Luckily, someone else from the 56th went into the shop for something similar, and the chap mentioned Robert's box... anyway, eventu-ally, here it is."

"It's beautiful." Emily ran her finger along the intricately engraved E on its lid.

"It's from a propeller... a German one. And there are a couple of other things you should have. These. Don't worry," Robert's mother gave an embarrassed laugh, "I haven't read any of them. If you hadn't been in London, I would have given them to you sooner."

"Don't worry, Mrs Buckley. I don't mind."

"He also said you were to have this, but it is the oddest thing." She handed Emily an envelope. "The letter's in German and there's a photograph inside too. How he got it and why he's kept it, I have no idea."

#

"And a letter from a German?" Emily's father said. "Have to ask him, I suppose." He returned his attention to his meal. "Alice has done us proud. This pudding is delicious. Can you pass me the potatoes, Clara?" Her father had been jovial since getting home and seemed genuinely pleased to see Emily, but he'd had other good news too.

"I have been chosen to take over the Chair," he announced. "I shall be installed at the next meeting of the Lodge."

Emily had always had a vague, rather confused view of what her father did when he went to his lodge meetings. She knew they met in the upper room of the Kingston New Inn in Hopwood Street, because Mr Barber had once mentioned seeing her father coming out from there. Her mother had never been forthcoming about what he did there, so Emily had turned to Aunt Eleanor. She had been disparaging.

"It's nowhere near as exciting or exotic as it sounds, Emily, the United Ancient Order of Druids. Your father does not rise before dawn on the summer solstice, paint himself with woad and cavort semi-naked around some pagan stones. A rather disturbing thought, I know." She'd smiled at Emily. "But no, it's a Friendly Society where he and other similar upholders of high moral propriety meet to their mutual advantage. They've even started one exclusively for women, but I've never been tempted. Your father sees himself as a pillar of the local community and hopes one day to sit in the Arch-Druid's Chair as recognition of that fact." As a result, Emily now understood why her father was in such a good mood.

"Congratulations, dear," her mother said. "I'm very pleased for you. Emily, could you eat any more?"

"Just a small piece, please."

"It does bring responsibility with it as well as influence, so I worry whether we should still be meeting in a public house. Not sure that Lieutenant Colonel Bullock would approve."

"Colonel Bullock, dear?"

"He's holding a meeting next week about the Wartime Prohibition Campaign at the Thornton Hall. He wants us to become the first city to hold a vote on prohibition. I'm sure he might be interested in my views, as he thinks along the same lines that I do about the scandal of turning food-stuffs into intoxicants in our current situation. I'm not sure what he'd think about our Lodge meeting above a public house."

"You'd have to find somewhere else anyway, wouldn't you, Alfred, if he's successful and all the public houses have to close? Why don't you wait and see?"

"Perhaps you're right, Clara. Wait and see."

"Emily, did I tell you Hammonds are advertising a beautiful display of curtains and window draperies? I thought you might help me…"

"Tramway conductresses, Emily."

Emily looked at her father.

"Your mother won't mind waiting a second, before she elicits your opinion on how to boost Hammonds' profit margins, will you, Clara? One of your mother's great virtues is that she is not like her sister, who, amongst her other eccentricities, has a large amount of material that she has bought because she believes it might just come in useful one day. My heart there-fore does not sink when she mentions new curtains, as she's bound to be sensible and frugal in her choice. Now, what did I want to ask you? Yes, London tramway conductresses."

Why would he want to talk about them, thought Emily?

"Perhaps you can enlighten me? One moment I'm reading about how their sangfroid is an excellent tonic during air raids, singing and joking whilst shrapnel's falling around them in showers, and the next I read that they're making outrageous demands."

"The threatened strike?"

"Exactly. As a resident, albeit only a temporary one, you must have an opinion."

Emily thought for a moment. "If you're replacing a man, doing his job, then being paid the same plus an extra pound a week over pre-war rates, doesn't seem unreasonable to me."

"So they're not holding Londoners to ransom in a time of national emergency?" He smiled at her. Emily hoped his mood of general bonhomie would last the whole of her stay.

"No. I don't think we should use the war as an excuse to deny people fairness. Isn't that what we are fighting against? And after travelling on tramcars I think people recognise their worth. So no, Father, I think their demands are reasonable."

"You may have a point, and thankfully there's been no threat to public transport here. I have myself been involved in an interesting correspondence about some of our conductresses." Emily looked at her mother, who raised her eyebrows. "Where will it all end? You'll be telling me next that all women should be paid the same as men, and down that road lies economic ruination for the country." He laid down his knife and fork. "Thank you, Emily. I realise your mother wishes to ask your advice on curtains, so rather than intrude on that, may I take a closer look at the box Robert sent you?"

#

Emily placed the letter back inside the box. If only the letter had been in French, she might have understood it. Aunt Eleanor's knowledge of German should mean that the letter's contents could be revealed. She yawned again and turned off her light. She lay down and closed her eyes, but couldn't help speculating on how the letter had come into Robert's possession. Why had he kept it? The girl's face in the photograph faded in and out of her consciousness as she drifted off to sleep.

March 15th, 1918
Westbourne Avenue

Dear Fish,

Thanks for forwarding Robert's letter and for yours too. The Northern Lights sounded magical. And no, I did not see them. I am jealous! Father said it was cloudy, so I wouldn't have seen anything anyway

I was relieved you weren't in London. It is worrying if they can raid us at any time of the month. A Zepp was here on Tuesday night but didn't amount to much. It's easier finding out about London raids in the papers than anything that happens here. Those poor people in Maida Vale! My parents were upset because Mrs. Lena Guilbert Ford, who wrote their favourite song, 'Keep the Home Fires Burning', was amongst the victims.

You asked if I was doing anything exciting. I am not sure if this counts as exciting but yesterday I almost became the proud owner of a duck and a rabbit! To my mother's horror, I bid for them in an auction – but sadly

I was unsuccessful, and neither Daisy the Famous Killingholme Duck nor Billy the French Rabbit will be making your acquaintance. You will be devastated! The auction was in aid of the Royal Naval Air Service. There were lots of other things going on too. Mother loved the excerpts from 'Fringes of the Fleet.' Do you know it? It's Elgar's setting of Kipling's poems to music. Do you remember seeing 'The Better 'Ole' at the Oxford? It's been adapted by Killingholme Squadron's Wing Commander and renamed 'Shell Shocks'. He could act as well as write, which was a surprise! The auction was the real highlight of the afternoon, though. If only Billy the French Rabbit could have talked, rather than merely twitching his nose and whiskers, then he would have told a poignant tale. He was the sole survivor of a warren devastated by German shelling of a French town, who was then found by an RNAS officer, fed on warm milk from a fountain pen and flown to safety in Angleterre away from the horrid Hun. The bidding was highly competitive, but thankfully both Billy and Daisy the Duck are now heading for new careers as mascots at other airfields and not as roasts or casserole in an oven.

Mother is obsessed with getting supplies of woollen underwear. I had to trail round town for ages with her. She wants me to look in London. Did you know the amount of actual wool is down to only fifteen to thirty per cent? No, neither did I, but it's something else to blame the Kaiser for.

Father has been remarkably even-tempered recently. I might be unduly optimistic but he seems to be treating me more as an adult. I hope being reasonable does not prove too much of a strain for him! We have endured occasional denunciations of some of his pet hates but perhaps I'm growing up (a bit!?!) and am able to tolerate them more. His relationship with my aunt is still unpredictable, but he no longer threatens me with not seeing her.

I have been up to see my old colleagues at Brooklands. It felt strange going back. They had a few neurasthenia cases there, though I don't think that they were as severe as David's. Mother says he is making slow progress. I wish I could get up to Edinburgh to see him.

Brooklands said they were happy for me to return, but don't worry, the myriad attractions of Byculla and the metropolis – and its victorious conductresses, no less! – will draw me back to London. There's talk of having to apply for a warrant for rail journeys. It's a good job I have next week's return ticket, so I shouldn't have any problem and will soon be back. How are you managing without me?

The
Mouldiwarp
made a little run
and a little jump
and Elfrida caught it.

P.S. I am unsure about your advance warning of smallpox vaccinations. I had the most dreadful boils last time I had it done.

P.P.S. I almost forgot. Robert's mother gave me something really interesting. I can't wait to show you!

March 23rd, 1918
Wood Green Empire Theatre

"I'm amazed you managed to get such good seats," said Emily, swivelling round and pointing upwards. "I was expecting us to be up in the Gods, rather than on the front row."

Fish nodded in agreement. "Connections, Mouldiwarp, connections. Or rather, my uncle's connections. It is rather fine, isn't it?"

Emily looked up at the proscenium. 'All The World's A Stage' stood out in gold leaf on the fine white plaster, with the deepest of red curtains fringed with gold hanging below. The whole theatre was impressive. The creams, the whites, the plush reds reminded her of the style of the Grand and the Palace at home, but this was far more opulent, and altogether newer and shinier. She studied her programme: 'Chung Ling Soo, The World's Greatest Magician, in a Performance of Oriental Splendour and Weird Mysticism, assisted by Miss Suee Seen, presenting in rapid succession the most Beautiful, Baffling and Interesting Series of Illusions ever submitted to the Public'.

"He was amazing in Bristol, so I hope he'll be as good tonight and you won't be disappointed," Fish said. "There's no guarantee he'll do *The Trick*, however. We'll just have to wait and see if his assistant announces it. He's never spoken a single word of English in all his years on stage, you know. Look! It's starting!"

It was nine o'clock exactly as the lights dimmed and the musical director of the Wood Green Empire signalled to his musicians in the orchestra pit to break into an overture of oriental melodies in honour of the star of the show. As the music faded away, the curtain rose on Tom Keno, the 'Pattering Comedian', and the first of five supporting artistes, to be enjoyed or endured according to taste. Emily thought that Ruby Roya, 'The Radiant Revue Girl', sounded the most promising.

By the time Will H. Fox finished his last comic monologue, rose from his piano, bowed and strode to the wings, Emily felt a palpable air of tension around her. "At last," she whispered to Fish as the front curtain fell. "I can't wait!"

The resounding sound of a gong reverberated through the theatre, and the curtain rose on an exquisite blue and white silken Willow Pattern backdrop. This opened to unveil a line of bowing Chinese. Behind them opened a succession of pagoda-like curtains, each revealing a new blue and white scene. It was as if the Willow Pattern were coming to life. Finally one last tent was left in the middle of the stage. With the kettledrums reaching a crescendo, this lifted to reveal a tall, handsome Oriental man in gold embroidered silk robe and rounded mandarin hat: Chung Ling Soo. He stepped forward, bowed, removed his hat and robe with a flourish, and stood there in silk trousers and tunic. He was almost bald, except for a long black braided length of hair at the back of his head. He was so close that Emily could see even the smallest change of expression. She looked at Fish and smiled; if his performance were to be as spectacular as his entrance, they were in for a treat.

Chung began simply: paper was torn into pieces then blown on to reform itself, a vase of ink was transformed into water, a coloured handkerchief disappeared from one side of the stage and reappeared on the other.

His chief assistant Kametaro made occasional announcements, reminding the audience that Chung Ling Soo never spoke English. Emily felt a nudge in her ribs. "Told you so," Fish whispered. Emily felt Chung hardly needed to speak, as each illusion was communicated by his lithe, almost mystical, movements. Each new trick was more amazing than the last. How had five large cases each with a bottle of stout inside, changed into one large bottle from which Chung's wife, Suee Seen, had emerged? It was impossible, yet she had seen it happen.

When Suee Seen shrieked as an arrow attached to a white rope was fired through her body to hit a bullseye behind her, Emily and Fish's own screams of surprise had been joined by hundreds of others. Chung led his wife to the front of the stage. Emily could see the rope went through her body. Chung tugged at the rope and it fell free. Emily turned to Fish and mouthed "How?" before joining in with the rapturous applause.

She had scarcely caught her breath before Suee Seen was transformed into a large orange tree. Moments later Emily had caught one of the oranges being flung into the audience. "Look!" said Fish. People further back in the audience were applauding because Suee Seen had materialised in the centre aisle. Emily was spellbound.

After Chung had performed the ever-popular Chinese Ring Trick, the stage was covered by a large silk curtain with an Imperial Chinese dragon embroidered on it.

"It's beautiful, isn't it?" Fish whispered, "That gold and green dragon!"

The atmosphere changed as a slow and menacing beat came from the orchestra pit, intensifying as drums and chimes from behind the curtain joined in.

"I think he's going to do *The Trick*," said Fish.

The curtain lifted to reveal a group of marching Chinese soldiers, the lights reflecting off their polished armour. Each struck a drum in time to the music and two carried long rifles. The soldiers parted into two lines to reveal bearers carrying a palanquin from which Chung, now in elaborate robes, emerged. Emily looked at his face. It was stony and impassive, as if he were a thousand miles away.

"Ladies and Gentlemen, if you please." declared Kametaro. "Chung Ling Soo now demonstrates how he was condemned by the Boxers during the rebellion, to be executed by firing squad! How he defied their bullets! And again, tonight, on our stage, just as in Peking many years ago!" Emily found that she was gripping Fish's hand. "Two gentlemen on stage, please. Two men who know something of guns, who have loaded bullets. Do we have any British soldiers in our audience? Any brave young men who know their guns, please? Surely you would be willing to step up here, on behalf of the audience?"

After some prompting from the girl sitting next to Fish, a soldier two seats away rose and made his way onto the stage, where he stood with a second man, looking rather sheepish in the spotlights. They examined the rifles, peered down the barrels, tested the triggers, before agreeing that yes, they were the genuine article. The girl next to Fish leant across and said, "I'm glad he didn't have to face the Hun with those. They look like a pair Noah took with him on his Ark." Each soldier then chose a large marble-sized bullet from a box and held it up before dropping it into a metal cup. "Could two gentlemen in our audience mark them?" Kametaro continued. Suee Seen descended from the stage and found two men to score lines into the soft lead with a knife. Some powder was scattered onto a small tray. "Real gunpowder? Is it real?" Kametaro asked. One of the soldiers smelt it and agreed it was real. Kametaro carried the tray forward and touched a lighted match to it. With a white flash and puff of smoke the powder exploded. "Yes, real powder." He poured a charge into each rifle and each soldier supervised as wadding was then tamped down with a ramrod. Suee Seen returned to the stage and both soldiers took a bullet, examined the marks and inserted them into each rifle barrel. Another cotton wad was rammed into place, and the young soldiers were escorted to the side of the stage.

"Ladies and Gentlemen, silence please! Silence for Chung Ling Soo," Kametaro intoned. "Two bullets! You have seen the bullets were marked. And you have seen the guns loaded. Now... silence! And watch closely. Watch, everyone!" Emily did not need telling. Her eyes were fixed on Chung Ling Soo as he moved to the right of the stage some distance in front of the curtain. He clasped a porcelain plate between his hands.

"It's what he catches the bullets in," Fish whispered. Emily glanced at the other side of the stage, where a firing squad of Chinese riflemen crouched before raising the rifles to their shoulders. Kametaro stood, sword raised, waiting for a signal to let it drop.

Chung Ling Soo took a deep breath, held the plate in front of his chest, breathed in again and nodded. Emily realised the muffled drumbeats which had been continuing in the background had ceased. For a few seconds there was absolute silence in the theatre. She held her breath. Kametaro lowered his sword. There was a violent crack from the rifles. The sound was still echoing around the auditorium as Chung Ling Soo staggered and twisted to his right, arching his shoulders as he did so. There was a crash as the plate he'd been holding smashed on the floor. His assistants, thunderstruck, remained rooted to the spot. Emily heard the stricken magician call out in perfect English, "Oh my God! Something's happened! Lower the curtain".

Emily turned to Fish. "Did you hear?"

"Yes, but look!"

As his knees began to buckle, Chung Ling Soo stumbled backwards and was caught by a technician, who lowered him to the stage. Emily realised that she and Fish, like many others, were now standing up. They had an unimpeded view of the horrors on stage. Chung Ling Soo's eyes were wide open, but his mouth was twisting in pain. The front of his robe was discoloured by a spreading dark stain. The paralysis that had gripped the other performers was released. Suee Seen ran on and crouched at his side, others rushed to lean over the broken figure. Confused shouting came from behind the curtain and moments later the white Bioscope screen descended to obscure the tragic tableaux.

Emily and Fish looked at each other in horror. Emily turned and surveyed the rest of the audience, where a shocked silence had given way to a cacophony of horrified speculation. A few people made for the exits, but most seemed unsure what to do. The projectionist must have been given a signal, as a War Office newsreel flickered into life on the large screen. From force of habit they sat back down to watch the film of soldiers somewhere in France.

"Fish... have you ever seen anyone shot before?" Emily said.

"No, never. I've seen the results many times, just like you, but no, never. And so close. What do you think happened?"

"Your guess is as good as mine, Fish. That poor man! A ghastly accident? Looking at him, I wouldn't say there was much hope."

Fish shook her head. "What did you make of what he said?"

"It's not so much what he said, but the fact that he spoke in English. It was so distinct, though I doubt if anyone beyond the third or fourth rows heard him." A few people passed in front of them. "Do you want to leave, Fish?"

"I'd be happy to just sit here for a while," Fish said.

"Me too." Emily still felt shocked. She looked up at the screen. "When death touches us..." She stopped, unsure whether to continue or not.

"Go on, Mouldiwarp."

Emily pointed at the newsreel. "It's as if death happens there. Set foot there and all the colours drain away. You end up marooned, living and dying in a silent, jerky, black and white world." Emily knew the tragedy she'd just witnessed was affecting her. She felt strange, odd. "It's an unreal world, but at the same time it's not, it's all too real." She paused. "I'm sorry, Fish. I know I'm not making much sense, and you've lost much more than me, so tell me to shut up if you want. Tonight the magician was shot in a world of noise and vibrant colour, but he'll be just as dead as many of those up there will be... dead in both worlds." She rubbed her brow. "Please don't look so worried, Fish. I'm okay."

"Are you sure?... I think I know what you're trying to say."

"If they could film in colour or you could hear? Would that change the way we see things? Would it affect us differently if that happened?"

"Tragedies affect us all in different ways," said Fish. "I know it's impossible to change it." She sighed. "It doesn't stop me from thinking... that only if I want it enough, want it not to have happened... so, so much... then perhaps it won't have happened. Ludicrous, but sometimes things just go round and round and round in your head. It's ridiculous, you end up blaming yourself for not changing something that's impossible to change." She shook her head. "And I brought you here tonight to escape into a pleasant world of illusion!"

"It's not your fault." Emily reached across to her friend and held her hand.

"Look, Fish." A group of Tommies on the screen were smiling and waving at the camera. "Do you ever think that's as much an illusion as earlier? Did I ever tell you that a couple of years ago a friend spotted someone up there whom she knew from the East Yorkshires? They were all laughing and smiling, waving as they marched along, just like them. 'Off to the Front' or 'Going up the Line', I think the caption said. A few months later, she met him when he was back home for a week, and said how surprised she'd been at how cheerful they'd looked, going off to fight. He told her the reason they were all so happy was they were filmed after they'd just left some bloody awful miserable hell-hole behind them and were setting off on leave. It was a distortion, perhaps a deliberate lie." She shrugged. "Since then I've been less sure about where to draw the line between reality and fiction. Here or..." The newsreel suddenly ceased. "I was going to say there." The first few bars of 'God Save the King' drifted out of the orchestra pit. Fish and Emily came somewhat hesitantly to their feet. As the anthem's last notes died away, the pointlessness of staying any longer became apparent, and they joined the general move for the exits.

As they crossed the foyer, Emily saw she was still clutching the orange that she'd caught earlier. For the first time she noticed the small red label tied to its stem. "Come on, we might just catch the ten past bus," she heard Fish say. She looked more closely; on the label was a portrait of Chung Ling Soo, the Marvellous Chinese Conjurer. She took a deep breath, and followed Fish out through the doors and into the cool of the night.

April 3rd, 1918
Trier

"You are doubtless wondering, gentlemen, why we are meeting like this on this dismal morning," the Kommandant announced.

Robert turned, and with a sense of foreboding glanced at Stan. They'd spent the last twenty minutes, standing in the cold, speculating about the reason for this special *Appel*.

"We all have other things we wish to do. I don't expect your sympathy if I tell you about the amount of paperwork sitting on my desk, but as you say... needs must. So!" He surveyed the ranks of British officers. "We could be here to celebrate the rapid advances the Imperial German Forces are making on the western front since *Die Kaiserschlact* was launched. You may look sceptical, but I assure you that your allied Armies, if not your Navy, are being pushed back at," he paused and smiled, recollecting a phrase from his long years in England, "at a rapid rate of knots. But it is not this remarkable progress that requires your attendance. No! It appears that some of you gentlemen are determined to depart... and leave some of you will, but not in the way you intended." He paused whilst a guard came and spoke to him. "I apologise, gentlemen. I should have told you that a search is being conducted in your quarters. It appears that some of you are dissatisfied with your beds. We have made them too comfortable. If there were too many wooden supports, why did you not ask for these to be removed?" He waited whilst his meaning sunk in.

"Which is worse, gentlemen? Having victory snatched from your grasp as you're about to cross the finishing line, or being told before you are under starter's orders that you are not to take part in the race? I think the latter is the easier to bear. I do not know when the starter was firing his gun, but the length of the course will shortly become clear. If it is five metres between the two fences," Robert could not resist a look, "and more than thirty from the nearest hut, and the stick that miraculously appeared poking up and down yesterday afternoon was some fifteen metres beyond the outer fence and perhaps five from the cover of the bushes, that suggests a minimum of fifty to sixty metres. Yes, gentlemen, it is easy for you to underestimate us. Some of us may be past serving at the front, but we can still be alert and have good eyesight. I may be wrong; perhaps the stick was being waved by..." he thought, "the English escapes me, *ein Maulwurf*... the little gentleman in the shiny black waistcoat, but that seems unlikely. If it is of any consolation, we have had our suspicions for some time. It is difficult to dispose of the products of your labours without leaving tell-tale signs. If it had been a French tunnel, I would have let events take their course, catching the escapees in the act... with the accompanying risk of casualties."

Robert tried to think. He was confident the smuggled contraband – the miniature compass, the map of the Dutch border, the rail timetables – were well hidden, but he had doubts about the civilian clothes. He felt dejected. Months of hard labour, under suffocating conditions, wasted, with only ten days before the planned break-out. They hadn't had any choice about pushing the rod up through the ceiling of the tunnel. It was a risk, but they had had to know how much further to dig. Robert had been sent out to wander near the fence and when he'd spotted it, his signal had been relayed back to the tunnellers. He had been shocked at how much they had veered off line.

Stan, next to him, sighed. Perhaps one of the guards they had bribed had let something slip. They were to have been the fourth pair out, and rather than lying low by day and travelling overnight as most others planned, they'd hoped to use Stan's German for a hundred-mile dash by train for neutral Holland. It was all academic. They had been discovered.

"As you are aware, attempting to escape is a crime under German law and where there is crime, there is punishment. I have to report your actions to my superiors, but my hands are not completely tied. I could be petty and stop various activities in the camp: your theatre, your showers and so on. I am reluctant to do this, and not only because I enjoy your dramatic productions. Your ingenuity in producing your leading ladies is quite remarkable, as are the make-up and the costumes. These skills do have other applications. Perhaps someone planned to reach the Netherlands dressed as a pantomime dame. Despite that risk, it is better that you are occupied... though patently not by exploring under the camp. In normal circumstances, escapees, after a period of solitary confinement, are sent elsewhere. Most of you know that I spent many years in England, and I was struck by your sense of fair play. Therefore, I give you a choice. If, let us say, a dozen of you were attempting to escape, then I can choose a dozen at random to transfer eastwards – or a dozen of you can volunteer. If your commanding officer gives me his word of honour that the number was less, I will even accept that. For anyone who is bored and desperate for a change of scene, I would stress that conditions in your new camp will be considerably harsher than your current surroundings. So, gentlemen, there you are. If you wouldn't mind waiting a little longer, then you will be dismissed and allowed to return to your quarters." He started to turn away, then stopped. "I would never, unlike some Kommandants, be rash enough to claim my camp is escape-proof. If I did that," he laughed, "I risk egg-on-my-face when someone sends me a postcard of windmills in Amsterdam. Good day, gentlemen."

May 9th, 1918
Byculla Hospital

Dear Aunt,

Thank you for the cuttings. I have not read them all yet, as these last couple of weeks have been so busy. I spent some time at Endell Street, and it's been work, sleep, work, sleep. Eat should be in there somewhere. There have been gaps, but it's all a bit of a blur. I have been dog-tired much of the time.

If our experience is anything to go by, the number of patients returning from France has increased. The crowds outside Waterloo and Charing Cross are as big as ever. The arrivals' stories share a common theme – pushed back for days over miles of territory laboriously gained over the whole war. One officer was in Paris when shells landed from that giant gun that can fire them seventy-five miles! He said it was most disconcerting for explosions to occur out of thin air.

I have managed one excursion since Wood Green, and again it was
thanks to Fish's family's theatrical connections. She was looking through
her uncle's copy of Kinematograph and Lantern Weekly when she spotted
the advertisement. Fish can be very persuasive. We attended a Private Trade
Screening of 'The Better 'Ole' at the Alhambra in Leicester Square! So I
am writing as a member of the Fourth Estate – well, not quite – I sat next
to a gentleman from the Evening News, so I bought the next day's copy
where he declared it 'the finest British picture ever produced'. And there
were 'many distinguished personages' there, but unless he meant Fish and
me I did not spot any. It was a jolly affair! The front stalls were filled with
Guardsmen, and as they took their seats the orchestra gave a stirring performance of Tipperary. I enjoyed the film, though I am not sure that you
would have been convinced by the final scene. Three Tommies march down
a country lane off to France and, cresting a hill, they disappear from sight
without a single glance back. Carry on regardless seemed to be the message. I read what you sent about conscription in Ireland, and this Countess
Markiewicz sounds an interesting person, but I'm not as sympathetic to her
views as you are. Did you meet her in your suffrage days?

The Nevinson exhibition has caused a furore so why am I unsurprised
you wish to go? Fish knew the quotation 'The paths of glory lead but to
the grave', but then she is keen on Gray. She wondered whether the painting was a lament for the dead rather than an attack on the war? If you are
here, and either of us have time, then we will go with you. Fish would like
to meet you again, though if I am as careless as I was the other evening then
neither of us will make it. I set alight some cotton wool we were warming
over a gas fire! Thank goodness we didn't need gas masks. Do you remember at Brooklands when the ovens caught fire and I had to put mine on?
How very stupid to go through all these years of war and then be burnt to a
cinder through my own folly.

Some patients talk about playing tennis if this weather ever ends. April
here was dull, wet and cold, though since the turn of the month we've lost
the rain. If I am unable to practice my forehand, I shall improve my bridge.
Edward said it was the ideal card game for me as a dummy was needed in
every hand, but I am finally getting a grip of it. Some officers enjoy playing
and though I haven't had much chance of late, when I did make up a four-

some you will be pleased that, with several outrageous finesses, I made four no trumps. Even Edward would have been impressed.

I was worried about Robert, as I had several letters returned last week, and have heard nothing in a while, but his mother wrote yesterday that an official notification of a camp move had arrived, so hopefully I'll hear more soon.

How is Mother? She wrote she is hopeful of good news about David. I wish he was near enough to visit. Is she losing faith in that spiritualist woman? There were hints that she might be. Do let me know of any exciting things you do or are planning, especially when it involves fleeing the provinces for the capital, even for a short while!

Your loving niece
Emily
xxx

P.S. Write even if you are leading the most monotonous of lives. I love getting your letters.

June 6th, 1918
Pearson Park

"How did you think he was?" Clara asked, sitting down on the bench next to her sister.

"Even forewarned, it was a shock," said Eleanor. "He's changed."

"I know. It's terrible. I've lost one son and now I feel I've almost lost another."

"Clara, I do understand, but he's only been back a week, so who knows? He is different, but then everyone you meet is." Eleanor sighed. "David has always reminded me of Alfred – a clear idea of where his interests lay and what he wanted to do. I could have seen him following a similar path, banking or finance, with all the advantages from Oxford? But now..."

"You can't see that now, can you?"

"I don't want to be brutal, but no, I can't. Talking to him, he's lost that air of confidence, that spark. Will he ever regain it? It's hard to imagine, after the awful experiences he's been through." She shook her head. "I wish I were being more encouraging."

"No. I don't want you to pretend just to make me feel better."

"But don't look so despairing, Clara. Think back six months."

"You're right... it was dreadful. That one visit particularly. It was Emily who got him talking again. Unintentionally, but she did. Eleanor, why am I telling you? You know all this. It's the way I've been... stupid."

"Clara, stop it. You're not being stupid. How are you meant to react?" There was a silence. Eleanor indicated the tea-room. "Shall we go in?"

Inside, Clara continued. "I was so relieved when we heard he was coming home."

"But he's not happy?"

"It's hard to understand. He barely says anything. That's why it was better your calling while I was out. I hoped he might talk to you. And then there's his classification; he's convinced he's capable of light duties in a home battalion. That's what he says he wants to do, but I can't coax him out of the house. And the weather's been so glorious. He'll sit outside in the garden, but when I suggest the park, he makes comments about being stared at and disappears up to his room instead. Is he afraid of meeting someone who'll accuse him of malingering? I'm at a loss as to what to do for the best." Clara shook her head.

Eleanor gave her sister a sympathetic smile. "Did the hospital give you any advice?"

"The hospital?" She raised her eyebrows. "They just said keep him busy, get him to talk, help him to help himself. Keeping him busy sounds fine, but it's so difficult. Perhaps I'm expecting too much too soon. You're right. It's only been a week."

"He told me a little about the hospital, Clara. It sounds a strange regime; people who hated noise given a room near the main road, those of a scholarly background not allowed in the library but having to do physical drill, and so on – but there again, he has made progress, so perhaps they know what they're doing." She took a sip of tea. "He gave me some old copies of their patients' magazine, *The Hydra*. It was sweet of him. He was quite animated when talking about the people who edited it." She picked one up, from the collection next to her. "I was reading one of them, last September's, while I was waiting. There are some powerful, affecting poems. David said a little about his nightmares and there's a line in one about seeing horrific sights... 'in all my dreams, in all my helpless sight'...It's harrowing. You should read it. I shall send a copy to Emily. It might convince some people of the sheer futility of all this."

"I will read it, Eleanor, but what's left to hold onto if it's all been futile? I don't want to sound like Alfred, but you'll be telling me next that the MP who hopes it all peters out in some inconclusive draw is talking sense."

Eleanor thought of saying that these horrors would ensure the world never embarked upon such a course again, but seeing her sister's agitation, she held her tongue. "Don't let your tea get cold, Clara. You mentioned Alfred. How does he feel about David?"

"Alfred's Alfred." She shrugged. "To be fair, he is trying. He's so certain about things, but he seems unsure of what to say to him, so he retreats into long descriptions of changes in Bank regulations or the financial imprudence of the Government. All very tedious, but there was a time when David would have been interested. They haven't had a normal conversation, not when I've been there. Alfred's even reluctant to give his opinions about the war, which..."

"Is unusual to say the least." Eleanor could not keep a hint of sarcasm out of her voice.

"And the little David has said about the war is tinged with bitterness. He won't say anything about his own experiences and Alfred doesn't want to spark off any unpleasantness. I think he wants to try and understand, but he'd also like David to explain why he's acting like that." She tried to smile at her sister. "In general, though, he's been in a sprightly mood, what with the German offensive running out of steam, and he's busy with his meetings. He's also been bucked up by the celebrations around the trial verdict in London. A vindication, he called it. A vindication!"

Eleanor rolled her eyes. Her unspoken sympathies for her sister were overwhelmed by a desire to speak her mind. "Trial! It was a sensationalist travesty... that loathsome creature Billing has got clean away with his despicable libelling of poor Maud Allan."

"Poor Maud Allan?" Clara scoffed. "Anyone who dances as lasciviously as that woman does must always be open to suspicion."

"For goodness sake, Clara, you're as prudish now as you were ten years ago."

"I take it you mean my refusal to go to her salacious performance of *Vision of Salome* with you? A farrago of obscenity, no less!"

"Oscar Wilde would find your assessment of his play somewhat overblown, Clara."

"Oscar Wilde? Eleanor, did you not hear how that degenerate was described in court?"

"As the greatest force for evil that has appeared in Europe during the last three hundred and fifty years? It makes him sound like a poisonous combination of Robespierre and Jack the Ripper. The whole thing's ridiculous!" Eleanor laughed bitterly.

"Eleanor, you must admit it was suspicious that Maud Allan was performing in private! Alfred believes that all manner of conspiracies could have been perpetrated there."

"Rubbish! Utter rubbish!" Eleanor said. "The only reason she danced in private was because of our Lord Chamberlain's outmoded diktat that public portrayals of biblical characters in plays are blasphemous. If it were in a Variety sketch it would not be! Completely unbelievable! I sometimes wonder whether we are still living in the nineteenth century. And how do you feel having evidence from a Criminal Libel case in your house?"

"You mean Alfred's copy of the *Vigilante*?"

"Yes. I've never understood the reason for the name change, as it produces the same malicious bilge whether it's the *Imperialist* or the *Vigilante*!"

"I am quite comfortable about the magazine, though I haven't read the article that's led to the trial."

"The Cult of the Clit..."

"Eleanor! We are in a tea-room. Someone might hear! Whatever you think, the Jury agreed that this Maud Allan is one of thousands of people in this Black Book who are open to blackmail, due to their lewd and unnatural behaviour. Margot Asquith..."

"Stop, Clara! Remember I loathe the woman. The idea that she, her husband and various Privy Councillors, Cabinet Ministers and members of His Majesty's Household belong to Billing's imaginary Unseen Hand conspiracy is preposterous. Who else will be revealed as plotters? Rapunzel, Rumpelstilskin or even Struwwelpeter... What?" She glared at her sister. "What's so funny? Why are you laughing?"

"I'm sorry, Eleanor. Here we are arguing and you mentioned Struwwelpeter. Don't you recall how frightened you used to be of Struwwelpeter? Shock-headed Peter? You were scared stiff! The memory of it all came back to me. You were so funny."

"I was never frightened!"

"I was there, Eleanor, and you gave a very good impression of being scared. But it did cure you of sucking your thumb. And don't deny it. Can you still remember it?"

"The story of little Suck-a-Thumb?" Eleanor nodded, and without hesitation began,

"One day Mamma said, Conrad dear,
I must go out and leave you here.
But mind now, Conrad, what I say,
Don't suck your thumb while I'm away."

She smiled at her sister. "Perhaps you can go on, Clara?"

"The great tall tailor always comes
To little boys that suck their thumbs.
And ere they dream what he's about
He takes his great sharp scissors
And cuts their thumbs clean off – and then
You know, they never grow again.

Your turn, Eleanor."

"I will be old and grey before I forget it, Clara.

Mamma had scarcely turn'd her back,

The thumb was in, alack! Alack!

And this is the chilling bit." Eleanor paused. "Yes, I admit I used to be terrified.

> The door flew open, in he ran,
> The great, long, red-legged scissorman.
> Oh! children, see! the tailor's come
> And caught our little Suck-a-Thumb.
> Snip! Snap! Snip! the scissors go;
> And Conrad cries out – Oh! Oh! Oh!
> Snip! Snap! Snip! They go so fast;
> That both his thumbs are off at last.

Last bit together, do you think, Clara?"

"Very well, little sister."

> "Mamma comes home; there Conrad stands,
> And looks quite sad, and shows his hands –
> Ah! said Mamma, I knew he'd come
> To naughty little Suck-a-Thumb."

As they finished they both burst out laughing.

"Look, you're still doing it," said Clara.

"What? I'm not sucking my thumbs. As we said, I was cured of that."

"No, look at your hands. It's what you always did when you were little."

Eleanor looked at her hands. Both thumbs were bent and tucked into her palms. She laughed again. "It was to stop the tailor getting them, wasn't it? Heinrich Hoffman should have written a cautionary tale about two sisters who argue. Losing their tongues, perhaps. And I'm sorry, I didn't mean to argue, especially with your being upset about David. I need to remember that you and Alfred just have different views on some things from me." She reached across the small table and grasped Clara's hand. "I did enjoy that, but we'd better not start on another poem, had we? We got one or two strange looks."

"True." Clara glanced around. "Edward liked those poems the most. *The Dreadful Story of Harriet and the Matches* was his favourite. I have a horrible feeling he used to frighten Emily with it. He changed it to...

> So Emily was burnt, with all her clothes,
> And arms, and hands, and eyes, and nose.

She once asked me never to buy her little scarlet shoes."

It took Eleanor a second or two to work it out.

"Ah, yes.

> And nothing else but these was found
> Among her ashes on the ground.

But what about David? Did he enjoy them?"

"He preferred the gruesome illustrations to the verse. But now," her voice dropped and shook a little, "he has his own plentiful supply of nightmare visions."

"Come on, Clara, dear," Eleanor said, standing up. "I thought you were brightening up. Let's take a stroll. It is such a beautiful day and sunshine does raise the spirits!"

Clara stood up. "Very well. We can go round the far side of the lake, but I mustn't be too long; Mrs Barber does for me on Thursdays." She sighed. "It's such a long time since Ivy left, and two afternoons a week isn't the same.

With David back now, I might see if she can manage more. Alice would find it a big help too. Did you say you are writing to Emily?"

"I was going to finish it later," agreed Eleanor.

"I don't want you to worry her, but perhaps you could hint at how difficult things are. I'd hoped she'd come home when her contract ended, but it'll be the beginning of August before she's back, as she's announced that she and a friend are going fruit picking, of all things, somewhere in the West Country."

"With her friend, Fish? I've met her. She's delightful."

"I'll take your word for it, but I'm not all together convinced that she's a good influence. Emily's becoming more and more headstrong." She gave Eleanor a pointed look. "I don't expect you to persuade her to come home, even though she takes more notice of you, but please mention it in your letter."

"I'll tell her how things are, Clara. She'll be sympathetic; it's not in her nature to be otherwise. But don't expect her to come rushing back. Give it a few weeks." Eleanor smiled at her sister. "Things may be better then." She paused. "If you need to get home, our paths divide here."

"Yes, I must. Thank you for visiting David. I do value your opinion."

"On some things," Eleanor laughed. "I was glad to, and I'll do what I can to help. Try and persuade him to come as far as me for tea. Perhaps next Wednesday, with you too? See how things go, and even if it's a struggle at times remember it might have been worse. And give my regards to Alfred... Don't look at me like that, I mean it."

"Very well, Eleanor, I shall."

Eleanor turned and walked away across the park through the summer sunshine.

July 7th, 1918
Wotton-under-Edge

Emily lay back and breathed in the heady scent of the flowers. She watched as a skylark rose into the cloudless sky above her. She shaded her eyes to follow it as it soared, its song continuing long after it had disappeared from sight.

"It's so peaceful up here. Just bees and birdsong," Emily said, as a second lark rose fifty yards away to compete with the first.

"I've been up here when there have been half-a-dozen or more," Fish replied.

Emily looked at her friend sitting a few feet away, hands clasped around her knees. "It's so beautiful up here, Fish. You're so lucky having a hill like this on your doorstep. All we've got are a few parks and everywhere is as flat as a pancake."

"You poor deprived thing, Mouldiwarp!"

"Deprived is the right word. Some of Robert's family live in Lincolnshire and always talk about their big skies, but give me mountains or hilly places like this any day."

"This has always been one of my favourite spots, especially at this time of year with so many flowers."

"I like the little bluey pin-cushioney ones."

"They're Devils-bit Scabious. The butterflies love them too."

"Yes, I've disturbed a small cloud of little blue ones with every step I've taken. You know, Edward would have loved it here. He liked anything to do with botany, butterflies, anything scientific, in fact. He was so funny at times. Father subscribes to..." she lowered her voice and said with mock seriousness, "*The Monthly Weather Report of the Meteorological Office.*" Seeing Fish's face, she threatened, "When I'm home I shall send you one! But if my father should need April 1912's to check its precipitation records, woe betide you if you've not returned it." She laughed. "Edward used to insist on reading bits out aloud. He'd always begin, in a serious voice, with "Issued by authority of the meteorological committee" and then go on to say "copious rainfall was accompanied by frequent thunderstorms" or "in the west, monthly aggregate showed a moderate excess." But what was strangest... how warm do you think it is today?"

"I don't know. Not as hot as earlier in the week. Eighty?"

"Eighty is an easy one." She thought for a moment. "Three hundred degrees. One of the few I can remember. Edward insisted on using degrees absolute. He'd say things such as there's a frost this morning, so it's only two hundred and sixty four."

"But why?"

"The Monthly Report only gave temperature readings in degrees absolute, not Fahrenheit. I haven't a clue why, but it was something that appealed to Edward. Today it must be about two hundred and ninety four." She glanced at Fish. "Are you all right? You've gone a bit pale."

"I couldn't come up here for quite a while," Fish started, before lapsing into silence.

Emily wasn't sure whether to say anything or to wait for her to continue. She pushed herself up and moved to sit closer.

"And I thought I was all right, that I'd got over it." Fish sighed. "It took me a year. It was August, two summers ago, before I could face coming up here again. When I did, I broke down like some silly schoolgirl in floods of tears. Time's meant to be a great healer but he hasn't helped a great deal yet."

Emily put her arm round her friend. "Was it my talking about Edward?"

"No, not really. We were up here on his last day of leave. Tuesday the fifteenth of June, nineteen fifteen. Two days before the Seventh Battalion sailed from Avonmouth. They landed on Gallipoli in July and by August the eighth he was..." Her voice tailed off. "Sorry. I didn't mean to get weepy."

"Don't be silly." Emily said, hugging her. "It's all right."

"You see St Mary's down there?"

Emily nodded.

"He pointed it out, looked at me and said perhaps I should practice walking down the aisle before he was here again."

"What did you say?"

"I think I just said 'Oh'. I didn't know what to say. I was a bit taken aback. I thought he might ask me, but I was still surprised when he did. And then he said how my parents were mellowing towards him now that he'd exchanged the precarious existence of an artist for his current occupation. And then he gave me this." She reached into the small knapsack she'd been carrying. Emily was expecting her to bring out a ring or locket, but instead she brought out a nine- or ten-inch long cardboard tube and handed it to Emily.

"There are two inside. I'd arranged to have them framed and then Chunuk Bair happened and I couldn't, so I put them away."

"Are you sure I should take them out?"

"Yes, go ahead. He said he'd do paintings another time, but he hoped I'd be happy with some pen and ink sketches for now."

Emily slid the drawings out of the tube.

"He said they're a pair." Fish smiled. "Fish in water and Fish out of water."

"It's where we were earlier, isn't it?" Emily said. "It's you paddling, just where the stream comes out from under the lane." She studied it. "He's caught the movement and the light reflecting on the water so well."

"I was meant to be tickling for trout, not that I've ever seen any there. For some reason he was convinced I could do it. My closest childhood friend, before we moved here, lived in a cottage with a tiny stream that ran through her garden to join a larger one. We used to feed the trout bits of bread and they became quite tame. We used to give them silly names." She smiled. "I told George, but he wouldn't believe wild trout are different. Set a Fish to catch a fish he said, but the only thing I've ever caught there are crayfish. He was hoping one would nip my toe, I'm sure."

Emily read the title. 'Stream in Coombe Valley – 12/06/1915'. She unrolled the second and held it out in front of her. "I like this even more. It's delightful. And it's only a few yards from here, isn't it? The church down in the distance. And he's captured you so well. You look vibrant, alive... Your hair's a little different."

"I had it longer then. I cut it when I started nursing."

"You ought to grow it again. It suits you. And you must have them framed. Not leave them in a cardboard tube."

"There are more. Sketches with his letters. But these two are the most precious. He'd done a painting of where we looked down on the strip lynchets earlier." Fish pointed back along the brow of the hill. "I wish I knew what happened to that," she said. "But he made a mistake on that one." She indicated the sketch Emily was holding. "Look at what he's written below."

"'Wotton Hill – 12/06/1915'. What's wrong with that?"

"This isn't Wotton Hill. That's the hill over there with the enclosed stand of trees on top. This is Coombe Hill. I always talked about going up the hill, so he'd always assumed... he had a tendency to assume things and that was the only thing that ever led to misunderstandings between us... but it's not important. And I do love the picture. And you're right. I must get them framed."

Emily gave her the sketches back and Fish rolled them up and returned them to their tube.

"The letter he sent before he sailed asked whether I'd understood him properly. He'd been worried how quiet I'd been before he left for Bristol. But that was because he was going away. I feel guilty that I wasn't more effusive." She looked at Emily. "Not something I usually have difficulty with! I wish he hadn't left it until that last afternoon. In a way that made the leaving harder."

"But he asked you again, that's the important thing."

"He signed that letter 'your private fiancé' but with a question mark. So I replied straight away and I started it 'my dearest fiancé' and added an exclamation mark. I told him if St Mary's wasn't available or if my parents hadn't mellowed, we'd elope to Gretna Green and then lead a bohemian lifestyle in some Parisian garret." She gave Emily a wistful smile. "I know he got that letter, but my last two were returned. The last thing I heard from him was one of those field postcards." She looked down the hill. "I do miss the church bells. There was a time when I would never have dreamt of saying that. The evenings they practiced used to drive me mad. On and on and on. But they'll all be extremely rusty... the bell-ringers that is."

"That's better, Fish," Emily smiled. "And with the way things are going, surely by next summer they'll be irritating you again."

"I hope you're right. I hate to say it, but we ought to be getting back. Mother said we'd eat at seven."

"It is strange!"

"What?"

"Hearing your mother call you Dora. I thought she was talking about someone else. And what she must she have thought when she got your letter saying Mouldiwarp was coming to stay?"

"She's used to it, but I think she despairs sometimes about some of my 'strange ways', as she calls them." Fish stood up and put the knapsack back on. "Come on, we'll go down through the woods and think of what we should do on Wednesday." She leant down, holding out her hand and pulled Emily up.

"Wednesday?"

"Your birthday. Don't pretend you've forgotten. We should spend some of your vast earnings. Stay at our haunted pub and see if a Roman centurion or a witch or a monk turns up to disturb us. Utter rubbish, but quite fun... I'm sorry, I forgot – doesn't your mother believe in that sort of thing?"

"As far as I know she's still seeing the medium, but don't worry, Fish, I think it's ridiculous too. And as to my birthday... the best treat would be a long soak in a hot bath. And mentioning my earnings, you have to admit I've improved."

"What, fourpence on Wednesday, sixpence on Thursday, a shilling... ow! Mouldiwarp!"

"You deserved it, Fish. Six and threepence, seven and sevenpence and a magnificent eight and elevenpence on Friday, so that's one pound two shillings and nine. And I am getting better, even if my back isn't." She rubbed it. "I hope it's raspberries, not strawberries. tomorrow."

"Beware! It could be gooseberries. Horrid prickly things. But either way you will look positively divine in that outfit of yours. The khaki breeches, the long tunic coat... the felt hat." Fish burst out laughing. "Heavenly!"

"What's wrong with the hat? I'll have you know that future generations will battle for possession of it. And I don't care, Fish, if it's only a halfpenny a pound for gooseberries. It's just such a wonderful change being here. Hopefully this weather will hold. It's a different world and a much nicer one." Emily stretched her arms above her head. "Thinking of other places, have you thought any more about the end of summer? About going back? What about the letter you had from VAD headquarters yesterday?"

"The one offering me a choice of any Military Hospital? Yours will have just been sent to your home. What do you think? Endell Street or even Byculla? Would you mind London again or would you prefer somewhere different?"

"No, London's fine, though I'm looking forward to a few weeks at home first. Mother's been desperate for me to return, and I can guarantee that she won't be keen on my going back to London. I'll doubtless be told what an invaluable help I am. How David will miss me and so on. And she's bound to mention the threat from German bombers, the Gothas and Giants. And if she'd known about my aunt's close shave... but there hasn't been a raid since Whit, so what do you think... three months up till the middle or end of November? And I might even send the letter before telling her."

"Agreed. Three months it is," Fish said. "The two musketeers. All for one and..."

"One for all. United we stand and..."

"Divided we... Careful. Mind the brambles."

Emily ducked underneath them and saw they were at the bottom of the wood. They turned left onto Adey's Lane, where the mixture of high hedges and overarching trees gave the impression of being inside a long green tunnel.

"Not sure what we're having... apart from strawberries," Fish said, "picked by the finest picker in this fair county."

"Thank you, Fish. A fine compliment, I think."

"What do you mean, compliment? I meant me!" Fish laughed. "Come on, slowcoach. We don't want to be late."

They linked arms and walked down through the lane's deep shadowy gloom.

Tuesday, August 6th, 1918
Field's Café

Emily looked at her brother. "How are you finding things, David?"

"What, things like being treated to tea at Field's by my sister? It's all very nice."

'You know I didn't mean that. When we were walking into town, you seemed..." She dried up, unsure how to put it.

He sighed. "I know you didn't mean that, Emily."

She waited for him to explain further, but he changed tack instead.

"Mother was pleased that you were getting me out and about. She must have told me half a dozen times this morning what a good idea it was." He paused for a few seconds. "Some people treat me like a simpleton, because of what happened. They repeat things," he sneered, "and speak more slowly. They give me sympathetic looks when they think I'm not looking. That's what I can't stand more than anything else. Their damned pity." His voice hardened in resentment. "Whatever you do, Emily, please don't do that.

Better to hate me for being an insufferable, ungrateful, unpredictable bore. Women who think I'm some sort of conchie look at me with contempt, but I prefer that to suffering their pity. So promise me you won't pity me, not even behind my back. If I want that I just look in the mirror." He laughed. "There, you see, Emily, I'm developing self pity into an art-form."

"I promise I'll try, but Mother..." Emily said, desperate to not let him see her concern.

It had been their first chance to talk alone since she'd arrived home late yesterday afternoon. The evening meal had been difficult. David had hardly said a word, picked at his food distractedly, before announcing brusquely that he was going to his room. Her mother, who had been giving her anxious glances, had looked crushed. Even her father, when not talking about the Germans retreating to the Marne, had been subdued. After helping to clear away, Emily had planned to tackle her mother, but the right moment had never arrived. After hearing her mother relate all the local gossip, at length, Emily had used the excuse of tiredness and gone up to her room.

After bedtime, feeling unsettled, something had drawn her out onto the landing. David's light had been on and she had tapped on his door, but there had been no invitation, no repetition of the conversation from eighteen months ago. She had returned to her room and finally, after much tossing and turning, fallen asleep.

At breakfast, David had been more amenable, and when she suggested a trip into town she'd been pleased when he'd agreed. He'd wanted to walk, which on such a lovely afternoon had suited her. He'd taken a meandering route, down past her old school, turning to cross the railway, past the Grammar School in Leicester Street – which reminded her of Robert – before cutting through a tiny snicket on Wellington Lane. Up to this point he had been unresponsive, volunteering nothing apart from the briefest yes and no answers. Emily had filled the gaps as best she could, wondering why he'd agreed to come, but once through the snicket he'd become animated.

"He wanted me to accompany him there," he'd indicated the Kingston public house on the far side of the road, "not because he's become a secret drinker, heaven forbid, but because he believes his wretched Druids' Society will stiffen my backbone. I said no, to his immense disappointment so... I'll have to continue being a spineless jellyfish."

Emily had started to say something, but he'd turned and set off. She'd hurried to catch him up, glancing back as she did. Wasn't that where Mr Barber lived, at number seventeen? She thought so, but David had already reached the corner of Freehold Street. "David, wait!" He'd paused long enough for her to catch up before marching off again, setting a pace she found difficult to keep up with. By the time they reached Spring Bank she was considering abandoning the trip, but he'd slowed and spoken again.

"Tell me about this fruit picking of yours, Emily."

She'd caught her breath, surprised by the sheer ordinariness of the question, but for the last stretch into town he'd seemed happy listening to her ramblings about her summer experiences, even laughing once or twice. It had hardly been a conversation, however. On arriving at Fields, she'd worried it would be too much of a trial for him, but the appearance of cups and saucers had revived some ingrained sense of etiquette on his part and an interlude of near-normalcy had followed, before the conversation had turned to his state of mind.

"...but Mother," continued Emily.

"Now don't tell me it's only natural for Mother to worry." Emily realised that was exactly what she'd been about to say. "I know it is. It's just so suffocating: her smothering disquiet, her concern overladen with an irritating false optimism. It's so... infuriating." He leant back and sighed, before picking up his teacup. She saw that he needed two hands to steady it. "Give Father his due, Emily, he tried, but he's now retreated into a dubious disapproval from which he emerges to make judgements or disparaging remarks." He twisted up his lip. "Pull myself together and other such helpful comments. The circuitous trip via the Kingston was because of him, and I'm sorry I shouldn't have dragged you there, but I'd been brooding about it all morning. Thoughts arrive – unexpected, unwanted, unbidden – and nag, nag away in my head for hours on end – a mental itch... like one in that part of your back that, no matter how you try, you can't quite scratch." He placed his cup back in the saucer. She saw he'd split some tea. "And sometimes," his voice wavered, "the itch transmutes into a long, rusty blade that's being forced in and out, slowly at first, then faster and faster, pushed in and out, deeper and deeper." His voice sounded despairing. He ran his hand across his brow, pushing his hair back. "I don't want to upset you, Emily, but it might have been better if you'd never visited me, better if you'd never made that mistake."

Emily looked at him, shocked at both how dark and forbidding he'd become and the speed with which he'd changed. She whispered to herself, "Jippo?"

"Jippo!" he laughed. "You annoyed something in my head that forced me out, and I still don't know why."

"But it was such a wonderful moment, David, that moment you spoke, and Mother was ecstatic when she heard, and you're better off..."

"Better off than I was? You would think so, wouldn't you, but I'm afraid you're wrong, though I've spent hours and hours trying to convince myself otherwise. Now I wallow in an unremitting nightmare. Then, Emily," his voiced slowed, "then, I... wasn't... always... aware. I moved in and out of a foggy miasma. I existed, but only vaguely. There was no need to speak to anyone, so why bother? It became easier not to. Just let myself drift. And then you pulled me out of it." He gave her a direct look. "Don't look so alarmed, Emily. I'm not blaming you."

"I'm sorry, I didn't realise I was looking alarmed," said Emily. Coping with this unpredictable emotional barrage wasn't easy. He might say he didn't hold her responsible, but did he mean it?

"Haven't the doctors said you'll improve in time? The Edinburgh ones?"

"Doctors?" he spat the word out. "Glad to be rid of me. They don't understand what any of us will be like. I'm fine for hours, then all of a sudden I'll fall off the cliff. It's being aware of that... waiting for it to happen, the ground disappearing under my feet, wondering how long before I hit the bottom." He looked haunted. "If I ever do hit the bottom, that is, that's what so awful."

"And what about the nights?" she risked saying. "I knocked. I saw your light was on."

"Did you? I didn't hear; I must have been dozing. And before you ask, I have a few good nights, but I rarely sleep the sleep of the just – the sleep of the damned, more like... I won't burden you with the unwholesome details," he paused, "so I prefer the light on. Easier to find my cigarettes when I do wake; the one thing that stills the jitters." He gave a shudder. "Talking of which, I could do with one now." He reached in his pocket and took out a packet, fumbling with it as he did, his hands trembling. "Damn stupid," he muttered something indecipherable under his breath, "bloody stupid shakes." He grasped left with right and with an effort of will forced his hands to still before extracting a cigarette. "Sorry, but you'd better light it for me." He gave her an apologetic thin smile. "I sometimes get warning signs. My heart races and feels lighter, and there's a rising feeling of sickness in my stomach. Then it all spreads up through my body and meets in my head in an overriding, engulfing, surging panic. I sometimes wonder about ending it all – but don't worry, I've no immediate plans to do that."

Emily picked up his matches, unnerved by what he'd said. She was aware her hands might shake too, but steadily struck one. David leant forward, lit his cigarette and inhaled deep down into his lungs. He closed his eyes for a few seconds before exhaling. "That's better. I hadn't realised how much I needed one. I'd have offered you one but... you're still not smoking?" She shook her head. "You ought to. You just need to persevere. It's worth it, they're an absolute godsend." He took another long drag. "But the nightmares arrive without warning. Not every single night, but most of them," he sighed, before adding, "So it can be a somewhat... dispiriting affair."

Emily had come across soldiers with various nervous conditions, but the personal nature of this, combined with David's bitter humour, was making it an unsettling experience.

"Have you spoken to Mother or Father?"

"No." He inhaled deeply again. "Can't or won't, I can't decide which. Either way it doesn't matter. I've no intention of doing so. I've talked a little to Aunt Eleanor, and now you, today, but apart from that I discuss it inside my head."

"You don't think it would be easier... if you tried to explain to them?"

"No!" He shook his head. "No!" He stubbed his cigarette out in an ash tray, took out another, lit it, this time without help, and lapsed into a sullen silence.

Change the subject, Emily told herself, you might retrieve things. "Did I say I'd heard from Robert? They had an inspection and a beastly Prussian ordered that the cricket nets, bats and balls they got from Holland all be burnt..." But even as she recounted the details, her mind was whirring, longing for the David she had started to feel closer to, or even for his older, long-lost boring self. It was impossible not to feel sympathy, but this new David was unnerving – the depths of melancholia and despair, and the rage that lurked beneath the surface. She understood why her mother found it difficult to cope, tiptoeing around, aware that one wrong step risked setting off an explosion. And his words had shaken her – better if you'd never visited me... better if you'd never made that mistake.

September 17th, 1918
Paragon Station

"Excuse me, do you mind if... ah, Eleanor, I didn't realise it was you under that hat."

Eleanor looked up to see her brother-in-law, an alarmed expression on his face.

"By all means Alfred. As you can see, I have the compartment to myself, but if you don't feel comfortable there are other empty ones along the corridor."

"No, no. This will be fine. Nothing like neutral territory," he said, sliding the door shut behind him, "for a meeting of..."

"Minds?"

"I was thinking more of adversaries," he said smiling, "but if hostilities do recommence, I've got my paper and I see you have a book, so we can always retreat behind them. As I'm only going as far as Howden, we shall hopefully survive the experience." He put his attaché case up on the rack and sat down opposite her. "I'm afraid I have interrupted you?" He indicated her book. "Something inspirational, I trust."

"Would I read anything else?" She smiled. "But Howden to Huddersfield is long enough to finish it, and I've read it before. It's excellent. I'd offer to lend it to you, but I'm returning it to a dear old friend... it wouldn't be your cup of tea, anyway."

He held his hand out. "May I?" She passed it to him "*Non-Combatants and Others*," he read out loud, " by Rose Macaulay. Hmm. A novel?"

"About a young woman's journey towards pacifism in 1915."

He handed it back. "You're right, not exactly my cup of tea."

Eleanor put her bookmark in place and returned Rose Macaulay to her bag. "How has David been this week?"

A troubled look passed across Alfred's face. "Not good. If anything, worse rather than better. Last night, Clara found him sleep-walking. And for days he's sunk in melancholia and when – or rather if – he does emerge, he's difficult. It's hard to know what to do. I realise you think I have all the subtlety of a bull in a china shop."

It was not often that Eleanor felt so sorry for her brother-in-law.

Alfred shook his head. "Clara does her best – she must have talked to you about it – but she's at a loss too. At least when Emily was home she brought him out of his shell a little. So to answer your question – How has David been?" He gazed out the window for a full minute before turning back to her. "The answer is unremittingly grim."

"Clara's found it hard, Alfred, I know."

"She's missed Emily these last couple of weeks. Pity the girl doesn't understand that she'd be more use here rather than gallivanting off back to London."

"I don't think she's doing much gallivanting. She's rushed off her feet, she said in her last letter. But you have to allow her a degree of independence."

"There we will never agree, Eleanor. I should have put my foot down when the subject of London first came up. Freedom and independence are all very well, but in my book responsibility and family duty outweigh them." He gave her a not unfriendly smile, "You, of course, have always encouraged a somewhat devil-may-care attitude to things."

Eleanor smiled in return. "I'm pleased you qualified my attitude with that somewhat, Alfred. When you don't condemn me entirely out of order it shows we are making progress."

"Progress? Perhaps." He removed his glasses and began polishing the lenses. "She showed us the photograph before she left."

"Of her climbing? I'm glad she did. Wasn't that exciting for her?"

"Driving a horse and cart down Whitefriargate at twenty miles an hour scattering everyone before you might be classed as exciting, but it doesn't mean it's desirable. Clara was meant to tell you how much we disapproved, but she hasn't. We were shocked... you were in loco parentis."

"Emily was perfectly safe, Alfred, and it was too great an opportunity to miss. I'd have leapt at the chance. Isn't it a good thing that she's finally felt able to show you?" The events on Bridlington beach passed through Eleanor's mind; would Emily tell her father about those at some point?

"She said she'd love another try. Completely incomprehensible to me, but there isn't the least likelihood of her joining the ranks of those unnatural women who became alpinists before the war. But," he replaced his glasses, "with all the things that have happened these last four years, Emily being pulled up a rock on a rope does not feel quite as significant as it once might. And who knows," he finished more positively, "by the time we see her again, the war might be over."

Eleanor was both a little surprised and also pleased at how reasonable he was being. "I hope you're right, especially after all the wasted opportunities there have been. Has your *Morning News* said anything about this latest offer? I meant to get one."

"About Austria's so-called peace advances? I think you'll find Germany hiding behind her draggled skirts. As to wasted opportunities, if someone offered me the opportunity to enter the lion's den..." Alfred left the sentence unfinished and unfolded his paper. "Ah, here you are – 'The Peace Dodge – Proposals Turned Down.'"

"Turned down? That is so disappointing. How long shall we have to wait for an agreement?"

"To wait, Eleanor? Until Germany's actions satisfy minimal standards of humanity, which is as unlikely as... snow in July." He handed the paper to her. "Look at this." He jabbed his forefinger at the banner headline, 'Germany's Bloodstained Hands'. "You'll find Mr Balfour's says it all."

Eleanor scanned the Foreign Secretary's concluding words - 'the German unworthiness to enter peace conversations. Germany with its outstretched hand still wet with the blood of the women and children done to death in the latest in the series of abominable crimes on the high seas.'

She returned the paper. "Yes, sinking the *Galway Castle* was appalling. Those poor women and children. But..."

"There's no but about it. When Germany crawls on her knees suing for peace, that will be the time to dictate, not negotiate, and then, Eleanor, we can discuss what happens next."

"Magnanimity or vengeance? I still have hopes that President Wilson will ensure that sanity prevails and overcome the objections of Clemenceau and Lloyd George."

"For all our disagreements, Eleanor, I admire you for retaining your faith in the underlying decency of human nature, even if disillusionment must be your constant companion. Take your friends Lenin and Trotsky – see how those scoundrels' myrmidons are busy cutting throats."

"I was always more sympathetic to the Mensheviks, Alfred, so I hold no brief for the Red Guards in Petrograd, nor Lenin and Trotsky. The massacres and wholesale executions are dreadful." She sighed and shook her head. "Events aren't turning out how I hoped. You're right, disillusionment is a risk." She smiled at him. "But better an optimist than a pessimist."

"A realist, Eleanor, a realist!" He looked out of the window again. "Here comes the rain." Within a few seconds it was driving against the carriage window. "I hope you're prepared."

"Always, Alfred. What else would you expect? I've never known a September like this, so much rain and so cold. I help with the Spring Bank Orphanage Band. They were meant to play last Wednesday at the third anniversary celebrations at Lees Rest Homes, but it poured, so rather than a medley of rousing tunes the residents watched slides of Victoria Falls instead. A poor substitute." She stared out of the window for a few minutes. It was a depressing sight; the far side of the river disappearing into the murk and, with the tide out, water and mudflats mingled into an unappealing brown melange. As the train moved away, a view of wet, sodden fields stretched to the horizon. She turned back to him. "Emily said it's been awful in London. The whole country seems affected. I dread to think what sort of harvest there will be."

"Did you know Clara went to see that La Somna woman at Hammonds?"

"'The most wonderful woman in the world,'" Eleanor said, "'demonstrating powers beyond the mind of man to fathom'. I've seen all the advertisements. One could hardly miss them."

"She had to queue for an hour before it was her turn. I told her to ask how long these dreadful conditions will last and if the sun will ever reappear, but Clara asked something else entirely." He didn't sound altogether surprised. "She seemed satisfied enough. The strange women you're attracted to, Eleanor, are of a different ilk from those that appeal to your sister."

"Was that a compliment, Alfred?" she smiled, before looking more concerned. "I thought that she'd stopped seeing the medium."

"Yes and no. She insists she has, but underneath she hankers after going again, still harbours hope," he said. "But enough of that. Did you enjoy the auction? Clara said you were bidding most enthusiastically."

"I was one of many who won the same plate of six potatoes, but like everyone else I put them back in, and I didn't win the marrow; that went for the princely sum of sixteen pounds. But more than one hundred and seventy pounds was raised for the St. John Hospital, which was excellent."

"I'm sure it is. I just wish Emily had found a place there." The train slowed. "My stop." He stood up and reached for his case. "Enjoy the visit to your friend."

"To Florence? I will. I'm glad we had a chance to talk, Alfred, and who knows, one day we might manage Lands End to John O'Groats in amicability." She smiled at him.

He returned her smile. "That, Eleanor, would be stretching credulity a little too far, I think." He slid open the carriage door. "As far as Leeds, perhaps. Good day, Eleanor."

"Good day, Alfred."

He shut the door behind him and Eleanor delved into her bag for her book.

Saturday, October 12th, 1918
London

The rhythmic clacking of the shoes reached her before the song. A fair-headed girl in a faded blue dress was skipping. Her friends, surrounding her, sang as they swung the rope. As Emily moved closer their words became clearer.

"I had a little bird."

Emily couldn't resist stopping to watch

"Its name was Enza."

A second girl moved in.

"I opened the window."

And joined her friend at the exact moment that all the girls in the group sang

"And in-flu-Enza!"

The two girls turning the rope increased its speed, and with each repetition of the rhyme another girl joined in, until four were skipping in time in the middle.

Emily had left Byculla twenty minutes ago and had been wandering the streets before coming across the girls. Their new skipping rhyme held her in an awful fascination.

> I had a little bird,
> its name was Enza,
> I opened the window
> and in-flu-Enza.
> I had a little bird,
> its name was Enza,
> I opened the window
> and in-flu-Enza.

The scourge's virulent reappearance in the second half of September had shattered any complacency that might have set in since July. A young Lieutenant she'd played bridge with one evening, three weeks earlier, had been chatty and gay, looking forward to being discharged. After a few hands, he'd started to complain of a headache and sore throat, and had even made a joke about their downfall in the last rubber being due to *la grippe*. Emily wasn't sure about the exact timespan but the speed with which he'd deteriorated was shocking. Mahogany spots had appeared on his cheekbones, then a lavender blueness had ominously spread from his ears across his whole face. He had struggled desperately for breath as he drowned in the liquid filling his lungs. He'd been dead by breakfast. It wasn't their only case and it was impossible not to be affected. She had the impression that young adults, who should be most resistant, were those most at risk, with recovery in the lap of the Gods. When Fish had woken one morning feeling achy, Emily had felt panic-stricken, but thankfully nothing had come of it. Fish had joked blackly that she had no intention of making the current shortage of coffins worse.

Heeding the Byculla doctors' advice about avoiding large crowds, where the bacterium could easily spread, Emily and Fish had abandoned their cinema-going, deciding that vacating the auditoriums every four and a half hours to ventilate them wasn't sufficient defence. Refraining from spitting on buses or in railway carriages was one piece of advice she was happy to ignore, never having been guilty of either habit. Finding the time and opportunity to get plenty of fresh air had proved harder. There was no shortage of other suggestions. Some said that cigarettes prevented infection, but the Lieutenant had been a heavy smoker and it hadn't helped him. Her mother had written that Alice was determined they should take Oxo two or three times a day, after seeing an advertisement claiming that 'Drinking Oxo reinforces the blood against the malady'. It wasn't clear whether she expected Emily to follow suit, but she had sent some deodar germicide and anti-flu handkerchiefs. Emily thought she had nothing to lose by using them, and she and Fish had also gargled religiously with salt and water and taken regular small doses of quinine.

"I had a little..."

The girls had stopped skipping mid-rhyme and were staring at her. Emily stood rooted to the spot looking at them. The girl in the blue dress was emboldened enough to come across.

"Miss? Why are you crying?"

"Am I?" She went to dab her eyes and realised she was still clutching the telegram. "I'm sorry, I didn't mean to spoil your game. Don't take any notice of me." She turned and walked away.

I had a little bird,
its name was Enza,
I opened the window
and in-flu-Enza.

Monday, November 11th, 1918

At ten past five in the morning, in a railway carriage outside Compiegne, three days of intense negotiation are concluded as Matthias Erzberger, head of the German delegation, accepts all the Allies' demands and signs the armistice agreement. The French Supreme Allied Commander, Marshall Ferdinand Foch, rejects his request for an immediate cessation of hostilities. The war is to continue for another five hours and fifty minutes.

\#

Emily's father left his desk, crossed to the window and peered down at the excitable crowd that had been waiting for news since early morning. As their numbers had grown, so had their enthusiasm. Had any of them been there, rubbing shoulders with David and Edward and celebrating outside the Mail's offices, all those years ago? He sighed. What had happened to that world? He removed his glasses, bent his head forward, and rubbed the bridge of his nose, then stood immobile for a minute before taking out his gold fob-watch from his waistcoat pocket. A little before ten to eleven. He was about to return to the report he was writing when the sound of exuberant cheering reached him. He opened the window and looked down. A newsboy was calling underneath.

"Kaiser's Downfall! Only a penny! Armistice signed! Only a penny!"

Half a minute later there was a knock at the door and one of his clerks appeared. "Eleven o'clock, Mr Walker! Less than ten minutes left! Isn't it wonderful? I've got you a copy of the paper."

"Thank you, Miss Rammell. Leave it on my desk, and please tell the staff downstairs that I shall give serious consideration to their request to finish a little earlier today."

#

At four o'clock, a little over an hour before the signing, thousands of American troops attack across pontoon bridges laid down on the River Meuse. The head of the American Expeditionary Force, General John Pershing, a vehement opponent of a ceasefire, believes the allies should 'strike harder than ever'. One of his commanders, General Charles P. Summerhall, tells his subordinates 'Get into action and get across! I don't expect to see any of you again, but that doesn't matter. You have the honour of a definitive success – give yourself to that'. By four-thirty, marines and infantrymen of the 89th Division take Pouilly on the river's east bank.

#

Emily's mother stood motionless, staring at the clock. Ever since Alice had returned from Princes Avenue, she'd felt distracted. Even sitting down for a cup of tea in the kitchen and letting Alice's excited ramblings wash over her had not dispelled this feeling. She couldn't blame Alice for being so enthusiastic, especially as the house had been a demoralising place these last few weeks, even with Emily's return. She shut her eyes. She wished Emily hadn't chosen today to go to Brooklands. She should be here. And then going into town too. And as for her talk of returning to London to complete the last few weeks of her contract!

The ticking of the clock resounded round the room, sounding louder than usual. The minute hand crawled towards twelve. The strange whirring noise that preceded the first chime began and then the first chime rang out. The country had been at peace for an hour. She counted the chimes, still unsure whether she could do it. As the last chime died away, her resolve strengthened and with shaking hands, she picked up Edward's letter.

#

At six o'clock, General Pershing receives the following instruction: 'Hostilities will cease at 11.00 hours on November 11th – Troops will stand fast on the line reached at that time which will be reported to Corps Headquarters – Strictest precautions will be maintained – There will be no intercourse of any kind with the enemy'. As heavy fighting continues, he informs his commanders of the ceasefire but offers no advice on how to act.

On some other parts of the Western Front, as the news arrives troops are told to stand down.

#

Eleanor hadn't expected to find the pavement artist where he'd been on the day of the raid, but even so she was disappointed. Until today, something had always held her back and now it was too late; he wasn't there, and instinctively she knew he would never return.

The milliner's and the dress shop were already closed, but a man was busy with a set of keys in the doorway of the shop she'd sheltered in. She was unsure if it were her rescuer, but when he turned she recognised him. He was a little older than she remembered, but it was the same man. Surprised, he made to raise his hat before realising that he hadn't got one on. He laughed at his mistake.

"You aren't the first gentleman I've seen hatless this morning," she said, laughing too, "perhaps you will start a new fashion... Mr Lightbourne." He looked astounded. "The air raid in July last year... I wouldn't be here now if you hadn't dragged me inside."

"Of course." She saw his look of recognition. He gestured to his head. "I should go back in for my hat, but it's such an exceptional day... so why not? Hatless!"

An overcrowded bus hooted at them as it went past. Three soldiers sat on the bonnet and a fourth on top of the driver's cab, his feet dangling over the windscreen. Two rather more elderly men hung on on either side of him. Everyone on the top deck was waving flags, some were singing, and Eleanor heard a bugle being blown.

"It's a wonder the driver can see anything," Eleanor said.

"It's such a long time since I've seen so many people so inordinately happy," Mr Lightbourne replied. "And where have they all got their flags from?"

"Hawkers are everywhere. I even saw people queueing to buy tickling sticks from one."

"Presumably you aren't currently armed with one, Mrs...?"

"Alsop. Eleanor Alsop." She smiled at him. "No, you have nothing to fear on that score, Mr Lightbourne. But I mustn't delay you further." She started to move away.

"No. I'm in no great rush. The only customer all morning just wanted to talk about events in France rather than buy anything, and then when all the maroons went off and the gunfire..."

"I was down by the river and thought it might be a final raid, but then everyone poured out into the street cheering. So..." Eleanor shrugged. "And as the guns died away the tugs joined in, and then the trains coming in to Charing Cross added their whistles. Not the most harmonious of choruses, but very welcome indeed."

"Two little red bugler boys popped up outside the Tube earlier." Mr Lightbourne laughed. "And not, for once, to send us to bed after the Gothas, but playing the all-clear from these dreadful years." He cocked his head. "And that's another sound that will take getting used to again."

"The bells!" she answered. They fell into silence, listening to the pealing. Eleanor looked around. Apart from the clearing where the building had taken a direct hit, there was little evidence of the raid.

"Other than what people recollect," she said. He gave her a strange look. "Sorry, I was thinking aloud and remembering those dreadful harrowing scenes. Look at it now."

A US military car with a Land Girl and a WAAC sitting on the bonnet drove past. Amongst those standing crammed in the back, Eleanor spotted an Indian turban and the bright blue uniform of a Frenchman. "My friend was unwell this morning, so I set out by myself and something brought me here. Maybe to pick up another memento from the artist." She pointed back along the street.

"He's not been there for months. Someone said he got anthrax from his shaving brush." He shrugged. "Perhaps he just took his talent in search of a better pitch... You're not from these parts, are you?"

"I lived in London for a time before the war," she smiled, "but no, I'm not. I shall give you a clue... I hail from one of the unholy trinity of Hell, Hull and Halifax."

He studied her as if giving great thought to his answer.

"I think the devil has knocked on my door once or twice before, Mrs Alsop, but I've never previously met anyone from the other two places."

Eleanor started to answer, then paused. "I must be taking up too much of your time, Mr Lightbourne. You must have someone to get home to."

"No." A fleeting expression of sadness passed across his face. "No. Not since nineteen fifteen." He looked at Eleanor again. "And you? Is there someone in Hell, Hull or Halifax?"

"No. I'm widowed too, but from much longer ago."

"At the risk of being overfamiliar, Mrs Alsop, this seems a remarkably intimate conversation for two complete strangers to be having standing in the street."

"Hardly complete strangers," she said. "My friends say I'm too forward." She looked at him, gauging his reaction. "As I hate to disappoint my friends, I suggest seeking out some sights together... as this *is* a remarkable day."

"Impulsive as well as forward, Mrs Alsop?"

"The denizens of Hell, Hull and Halifax are all renowned for it, Mr Lightbourne."

He smiled. "Some sights it is then. Bus or tube?"

"If we can get on one, a bus would be more exciting, don't you think?"

"Excellent. So is it Hull or Halifax?"

#

At nine o'clock, in Bois la Haut near Mons, Brigadier Alex Ross of the Canadian 28th battalion orders discretion in engaging the enemy in heavy fighting, but despite this he also orders his battalion to take the village of Havre and also attempt to reach the Canal du Centre.

#

Fish rubbed the back of her neck and sighed. The headache she'd woken up with had intensified and even the morning's news hadn't relieved it. She felt quite subdued, envying the impromptu band that was touring the wards playing an enthusiastic, if erratic, 'Tipperary'. If they were at the joyful end of the spectrum, the reaction of one young Lieutenant was at the other. As she'd changed his dressing he'd been tearful, telling her over and over again "He hadn't lived yet, he hadn't lived yet." Fish knew the *he* was the best friend with whom he'd joined up. No, like George, he hadn't lived yet. She sighed again and murmured to herself. "A glorious victory, but a bittersweet peace." She rubbed her neck again. "I wish you were here too, Mouldiwarp."

"Nurse! The war may be over, but our work isn't, so daydreaming is best saved for another time. You do have something to do, I take it?"

"Yes, Matron, I was..."

"Then I suggest you get on with it. And then tell the officers in your ward that by way of celebration we shall be having ham and eggs for lunch."

"Yes, Matron." Fish hurried off before any other of her shortcomings could be brought to her attention.

#

At nine-thirty, Private George Edwin Ellison, from Leeds, is shot near Mons. Having fought in the first battle of Mons in August 1914, he is the last British soldier to die in battle in the First World War.

#

"*Ich kann Ihnen keine Fahrkarten verkaufen. Dank Ihre Freunde glaube ich nicht, daß Sie weiter als Leipzig kommen würden. Es ist unmöglich.*" The station master looked at them with contempt. "*Sie sollten lieber laufen.*"

"I take it that was a no then, Stan?" Robert said, as they left the small railway station.

"It was a hare-brained idea anyway," Stan laughed. "He suggested we walk! Pity the Rhine's so far away. We could have hired a boat and sailed home."

"You must be joking! Us? Sailors? We'd be better off finding Richthofen's home and seeing if there are any LVGs lying round the back garden." He slapped his friend on the back. "Don't worry, if there's only a Fokker, you can sit on its tail on the way home." He grinned. The elation that Robert had felt all day showed little sign of dissipating. "So what now? Back to the camp? A wander round town?"

"Town, I think. Lead on, Stanley!"

Rumours had been spreading for days. Nearby, gunfire had been interpreted as either mutinying troops decoupling a train engine and refusing to go on, or a Bolshevik uprising, or both. The Kaiser had fled, been arrested or killed. It had been difficult to know what to believe. The one thing that everyone had been certain of was that the war was ending on Monday. That morning's bugle call for parade had been ignored. Some of the guards had disappeared. Others remained and were trying to barter items. Robert had acquired an Iron Cross in exchange for a small bar of soap.

They'd walked out unhindered through the gates where a sentry, who was still on duty, had told them to be careful in the town. Once outside they'd hugged and danced round in a circle like dervishes, until forced to stop for breath. It had been then that the idea of buying train tickets to London had come to Robert. But now, a few minutes after leaving the station, the guard's warning came back to them. They rounded a corner to find a small group of people arguing over the carcass of a horse. Two men hacked at it with knives whilst several women tried to pull off pieces of flesh. A third man, presumably the owner, was trying to stop them. As they watched, the atmosphere became ugly, and as others were drawn into the dispute the first blows were exchanged.

"Best give them a wide berth, Stan."

They skirted the melee and walked on.

"Did you notice?" Stan said. "Their faces?"

Robert nodded. "Pale as hell. They were starving."

In the town square a small group was putting up a banner across the front of a large building. "*Willkommen die sieglosen Helden.*" Robert looked at Stan.

"Something along the lines of... welcome home to the unconquering heroes."

The German holding the ladder shouted at them in an unpleasant way.

"Afraid my extensive vocabulary of swear words doesn't quite stretch to all of that." Stan addressed the German. "*Vielleicht können Sie das wiederholen, nur etwas langsamer. Und Sie scheinen es schwer zu haben.*" He pointed to Robert and himself. "*Brauchen Sie Hilfe?*" And then he repeated in English, "Do you need some help?"

This time the invective in the German's reply was clear. The man at the top of the ladder spat in their direction and said something to his companions.

"Maybe we should move on, Stan. They might be a pretty elderly bunch, but you never know. I'm sure they weren't expecting you to respond. Did you catch any of his reply?"

Stan smiled. "They declined my offer of assistance. I don't know about you, but I'm getting a bit peckish, and given the reaction of our friends over there I'm not sure what reception we'd get in a local cafe, so it has to be the delights of the camp canteen?"

"Right. Home, Sweet, Offiziersgefangenenlager Schweidnitz it is then." They laughed and set off back together.

#

At ten-thirty, the all black 92nd Division of the 167th Field Artillery Brigade launch their final charge. Their Operations Officer, George K Livermore, later speaks of 'the little crosses over the graves of the coloured lads who died a useless death on that November morning.'

#

"I'm sorry. I didn't mean to knock you." Emily apologised to the munitionette she'd nearly sent flying, before realising that she recognised her. "It's Ivy, isn't it?"

The young woman took a few seconds to respond. "Miss Emily? My goodness, you've changed! I didn't recognise you."

Emily blushed. "Were you watching? How embarrassing."

Ivy laughed. "I thought you were all doing an excellent cakewalk. I couldn't make out what you were all singing, though. You weren't the one ringing her bell, were you?"

"No, I wasn't. It was all a bit of a mishmash. It wasn't rehearsed! And then I lost my footing at the end." Emily looked around at the crowds. "I seem to have lost my friends. Never mind! We've been out for hours."

"Everyone's a bit giddy, not just you. I had to join in with a game of ring-a-roses with about twenty children. Look at that Tommy!" A soldier was performing an impromptu sword dance. Emily and Ivy found themselves clapping in time with the crowd. Eventually the soldier stopped, picked up the cane and hat he'd been dancing around and moved away.

"Did you see the man covered head to toe in flags?" Emily said. "He came up to me, twice."

She paused, swayed, and added a slight slur to her speech. "My name is George and I'm... camelflagged." They laughed together. "He was as old as my father." Mentioning her father, Emily felt a slight twinge of guilt that she hadn't gone home, but when she'd left Brooklands she'd sent word that she didn't know when she would be back.

"It still feels queer that it's finally over," Ivy said. "It'll take a bit of getting used to. And I'm not sure how long I'll be needing these." She indicated her jerkin and trousers.

"Would you go back into service?"

She shook her head. "No, never. Don't get me wrong, I was happy enough at yours, but even though it's been hard work at Rose Downs I've enjoyed working with the other girls there. Rose Downs might give up munitions now, but it'll make something else instead. Then when my Bert's back, there'll be bairns." She pointed at a group of lads swarming over the statue of Queen Victoria. "Though mine won't be behaving like Red Injuns."

Though a half-moon hung in the darkening sky, Emily realised it wasn't that making the boys on the statue stand out so; it was the lights blazing out from the buildings. "It's the strangest thing, Ivy. The lights! Who'd have thought it? In shop windows too. And that tram over there all lit up. I hadn't even noticed!"

"And look at Willis's." Ivy pointed down Carr Lane at the department store's illuminated large clock. Emily instinctively turned and looked up at the Dock Offices, but its clock was still in darkness.

"I heard the shop windows being lit up is just for today," Ivy continued, "though I saw someone scraping paint off the street-lamps earlier." Her next words were drowned in the racket of buzzers, sounding for the second time that day. Accompanying shafts of light swung backwards and forwards high above the city. The display lasted several minutes and, as the last searchlight dimmed, cheers resounded around them.

"It's grand," continued Ivy, when she could make herself heard, "to think that Hull will never hear an air raid warning or an all-clear again. Mind out!"

Emily ducked, dodging the fireworks being thrown into the air. A nearby, less fortunate woman screamed blue murder at everyone and no-one in particular when sparks set her feather boa alight. She stamped on it, before spotting a man throwing crackers into the dock from the top of Bridge Chambers and moving off to vent her fury on him.

"Apart from her, I've never seen so many people in such gay spirits. The whole of Hull's shut up shop and come down here to celebrate." Ivy pointed up at military bandsmen assembling on the City Hall balcony, "We're to be musically entertained too." She paused and looked directly at Emily. "I'm still in touch with Millie next door, so I heard about your brothers. And for the flu to take David, after all he'd been through!" She shook her head, "Your poor parents." She reached out and gave Emily's arm a sympathetic squeeze.

"Thank you, Ivy, it's kind of you to say that... of course I know I'm not the only one here who's lost loved ones." She sighed, "David was so troubled, but it was still a terrible shock."

"But you'll have Robert coming home to look forward to. A pair of love-birds, I heard." Although embarrassed, Emily couldn't help smiling.

"And you'll be slipping some of those ribbons on for him, I'm sure." Ivy laughed and pointed at a woman with a paper ostrich feather in her hair, who was dancing by the statue. The woman held one hand out as if signalling danger, and to screeches of delight from her flapper friends pulled up her skirt and petticoats with the other hand to reveal red, white and blue ribbons tied above her ankle.

Emily laughed. "We'll see. He's in Germany, so who knows when he'll get home. But you're right, I can't wait."

"Ivy!" A young munitionette shrieked from behind Emily. "I was wondering where you'd got to."

"My friend Rose," Ivy explained.

"The others are all meeting up at Powolny's," the newcomer said.

"Goodness, we are going posh! We might just about afford the soup. Are you sure they'll let the likes of you in?"

"Cheek! If you can't celebrate for this, you can't celebrate for anything, can you?" She looked at Emily.

"It is very nice in Powolny's," said Emily.

"There you are, Ivy. Your young friend thinks it's very nice in Powolny's, so are you going to come? This'll be going on for hours yet."

Ivy smiled at Emily. "It was lovely bumping into you. You just come here, my little Miss Emily." Ivy embraced her, before adding, "And you look after yourself."

"And you too, Ivy."

"And give my regards to everyone in Westbourne Avenue."

Emily watched as Ivy and Rose pushed their way through the crowd in the direction of Bond Street and Powolny's.

#

At sixteen minutes before eleven, a runner catches up with the American 313th Division and reports the armistice has been signed. Brigadier General William Nicholson decides: 'There will be absolutely no let-up until eleven a.m.'.

#

"It's not as if we can hear a word, not that that matters," Eleanor said. She peered at the distant figures on the balcony. "Is the Queen waving a Union Jack? It's a shame we couldn't get any closer."

"You'll be able to read about it in the morning's papers. We should be up there, for the best view." He pointed at the airship circling above them and laughed. "Did you ever chain yourself to Buckingham Palace railings then?"

"No... it looks as if they're going back in."

The chant of 'We want the King' broke out again around them.

"Where to next, Eleanor?"

"Trafalgar Square should be fun, Bill. What about making for there? Oh look, they're coming out again." The rest of her words were lost as the cheering around them reached new heights.

#

At two minutes to eleven, Private George Lawrence Price is killed in street fighting near Mons. The Canadian is the last British and Commonwealth soldier to be killed. The Commonwealth War Graves Commission records eight hundred and sixty three deaths on 11th November, though this includes some men dying from wounds received previously.

#

Clara's hands shook as she opened the envelope. To her surprise there was a second envelope inside addressed to Emily. She put it to one side and carefully took the first letter out.

Dear Mother and Father,

Sorry I haven't been able to write much recently as...

The familiar untidy handwriting, as fresh as if it had been written yesterday, made her gasp. She reached for the chair behind her, sat down and took a deep breath before continuing to read.

...the Boche have been keeping us a little busy of late. But it's quiet now, so we've been sent back for some rest. How long we'll be here I don't know. There are rumours of a big push, but rumours being rumours I might still be sitting with my feet up in some estaminet by the time you are reading this. Or I might have been sent up the line. If I have, don't worry if you don't hear for a while. I'll send a card when I get a chance.

Thanks for the parcel. The cake was scrumptious. Sometimes the food is a bit hit and miss but quantity and quality have been pretty decent recently though I do crave a bit of chocolate. So perhaps you could...

She wavered, her eyes misting over. She took another deep breath...

#

At one minute to eleven, an American of German descent, Private Henry N. Gunter of the 313th Division, becomes the last allied soldier to die. His unit had been ordered to take a German machine gun post. His divisional record later states 'Almost as he fell, the gunfire died away and an appalling silence prevailed.'

#

She hadn't shut the door when her mother came into the hall. Emily spent a few minutes describing events in town before asking about her mother's day. It was then that her mother had produced it.

"I'm sorry, Emily. I shouldn't have left it so long. I never thought that there might be two letters. It's for you... from Edward."

Emily was completely taken aback but managed to hold out her hand.

"I haven't read it. Not yours, anyway." She passed it to Emily. "I almost opened the envelope after David's funeral," she shook her head, "but I couldn't. Not then. But then, this morning, the world's changed, hasn't it? I had to do it, now or never."

Emily struggled, but managed a hesitant reply. "How are you?"

"A bit weepy earlier, but better now, I think, I don't know... No, I do feel better, now that I've finally grasped the nettle. And your father's relieved I have too."

"But what did Edward say?"

"That's the funny thing – there was nothing special in it. No," she shook her head, "that's wrong – it was special, very special, but the contents were so ordinary. A little bit about what he'd been doing; a list of things he wanted sending out... chocolate, socks, newspaper. Completely unremarkable. But somehow..." she ran out of words, "anyway, perhaps there's more in yours, not that you have to tell me." She smiled, desperate to know Emily's news. "There's a few bits and pieces in the kitchen if you're hungry, but you look tired, dear, so why don't you go up? We can talk about it in the morning."

"Yes, I might get something later, but I'll go up first." She stopped on the third step and turned. "And Mother, I'm so glad you've finally read it."

#

At a few minutes after eleven a Leutnant Tomas approaches some American troops to tell them the war has ended and they can have the house he and his men have been holding. Due to a communications breakdown they are unaware of the armistice and shoot him. He is the last soldier to die in battle on the Western Front.

#

Emily pulled back her bedroom curtains. Light streamed out from the back windows of the houses on Marlborough Avenue. On her right, the apple tree in Robert's garden stood bare and leafless. As she gazed at it, images from the evening came back to her – the impromptu American jazz band playing Dixie in Whitefriargate, the young American sailor who'd told her "Gee, I wish I was in New York City right now", the ridiculous cardboard trumpet she'd bought, the boys burning green and red powders which she could still smell, the crowds and the ever more furious fun.

She turned away from the window and started to run her fingers along the edge of the envelope in her hand.

Dear Emily,

A few days' recuperation has left enough time to write a few letters, so here you are, dear irritating little sister – here is yours.

Thanks for your most recent missive. After your previous exciting exploits at Brid I expected to hear that the Time Traveller himself had whisked you off somewhere else. I know he will return to Richmond, not Hull, but my imagination is allowed some poetic licence, so let his Machine now travel in space and time. If he does call, where and when would you want to visit? Do let me know and I shall see what I can do, though if your wish is to meet Morlocks there's no need for a Time Machine, as they are abundant in this dystopia around me.

I wish my H.G. Wells collection wasn't gathering dust on my bookshelf. No, I'm sure there is no dust there, and God knows what they might get covered in here. Perhaps you could select one to send me? I have been thinking of Wells' books a good deal recently, especially War of the Worlds. For this last month, Mars has been highly conspicuous after sunset. It's being overtaken by the sun, but it's still excellent. The other evening, as I stared at it (by the way, send my telescope too – just joking!), I imagined bright flashes emanating from the red planet's surface. And this time Martian cylinders, rather than landing in Woking, have landed here in France instead. The Hun's Flammenwerfer are adequate replacements for heat and death rays, and when there's a gas attack, even with the colour being wrong, it might almost be Martian black smoke rolling towards you. As yet red weed hasn't sprouted up smothering no-man's land, though that might be no bad thing. I'm sorry, this is getting too gloomy – I shall continue on a brighter note – always remember that after all that death and horror 'War of the Worlds' does have a happy ending. I love Wells' last line – its hope is something to cling onto, amongst all this.

I do find stargazing relaxing. There's a Boche intent on disturbing our sleep by sending off salvoes every so often, but thanks to him I observed my best-ever meteor shower – radiating outwards from near Bootes. Can you remember how to find Arcturus?...

Emily smiled. Astronomy, more than any other passion, brought out Edward's oddest behaviour. When a new garden shed was being bought he'd argued at length for a flat rather than pitched roof. Having no interest in sheds, she had not followed his argument, and it was only when she came across him wrapped in innumerable layers of clothing on a bitter December evening that she understood. He had gone outside, climbed onto the roof, and lain there for the best part of an hour examining the heavens through a battered old pair of opera glasses. On subsequent evenings, he'd suggested she join him, an offer she'd declined, but despite this it had proved impossible not to accumulate some information.

"Find the Plough, follow it down and the bright orange star it points to is Arcturus," she whispered.

...It's Bootes' brightest star. You use the Plough to find it. Remember? The meteors were yellowish, here for a moment before they were gone, bursting in spectacular light flashes. It's all very confusing as the Bootids are generally seen in January, not the end of June, so most strange. Doubtless you are equally perplexed and will be heading up to the attic to scour the heavens through my telescope. When I'm home on leave, I shall offer lessons about the cosmos at very reasonable rates!

I have started a nature journal but I shall not be recording those unwanted visitors that proliferate in abundance, merely the welcome, the common and the unusual. I saw a butterfly the other day, a Red Admiral. Its colours were so vibrant that it must have just hatched, but it was the contrast with its surroundings that struck me most. The sun was shining, yet the landscape was dull and depressingly monochrome – browns, greys, more browns. And there it was, so colourful, a tiny fragile shimmer of red, black and white flitting above the fire-step and up in between and around the barbed wire. I couldn't understand what the appeal was – there are a few skeletal tree stumps but nothing for nectar, and not even a lowly clump of nettles to lay its eggs on. I watched it for several minutes, willing it to turn back, but it would not be persuaded, and the last I saw of it it was venturing over the top. I hope it found something worthwhile on the other side. The naturalist was tempted to peek, but a Red Admiral hardly merits giving a sniper a chance. Now if it been Nymphalis antiopa – 'The Grand Surprize' – then I might have risked it. Perhaps if the Time Traveller calls on me, rather than you, I shall request a trip back to Cold Arbour Lane in 1748 to see the two specimens famously caught there. Who knows, I might be lucky enough to see a Camberwell Beauty here – but don't worry, I won't stick my head above the parapet no matter how excited I feel – after all, the Americans call them Mourning Cloaks.

Has Robert returned? I sometimes look upwards and wonder. Such fragile things. Almost like the butterflies. Myself, I prefer to have my feet firmly on the ground.

Do write. I soak up news most voraciously. I'm not sure how long I'll be here as we can be sent back up at a couple of hours notice, but it's nice to have something to hold onto, to look forward to, so please do write.

Look after yourself, my irritating little sister,
Edward
xxx

P.S. Jupiter is especially good in Aries in the early hours. You can't miss it.

\#

At midnight, forty minutes after the moon has set, the Guildhall clock in Alfred Gelder Street strikes twelve. The first complete day of peace is just about to

begin. Official figures record over ten thousand men killed, wounded or miss-
ing on the day of 11th November 1918. The Americans alone suffer over three
thousand casualties.

November 12th, 1918
Westbourne Avenue

Dear Edward,

I never write letters at half past one in the morning, but today will be an exception. It's a couple of hours now since I read your letter. It was delayed, but I was so pleased to hear from you.

Part of me feels silly writing this, but I know you won't mind. You wanted to hear the news and it could hardly be more momentous than today's. The war is over! I was in town. You'd have really enjoyed it – crowds of riotously giddy people who doubtless will still be celebrating tomorrow – but for you and David, and so many more, there aren't going to be any tomorrows, are there? I hope that hasn't shocked you. About David... it's why I'm at home. He survived the German's bullets but the Spanish flu took him. He was changed, though, by the war. Tortured. Not physically, but his mind wasn't the same. There were times when you wouldn't have recognised him. I'm not sure he recognised himself. It wasn't all grim, though –

there were moments of joy when we thought he was making a recovery, but the bright spots were just so many false dawns. And then the wretched flu swept across the country. I don't know if he fought against it or, more likely, just gave into it and slipped away. Mother was in a daze. It's all been a terrible strain for her. All those months of worry and then last month this blow. But I'm convinced finally reading your letter has helped her. She seemed relieved when I came in. More her old self. I could tell she's desperate to know what you've written to me, but that will wait till morning.

Father's much the same, immersed even more in the bank and his blessed Druids. In some ways he's mellowed. Sadly there is no fresh correspondence of his to the Mail to report. Perhaps this peace will give him new opportunities to put pen to paper. You will be relieved that he hasn't yet lost his tendency to be a bit pompous. There was a worrying period when he and Aunt Eleanor had a major disagreement – over politics, the war and so on. She doesn't call as much as she used to, not when he's at home anyway, but I've hardly been here much either. I worked as a VAD for a while at Brooklands on Cottingham Road, but this last year I've been down in London. I can hear your gasp of amazement! I've loved it and I've made the most wonderful of friends there. She's called Fish (I'll explain some other time). You would love her. She has the same sense of humour as you. I wish you could meet her. I hope you don't mind if I show her your letter. I haven't told Mother yet, but I've decided to go back to London. I've been up here long enough. The hospital were very good about letting me come home after David's death, but my contract runs into early December and I want to complete it. So I'm no longer a poor provincial mouse but a distinctly metropolitan one. I exaggerate only slightly.

Robert was shot down and captured and is somewhere in Eastern Germany, but will be coming home now. I can hardly wait, but wait I shall have to. They say absence makes the heart grow fonder – I just pray that we are as close as I think we've become and that when we are reunited it's not some shimmering mirage.

When I finished your letter I couldn't settle. I had to examine your H.G. Wells collection. It and the rest are definitely not gathering dust! I took the liberty of rearranging one or two that had escaped the rigid alphabetical constraints you always enforced on them. I hope you approve. You're right, Wells never appealed to me, but it would be so boring if we all adored the same thing. Aunt Eleanor always says try something new, so sitting on your bedroom floor I made a very early New Year's Resolution to work my way through your bookshelves. My first choice has to be Wells – I took some time to decide which, but to suit today I've settled on 'The World Set Free'. I would happily have sent one of his to you, but... I am reconciled to a diet of Kipling (yes) Rider Haggard (unsure) Verne (no). So I have decided to take back to London the fourth from the right (top shelf), the seventh from the left (third shelf) and the one at the extreme right (bottom shelf). I shall even resist looking at my random choices until I get there.

After what you said, I had to read the last chapter of War of the Worlds. I can see what you meant about the hopeful last line – 'And strangest of all, is to hold my wife's hand again, and to think that I have counted her, and that she has counted me, among the dead.' But reading that and thinking of you just made me feel sad. The lack of hope. Sorry.

After that I was about to go to bed, but I looked out of your window. The sky was clear, and much to my amazement – and yours, I imagine – I went outside. Don't worry, I'm not stupid. I put something on, or rather I put a lot on and crept downstairs.

'Let your eyes adjust'. Wasn't that what you said? It only took a few minutes. The Milky Way was magnificent. And no, I did not lie on the top of your blessed shed!

I could not find Mars. Planets are wanderers, you said. I never understood why, though I shall always be grateful for that demonstration you did in the garden when you laid out lots of fruit with one of your balls in the centre. The park would have been better, you said, as you seemed to be having problems with scale. It was a pity Alice came out to reclaim Venus and Saturn for a pudding she was making. You even attempted once to explain retrograde motion to me (have I got that right?) and I willingly confess that I still have no idea what you were talking about. You said you would be lecturing on the cosmos – well, your first lecture should be 'Planets – wouldn't life be simpler if they stayed in one place?' So although I couldn't find Mars, I think Jupiter was there, to the north-east, in your star sign, Gemini. I was boring old Cancer, a horrid crab, and you were one of Castor and Pollux, the heavenly twins. You were convinced you were Castor, but I'm afraid you weren't, were you? You were poor vulnerable Pollux, and sadly, when you needed him, Castor did not turn up at Guillemot to share his immortality with you.

I'm sorry, I had to stop writing for a little while. Yes, I'm sure it was Jupiter. It wasn't twinkling.

And I found Arcturus but no meteors, Bootid or otherwise. Or butterflies.

It's well after two now and I am finally feeling sleepy so I know you won't mind if I finish. I've read this letter through and it seems to be just a collection of disjointed ramblings, but carpe diem – if I left it until morning then you would have waited forever for this. I'm sure I've missed out lots of important things and I could write again, but I think that's unlikely,

love and memories,
from your irritating (though surely not always) little sister
Emily
xxx

P.S. If the Time Traveller ever calls, I shall return with him to 1748 and find your Camberwell Beauties for you.

December 14th, 1918
Beverley Road

"So there you are then," said Emily, "you managed it under your own steam. No wheelchairs or special sedans transporting you from your death bed." She beamed at her aunt. "And how was it?"

"I never realised it would be so difficult when the only choice lay between a Liberal and a Coupon Conservative. Four constituencies in the city, and the only one without a Labour candidate. Even your Father could vote Labour," she smiled, "not that seems the most likely of things to happen today! If I'd had a hundred and fifty pounds deposit to lose, I'd have sponsored one myself."

"Or stood yourself?"

Her aunt laughed. "Exactly. If only I'd thought of that. Perhaps next time. Member of Parliament for Kingston-upon-Hull Central has a fine ring to it. But even with having to wait until after Christmas for the count, this result is a foregone conclusion. Sir Mark Sykes will be my MP, if not yours."

"So what did you do?"

"Hold my nose whilst deliberating between the devil and the deep blue sea?" She paused. "Or spoil my ballot paper with some pithy comment?"

"And?"

"And what?"

"What did you do, Aunt?"

"Emily, William Gladstone introduced the secret ballot more than forty years ago so you'd hardly expect..."

"Aunt!"

"How about a cup of tea and you can tell me about your plans, now you've finished, and we can discuss what you would have done."

Emily could see she was unlikely to extract any further information.

"A cup of tea it is then, Aunt."

#

Reaching her garden gate, Emily began to lower her umbrella. It was then that she felt his arms envelop her and grasp her tight.

"Rob..."

One hand moved up and gently covered her mouth whilst the other remained firmly clasped around her waist.

"Ssh."

She was desperate to turn round. To see him. But he would not release her. She could hear him whispering close to her ear.

'Twas brillig and the Slithy Quirk did drone and burble in the blue,

all floppy were his wing controls and his observer too,

beware the wicked Albatros, the O.C. Quirks had told him flat..."

His grip had lessoned and she was able to turn.

"...beware the Hun-Hun bird and shun..."

Seeing her properly for the first time, he hesitated.

"...and shun the frumious Halberstadt," she completed for him and laughed. "Robert, you beast, why didn't you let me..." She was unable to finish, as the breath was squeezed out of her once more.

After a full minute he released her.

"What will the neighbours think? Here in the street?"

"If we take two steps here," he picked her up and swung her around, "we are now safely confined in the privacy of your front garden." He laughed.

"But why didn't you let me know? And what if I hadn't been here? I only got back on Thursday."

"It's all been so unsure and it was only last night that I was certain. I called on your mother and she said you'd be back by one, so I've been over there, leaning on the fountain's railings, waiting for you. I was watching you walking closer; you seemed in a dream-world under that umbrella of yours. So I thought I might as well creep up and..."

"Scare the living daylights out of me?" She smiled broadly, before looking at him closely. "But you're soaked." She saw his lapel and smiled. "You've still got it."

"Of course."

"But it was lovely earlier, and you've been standing outside in this? Harebrained! I wait two years and then you come back and I lose you when you catch pneumonia!"

"Emily!" He put his finger to her lips. "It's only a bit of rain. And anyway," he grinned, "I was worried you wouldn't recognise me. But you're right. We ought to get in and I can change. Shall we go into my house then?" He took her hand and started moving towards the gate.

She pulled him back. "This is a very efficient umbrella, and just large enough for two, so we could risk a little stroll around the fountain."

He reached forward and pushed a wisp of hair out of her eyes. "How many times?"

She smiled. "As many as it takes?"

The rain intensified and she pulled him closer. They walked out of the garden towards the fountain.

September 17th, 1921
Bitter Harvest Moon

Emily looked out from the promenade deck of Victoria pier. It was a beautiful evening, yet to her the Humber had never looked bleaker. A number of trawlers catching the high tide passed wraith-like through her field of vision. Movements closer to hand seemed more real. A couple keen to make the *Killingholme*'s sailing to New Holland hurried towards the Great Central Railway ticket office. Arm-in-arm, they looked so happy, she thought.

She ought to be moving, but she hesitated. She looked eastwards, to the right of the confluence of Hull and Humber, out beyond King George's Dock. The moon had yet to rise. She turned through one hundred and eighty degrees. A vessel moved out of Humber Dock, silhouetted against the setting sun.

She breathed in deeply and glanced down. A spider was meticulously weaving its web in the gaps between the rails. She studied it for some time then looked skywards again, imagining the sun hauling the moon up into the sky from beyond the far horizon, pulling it on a thin gossamer thread, a thread that bisected the centre of the spider's web.

Her attention was taken by the water again. If they'd been underway they might have passed the point, out nearer New Holland, where today sun and moon simultaneously seemed to sink into and rise from the river. It was an illusion that the receding distant flatness of the lands beyond made easy to imagine. She let out a long sigh. It had been two years and a week ago, returning from his aunt's house, that she'd seen that. She looked at her watch. No. Two years and one week ago... "In twenty-seven minutes' time," she whispered.

She lingered as long as possible but finally the plumes of smoke drifting towards her and a warning whistle stirred her into action, and she joined the other stragglers about to board. Most of her fellow passengers headed for the area of covered accommodation. She knew where she needed to be; on the port side, well forward of the *Killingholme*'s giant paddle. She checked her watch. Almost seven o'clock.

The ferry began to gather speed as it left the pier and headed upstream. Emily knew these first few moments might prove difficult and when they were a few hundred yards out she shuddered and a sick and giddy feeling ran through her body. She shut her eyes. Concentrate, concentrate! It will pass.

"Are you all right?"

She opened her eyes. An elderly woman was peering at her, a concerned expression on her face.

"No. Thank you. I'm fine, honestly."

"Well you don't look fine to me. Come and sit down a minute. I insist."

Despite her mild protestations Emily allowed herself to be led inside. "Just for a minute then. But I do need to be outside. It must be five past. The moon is rising..."

"The moon's not going anywhere. Not any time soon anyway. You sit there. I'll find you a glass of water." With that the woman disappeared.

Not wishing to risk the woman's disapproval Emily resisted the urge to go back outside. She rubbed her forehead. The last three weeks had passed in agonising confusion. Perhaps she shouldn't have come, but the idea had struck her two weeks ago last Wednesday and she couldn't resist it. She'd been sitting in Howden Minster, amongst all those people. Though she'd had doubts, she felt it was something she had to do.

The woman returned after a few minutes. "Here you are, dear. You drink this." She passed Emily a cup of tea. "Get some colour back into your cheeks. And I found some chocolate too. You've such a pretty face, and ghostly white doesn't suit you." She paused and looked enquiringly at Emily.

"Emily... And thank you for the tea." She took a sip. Hot and very, very sweet. She managed not to grimace.

"That's better, Emily. You were having quite a turn just then. I was rather worried. Going to visit relatives, are you?"

"No." She shook her head. "Just there and straight back."

The concerned look returned to the woman's face. "I hope you don't mind me saying, but that does seem a strange way to spend a Saturday evening. And by yourself too. Shouldn't you be enjoying yourself somewhere?"

"It had to be tonight. It was important." Her voice almost a whisper. "Tonight. The harvest moon." She hesitated before continuing a little more strongly. "And I *have* to be outside on deck at some point, though I can wait a bit longer... there's always the way back." She took a deep breath. "It was just over two years ago."

"What was, dear?"

"When he gave me this." She held out her hand.

"What a lovely ring." The woman examined it. "And so unusual. It's blue, it's almost transparent."

"It's a moonstone."

"And it shimmers when you move your hand. It's exquisite."

"He said he would have given it to me on a blue moon – you know, the extra full moon you get some years – but there wasn't one till the following summer and he couldn't wait that long. So he said he'd settle for the Harvest Moon instead. I'm sorry, I don't know why I'm telling you all this. You can't be interested."

"Please don't look so worried, dear. You just carry on."

"If you're sure?' The woman smiled and nodded. "So I said yes to him. I'd always expected to. Since the middle of the war anyway. I remember joking that it was a good job he hadn't given me *the* Moonstone. You've read the Wilkie Collins?"

The woman shook her head.

"My aunt gave me the book." Emily smiled at the memory. "She was worried it might not be suitable, that I was too young, but I loved it. It was so exciting. The Moonstone's a sacred diamond that's been stolen from an Indian temple. Whoever owns it, and their descendants, are cursed in perpetuity as a result."

"It sounds quite shocking. You'd hardly want that as a gift."

"No, you wouldn't, I agree. That Moonstone is a deep golden yellow that waxes and wanes but is always at its brightest when the moon's full. So, for colour, tonight's a perfect match. But I was more than happy to settle for this one." She ran her fingers backwards and forwards across the stone, staring at it. "I asked him what he would have done if it'd been raining." She tried but failed to keep an overwhelming sadness out of her voice. "He laughed and said he'd placated all the Gods and arranged for a beautiful evening... not only that, but they'd agreed that nothing could ever come between us."

"That sounds lovely, Emily. What has happened to make you so upset?"

"The R38. That's what happened."

The woman reeled back and gasped, a look of total shock on her face. "You don't mean...?"

Emily nodded, struggling to hold back tears.

"But you poor thing! How simply awful."

"He was a flyer in the war, but he always had an obsession about balloons and airships even when we first met, and then he had an opportunity, based at Howden too, so who was I to try and dissuade him? To encourage him to get a job behind a desk like his father and mine, rather than fly in the world's largest airship?" She paused, took out her handkerchief, and blew her nose. "He was so frustrated the two weeks before the final trial, whilst they waited and waited for the weather. And then that would be it. The Americans would fly it home and his future was less certain."

"I saw it early on the Tuesday morning."

"You did? I was on the pier. Up at the crack of dawn to get down there. I like to think he saw me waving. But probably not," she shrugged.

"But you weren't there on..."

"On the Wednesday? No, thank God. I was spared that. Someone dropped a letter overboard tied to a piece of silk which landed in Anlaby Road but it wasn't for me." Her next words were tinged with bitterness. "And I've heard enough about it since to last me a lifetime."

Shortly after five thirty-five p.m. on the 24th August 1921 the R38, nearing the completion of its fourth and final test flight, passed over Alexandria dock and headed for the Humber. Having been bought by the USA, there were pressures to get the airship signed off as airworthy and handed over to its American crew as soon as possible. Corners were cut. Trial flight time was reduced from one hundred and fifty hours to fifty. Deficiencies in the design and earlier technical problems were ignored. Key decisions in the chain of command were taken by men of high rank but little knowledge of airships, while advice from officers of lower rank but with greater experience was ignored.

Having only been flown in favourable weather up till then, at five thirty-seven p.m. the airship began a series of sharp turns meant to simulate flying in violent, turbulent weather, a manoeuvre only recommended for this type of airship above seven and a half thousand feet. The R38 was at approximately two and a half thousand feet and a few hundred yards off Victoria pier. The strain between air-frames nine and ten caused girders to rupture and the middle of the craft to rise upwards, whilst the nose and tail sank downwards. The hull jackknifed and broke into two. A lethal cocktail of a highly ignitable, vaporised mix of petrol and air, the rupture of hydrogen gas cells, and some form of electrical spark led to disaster for the airship and death for most of its crew.

"I heard it at home," Emily continued. "You would have had to be stone deaf not to. And all those hundreds of windows blown in across the town." She shook her head.

"My sister," the woman started... What was she going to say, that her sister saw the crease run diagonally back from middle to rear, the cloud of vapour envelop the ship, changing it from silver to dark grey, saw it breaking into two, heard the huge explosions, witnessed the poor souls who parachuted from it into a river transformed into a fiery Hades and listened as the crowds' screams of anguish gave way to an awful, dreadful silence. No, she could hardly say that.

"No, it doesn't matter. But you, you poor thing." A change in the background noise as the paddles slowed suggested they were nearing New Holland. "I feel guilty leaving you. Will you be all right? You could come with me and we could send a telegram." The woman stopped.

"No. You've been very kind but no, thank you. And I will be all right, I promise."

"If you're sure, then. Let me give you my details." She rummaged in her bag and handed Emily a card. "I'll be back home in three or four days and I'd love to hear that you are all right."

She smiled and reached for Emily's hand before standing up. "And it is such a beautiful ring. Do treasure it."

Twenty-eight British and sixteen Americans died on the R38. There were five survivors.

Emily looked around. Far fewer people were about on deck for the return journey, only one or two, and none in close proximity. She felt calmer, relieved that this time she hadn't drawn attention to herself. Was she calm? No, calm was the wrong word. More confident, assured? But perhaps this would prove nothing more than a meaningless gesture. Apart from the breeze created by the movement of the ferry, it was a perfectly still evening. The glorious sunset's red afterglow had all but disappeared, and the sky had darkened rapidly. The moon was higher but was still in thrall to the horizon, and displaying those exaggerated proportions only possible on these rare evenings.

The minutes lengthened as Emily stared at it. As the moon's deep, blood-orange colour melted into burnished gold, she imagined it growing to encompass half the sky. The idea was suddenly too disturbing and she shook her head, concentrating instead on the reflection in the river. The watery image was different; its intense shimmering lemon yellow was haunting. She'd stood here before, spellbound, but that covenant had been broken. This image held no hope. It was bitter. A bitter harvest moon.

She knew it was illusory but she could hear his voice. It was after he'd given her the ring. He'd promised her everything on the far side of the moon. She'd laughed and said how could he possibly know what was there, and what if she hated it rather than loved it? That was the beauty of it, he'd replied. Once a month, when it was in total darkness there, you were granted a wish. She'd looked at him with a mixture of amusement and scepticism. And once a year, he'd continued, at a Harvest Moon, the magic was especially strong and your wish was guaranteed to come true. He'd then laughed and added that you were only allowed one wish, so best not to waste it. All you needed was an imagination. It was all there, waiting, on the far side of the moon. She'd started to say something, to make a wish, but before she could, he'd pulled her close and kissed her hard.

She gripped on to the rail. It *would* be dark out there tonight.

"I don't care what's there, but I never made one," she whispered. "I wish... I just want..." She could not finish the sentence. Instead, she reached inside her bag and felt for the coldness of the bottle. She took it out and held it between her hands. She'd checked the top fitted earlier but that didn't stop her checking yet again. She was surprised that her hands weren't shaking.

"He shouldn't have taken them, it wasn't fair to you, or to him. My aunt knew of the photograph – the Berlin park – the Märchenbrunnen. The fountain of fairy tales, she said. But there were no happy ever afters, were there? And, dear Erica," she made a half-hearted attempt to laugh, "we're both in the same position now. It's been four years for you. I wonder, do you still think of your Werner every day, or has a Fritz or Max turned up and taken his place?" She ran her fingers round its edge. "I've added my own little note. I hope you don't mind." And with that she threw the bottle with all her strength towards the moon.

She tried to follow the arc of her throw but quickly lost it, and the moon's reflection was not noticeably disturbed. The noise from the paddles masked the sound of any splash, but with the tide on the turn there was a reasonable chance it might make it out into the North Sea and then who knows? "Gothenburg, not Goole."

She reached into her bag again, knowing this would be immeasurably more difficult. She wasn't convinced she could go through with it, but after a full minute of letting it play through her fingers, she gained enough resolve to take it out.

Its pin was rather more worn, the ribbon's colour more singed and faded, but it was undeniably the pin she'd fastened onto him that June morning in nineteen fifteen. His guardian angel. Carefully she attached the pin to the remaining remnant of original ribbon. One part of her knew that regret was an insidious and pernicious emotion with no redeeming features, but what price rationality when you could sink into the morass of *what if* and *if only*? Logically she knew that the red ribbon had *not* kept him protected in his blessed plane, had *not* saved him when he was shot down... but... but... when he'd received the news after all that frustration that the test flight was finally happening, if he hadn't been so excited, rushing around madly... what if before giving her that final kiss he'd noticed it where he'd dropped it on the floor. If he'd picked it up and taken it with him, would he have somehow found himself in the airship's tail? If he had, then five survivors would have become six. No, perhaps she should embrace fatalism instead.

She threaded the ribbon between her fingers. Caressing it. One airship brought it to her and a second would see it released. She hesitated, but then the ribbon started to slip away. She looked up. The metaphysics of magicians, to make this moon drop from its sphere, to do whatever she commands, to sell her soul to bring him back. To sell her soul.

She started. She clutched for it, but it was too late. It was lost. She felt a momentary, overwhelming, bitter regret. She couldn't see it. It was gone and so was he. Neither would be returning. They were gone forever.

A powerful urge to follow swept over her.

"You promised to take me anywhere. Take me to the far side of the moon, Robert. The dark side." Her right foot moved towards the lowest rail. Whatever shall be, shall be. *Climbing.* This time the rope didn't stretch out in front – it hung limply behind her. There would be nothing and no-one to hold her. *Excellent, Emily. First rate.* And if she fell, she would fall through the clouds before landing safe and sound in the cockpit next to him. It was the only way to be with him. She started to push herself upwards. *You're a natural. Just feel the rock.* Feel the rock? Her head jerked back. It wasn't warm firm granite beneath her fingertips; it was damp, cold, clammy wood. Startled, shaken, Emily stopped. She stared down at the moon's reflection before raising her head to examine it, hanging there, suspended in the sky. Slowly and deliberately, she placed her feet back down onto the gently vibrating solidity of the deck. She took a long deep breath, turned away from the moon and looked northwards in the direction of home. She sighed. Home? It was hard to imagine she would ever think of it as that again. She shook her head, trying to clear it. No, she must return, if not forever, for now, at least. As the boat edged ever closer, the lights of Hull burned increasingly brightly – bright lights seen through a film of tears.

Postscript

Emily sat at her desk and, though she knew it by heart, she read the short letter once more. It all seemed so very long ago. She put it down, leant forward and took out a piece of writing paper. Were circumstances more propitious now? Would they still look on any application most favourably? Was she still interesting? She smiled. Nil desperandum. There was only one way to find out. She picked up her pen and began to write.

#

An Historical Note

The illustration above is from an old photograph of Bridlington beach that I picked up in a junk shop on Hessle Road, Hull. I immediately knew that in the girl on the left I had found my main character, Emily.

Descriptions of Hull are based on a variety of primary and secondary sources. Thanks to the excellent facilities and staff at the Hull History Centre I was able to access news items, reviews, leading articles and advertisements from the Hull Daily Mail and Eastern Morning News. Extracts from letters that appeared in these newspapers under monikers such as 'Middle Class' were used verbatim as Emily's father's letters.

The initial chapters when Emily was a young girl combine episodes from 1907-10. Incidents such as the balloon crash in New Holland, Professor Gaudion's parachute jump, the concerts in Bridlington, the shopkeeper's prosecution, the suffrage vanners, and associated events happened as described but have been amalgamated into one summer.

The Abraham brothers were climbing in the Lake District during 1914. It is not known whether they climbed on the day of Emily's visit. The first ascent of Troutdale Pinnacle was in May 1914 by Mallinson and Mawson (who were also Keswick photographers).

The riot in the aftermath of the Zeppelin raid, combines several accounts from across Hull: a piano was pushed out of an upstairs window, but there is no evidence of an impromptu concert first. A description of Edwin Davis's department store after the bombing mentions red ribbon seen amongst the devastation being 'guarded' by a policeman. The 'finely dressed woman' is Mrs Strickland-Constable. Her diaries, written in exercise books, record the visit. She was in charge of Brooklands Military Hospital for part of 1917.

It is true that an RFC officer landed on a South Coast beach to meet his girlfriend. It is unrecorded whether he took her up in the air, but there were many examples of people being given joy-rides in their planes.

Original games of Panko do come up for sale occasionally. Eleanor's actions and views are based on contemporary accounts quoted in books such as Jill Liddington's excellent *Rebel Girls*.

Events in France were possible, but not necessarily factual. The 56th Squadron flew sorties on the days described. The chapters about flying would have been impossible to write without Peter Hart's superb books about the RFC. His quotations from the memoirs of RFC pilots, including those who were also POWs, underpinned this section of the novel. The shooting down of Robert's plane was based on the account of Captain W.E. Johns, of Biggles fame, being shot down. The Major who interviewed Robert was inspired by a well-documented case of a German of Argentinian extraction, who began his questioning of RFC prisoners by talking about polo. The Kommandant at Trier was described as *a decent sort* and spoke excellent English, but no escape attempt was discovered at Trier. The camp Robert was sent to in Schweidnitz was near Richthofen's birthplace. Letters from Robert and Edward include more than the censor may have allowed.

Thank God I'm not a boy, Dora Willatts' account of working as a nurse in Hull was a vital source in writing about Emily's experiences as a VAD at Brooklands and Byculla.

An American, William Ellsworth Robinson, copied the act of a Chinese magician called Chung Ling Foo. He moved to Europe and took the name of Chung Ling Soo, and his wife Olive became Suee Seen. Weeks of wild speculation followed the tragedy, fuelled by sensational revelations of bigamous marriages, mistresses and marital infidelities. The inquest decided his death was the result of failing to clean one of his trick guns. The build-up of gunpowder was sufficient to fire the fatal bullet. He was the sixth magician to die performing 'the bullet catch'.

There is some uncertainty about when exactly Brooklands Military Hospital opened but J.R.Tolkien spent several weeks recuperating there in 1917. Wilfred Owen and Siegfried Sassoon were patients at Craiglockhart hospital in Edinburgh.

Where the weather is specifically mentioned then it was as described on that day (similarly with moonrise and tide times). There was a spectacular Auroa Borealis display across Southern England on the night of the bombing raid, as described by Fish. On that night it was cloudy in Hull. The weather throughout September 1918 was atrocious, which partially explains why London was spared bombing with the new deadly Elektron Incendiary Bombs, though the German High Command may also have been concerned about reprisal raids.

I did not check what the weather was like on the nights of the Harvest Moons as I did not wish to discover that the events described could not have happened!

I have tried to make the novel as historically accurate as possible and apologise for any inaccuracies that there might be.

Bibliography

I gratefully acknowledge the help that these sources have provided and without which I could not have written the novel.

Hull and Bridlington
  Illustrated history of the Avenues
  Chris Ketchell

This Dear, Dear Land:Zeppelin raids on Hull
John Hook
Hull Pals
David Bilton
Keep the Home Fires Burning
John Markham
Grandfather's adventures in the Great War
Cecil Slack
Thank God I'm not a boy
Dora Willatts
Personal diaries
Mary Strickland Constable
Overalls & Sashes: Reminiscences of French Convent
Irene Megginson
Dorothy Denton's Diary
Dorothy Denton
Elaine
Elaine Cussons
Golden age of the Yorkshire seaside
Malcom Barker
Bridlington
Ian & Margaret Summers
Hymers College:The First Hundred Years
Newland High School-Central Secondary 1907-1957
Aspects of Hull
Streets of Hull

Women and Suffrage
     Rebel Girls:Their fight for the vote
     Jill Liddington
     Status of Women in University/Higher Education
     Carol Dyhouse
     Bluestockings
     Jane Robinson
     Votes for Women:Virago book of Suffragettes
     Joyce Marlow
     The Women's Suffrage Movement: 1866-1928:
     Elizabeth Crawford
     The Strange Death of Liberal England: 1910-1914:
     George Dangerfield, David Marsland

Sylvia Pankhurst: A Life in Radical Politics:
Mary Davis
Feminism: A Very Short Introduction
Margaret Walters
The British Women's Suffrage Campaign: 1866-1928
Harold L. Smith
Mrs.Warren's Daughter
Sir Harry Hamilton, Johnston
My part in a changing world
Emmeline Pethick Lawrence
Unfinished adventures
Evelyn Sharp
Prisons and Prisoners:some personal experiences
Constance Lytton

Climbing

Because it's there
Walter Unsworth
British Mountain Climbs
George Abraham
Scrambles in the Alps
Edward Whymper

General

Castle Blair
Flora L Shaw
Lost voices of the Edwardians
Max Arthur
Forgotten voices of the Great War
Max Arthur
Panorama 1900-1942
Harold Herd
The Trench
Richard Van Emden
Falsehood in Wartime
Arthur Ponsoby
World War One: Day by Day
G Hodges

Tommy's War
Thomas Cairns
Combatants and non-combatants
Rose McAuley
Echoes of the Great War
Rev Andrew Clarke
Managing dissent in First World War Britain
Brock Millman
Civilian Life in WW1
Peter Cooksley
How we lived then: 1914-18
Dorothy S Peel
Life's enchanted cup
Dorothy.S Peel
When the lamps went out
Ed. Nigel Fountain
Scrimgeour's small scribbling diary
Alexander Scrimgeour
Dear Friends: Liebe Freund
Rosamund Ridley
Home Front 1914-18
Ian Becket
Diary of a dead officer
Arthur Graham West
Struwwelpeter
Heinrich Hoffman

Prisoners of War
The ethics of escape
S.P.Mackenzie
First World War Central Power Prison Camps
Kenneth Steuer

Medical
The shock of war
Caroline Alexander
Memoirs & Diaries of a Casualty Clearing Station
John A Hayward

War in the Wards: Social construction of medical work
Janet Watson

<u>War in the Air</u>
Fighter Heroes of World War One
Joshua Levine
Aces Falling
Peter Hart
Bloody April
Peter Hart
The First Blitz
Kenneth Poolman
Zeppelin Nights: London in the First World War
Jerry Head
Memoirs of an Old Balloonatic
Goderic Hodges
Zeppelins of World War 1
Wilbur Cross
Zeppelin History of German Airship
Christopher Chant
Royal Flying Corps in WW1
Ralph Barker
German Air Forces 1914-18
Ian Sumner
Zeppelin fighter
Arch Whitehouse
Fighting Fury
James McCudden
A few of the First
Bruce Lewis
Cavalry of the Clouds
Alan Bott
Icarus Over the Humber: The Last Flight of R.38/ZR-2
Tom Jamison
Lewis Carroll parody
William Bond

A list of online sources can be obtained from the author at hullsaddler@hotmail.com For anyone interested in local history in Hull, I would recommend https://www.paul-gib-son.com/ . I would also like to thank Paul for use of the Westbourne Avenue fountain photograph.

Printed in Great Britain
by Amazon